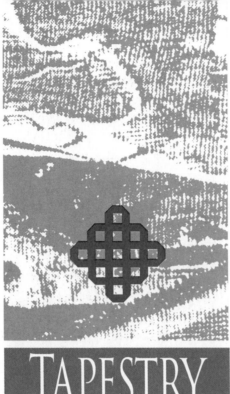

TAPESTRY

THE NEWBURY HOUSE GUIDE TO WRITING

TAPESTRY

The **Tapestry** program of language
materials is based on the concepts
presented in ***The Tapestry of
Language Learning:*** *The Individual
in the Communicative Classroom* by
Robin C. Scarcella &
Rebecca L. Oxford.

❖

Each title in this program focuses on:

❖

Individual learner strategies and
instruction

❖

The relatedness of skills

❖

Ongoing self-assessment

❖

Authentic material as input

❖

Theme-based learning linked to task-
based instruction

❖

Attention to all aspects of
communicative competence

TAPESTRY

THE NEWBURY HOUSE GUIDE TO WRITING

M.E. Sokolik

Heinle & Heinle Publishers
An International Thomson
Publishing Company
Boston, Massachusetts, 02116, USA

I T P

The publication of *The Newbury House Guide to Writing* was directed by the members of the Heinle & Heinle Global Innovations Publishing Team:

David C. Lee, Editorial Director
John F. McHugh, Market Development Director
Lisa McLaughlin, Production Services Coordinator

Also participating in the publication of this program were:

Director of Production: Elizabeth Holthaus
Publisher: Stanley J. Galek
Senior Assistant Editor: Kenneth Mattsson
Manufacturing Coordinator: Mary Beth Hennebury
Full Service Project Manager/Compositor: PC&F, Inc.
Interior Design: Maureen Lauran
Cover Design: Maureen Lauran

Manufactured in the United States of America

ISBN: 0-8384-4681-7

Heinle & Heinle Publishers is an International Thomson Publishing Company.

10 9 8 7 6 5 4 3 2

For Michael
and
For everyone, past and present,
at Blacksmith Angus Farm

PHOTO CREDITS

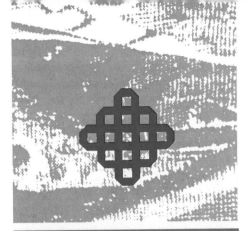

WELCOME TO TAPESTRY

*E*nter the world of Tapestry! Language learning can be seen as an ever-developing tapestry woven with many threads and colors. The elements of the tapestry are related to different language skills like listening and speaking, reading and writing; the characteristics of the teachers; the desires, needs, and backgrounds of the students; and the general second language development process. When all these elements are working together harmoniously, the result is a colorful, continuously growing tapestry of language competence of which the student and the teacher can be proud.

This volume is part of the Tapestry Program for students of English as a second language (ESL) at levels from beginning to "bridge" (which follows the advanced level and prepares students to enter regular postsecondary programs along with native English speakers). Upper level materials in the Tapestry Program are also appropriate for developmental English courses—especially reading and composition courses. Tapestry levels include:

Beginning   Advanced
Low Intermediate   High Advanced
High Intermediate   Bridge

Because the Tapestry Program provides a unified theoretical and pedagogical foundation for all its components, you can optimally use all the Tapestry student books in a coordinated fashion as an entire curriculum of materials. (They will be published from 1993 to 1996 with further editions likely thereafter.) Alternatively, you can decide to use just certain Tapestry volumes, depending on your specific needs.

Tapestry is primarily designed for ESL students at postsecondary institutions in North America. Some want to learn ESL for academic or career advancement, others for social and personal reasons. Tapestry builds directly on all these motivations. Tapestry stimulates learners to do their best. It enables learners to use English naturally and to develop fluency as well as accuracy.

Tapestry Principles

The following principles underlie the instruction provided in all of the components of the Tapestry Program.

EMPOWERING LEARNERS

Language learners in Tapestry classrooms are active and increasingly responsible for developing their English language skills and related cultural abilities. This self direction leads to better, more rapid learning. Some cultures virtually train their students to be passive in the classroom, but Tapestry weans them from passivity by providing exceptionally high interest materials, colorful and motivating activities, personalized self-reflection tasks, peer tutoring and other forms of cooperative learning, and powerful learning strategies to boost self direction in learning.

The empowerment of learners creates refreshing new roles for teachers, too. The teacher serves as facilitator, co-communicator, diagnostician, guide, and helper. Teachers are set free to be more creative at the same time their students become more autonomous learners.

HELPING STUDENTS IMPROVE THEIR LEARNING STRATEGIES

Learning strategies are the behaviors or steps an individual uses to enhance his or her learning. Examples are taking notes, practicing, finding a conversation partner, analyzing words, using background knowledge, and controlling anxiety. Hundreds of such strategies have been identified. Successful language learners use language learning strategies that are most effective for them given their particular learning style, and they put them together smoothly to fit the needs of a given language task. On the other hand, the learning strategies of less successful learners are a desperate grab-bag of ill-matched techniques.

All learners need to know a wide range of learning strategies. All learners need systematic practice in choosing and applying strategies that are relevant for various learning needs. Tapestry is one of the only ESL programs that overtly weaves a comprehensive set of learning strategies into language activities in all its volumes. These learning strategies are arranged in eight broad categories throughout the Tapestry books:

Forming Concepts
Personalizing
Remembering New Material
Managing Your Learning
Understanding and Using Emotions
Overcoming Limitations
Testing Hypotheses
Learning with Others

The most useful strategies are sometimes repeated and flagged with a note, "It Works! Learning Strategy . . ." to remind students to use a learning strategy they have already encountered. This recycling reinforces the value of learning strategies and provides greater practice.

RECOGNIZING AND HANDLING LEARNING STYLES EFFECTIVELY

Learners have different learning styles (for instance, visual, auditory, hands- on; reflective, impulsive; analytic, global; extroverted, introverted; closure-oriented, open). Particularly in an ESL setting, where students come from vastly different cultural backgrounds, learning styles differences abound and can cause "style conflicts."

Unlike most language instruction materials, Tapestry provides exciting activities specifically tailored to the needs of students with a large range of learning styles. You can use any Tapestry volume with the confidence that the activities and materials are intentionally geared for many different styles. Insights from the latest educational and psychological research undergird this style-nourishing variety.

OFFERING AUTHENTIC, MEANINGFUL COMMUNICATION

Students need to encounter language that provides authentic, meaningful communication. They must be involved in real-life communication tasks that cause them to *want* and *need* to read, write, speak, and listen to English. Moreover, the tasks—to be most effective—must be arranged around themes relevant to learners.

Themes like family relationships, survival in the educational system, personal health, friendships in a new country, political changes, and protection of the environment are all valuable to ESL learners. Tapestry focuses on topics like these. In every Tapestry volume, you will see specific content drawn from very broad areas such as home life, science and technology, business, humanities, social sciences, global issues, and multiculturalism. All the themes are real and important, and they are fashioned into language tasks that students enjoy.

At the advanced level, Tapestry also includes special books each focused on a single broad theme. For instance, there are two books on business English, two on English for science and technology, and two on academic communication and study skills.

UNDERSTANDING AND VALUING DIFFERENT CULTURES

Many ESL books and programs focus completely on the "new" culture, that is, the culture which the students are entering. The implicit message is that ESL students should just learn about this target culture, and there is no need to understand their own culture better or to find out about the cultures of their international classmates. To some ESL students, this makes them feel their own culture is not valued in the new country.

Tapestry is designed to provide a clear and understandable entry into North American culture. Nevertheless, the Tapestry Program values *all* the cultures found in the ESL classroom. Tapestry students have constant opportunities to become "culturally fluent" in North American culture while they are learning English, but they also have the chance to think about the cultures of their classmates and even understand their home culture from different perspectives.

INTEGRATING THE LANGUAGE SKILLS

Communication in a language is not restricted to one skill or another. ESL students are typically expected to learn (to a greater or lesser degree) all four language skills: reading, writing, speaking, and listening. They are also expected to develop strong grammatical competence, as well as becoming socioculturally sensitive and knowing what to do when they encounter a "language barrier."

Research shows that multi-skill learning is more effective than isolated-skill learning, because related activities in several skills provide reinforcement and refresh the learner's memory. Therefore, Tapestry integrates all the skills. A given Tapestry volume might highlight one skill, such as reading, but all other skills are also included to support and strengthen overall language development.

However, many intensive ESL programs are divided into classes labeled according to one skill (Reading Comprehension Class) or at most two skills (Listening/Speaking Class or Oral Communication Class). The volumes in the Tapestry Program can easily be used to fit this traditional format, because each volume clearly identifies its highlighted or central skill(s).

Grammar is interwoven into all Tapestry volumes. However, there is also a separate reference book for students, *The Tapestry Grammar,* and a Grammar Strand composed of grammar "work-out" books at each of the levels in the Tapestry Program.

Other Features of the Tapestry Program

PILOT SITES

It is not enough to provide volumes full of appealing tasks and beautiful pictures. Users deserve to know that the materials have been pilot-tested. In many ESL series, pilot testing takes place at only a few sites or even just in the classroom of the author. In contrast, Heinle & Heinle Publishers have developed a network of Tapestry Pilot Test Sites throughout North America. At this time, there are approximately 40 such sites, although the number grows weekly. These sites try out the materials and provide suggestions for revisions. They are all actively engaged in making Tapestry the best program possible.

AN OVERALL GUIDEBOOK

To offer coherence to the entire Tapestry Program and especially to offer support for teachers who want to understand the principles and practice of Tapestry, we have written a book entitled, *The Tapestry of Language Learning. The Individual in the Communicative Classroom* (Scarcella and Oxford, published in 1992 by Heinle & Heinle).

A Last Word

We are pleased to welcome you to Tapestry! We use the Tapestry principles every day, and we hope these principles—and all the books in the Tapestry Program—provide you the same strength, confidence, and joy that they give us. We look forward to comments from both teachers and students who use any part of the Tapestry Program.

Rebecca L. Oxford
University of Alabama
Tuscaloosa, Alabama

Robin C. Scarcella
University of California at Irvine
Irvine, California

PREFACE

The Newbury House Guide to Writing is intended for students from all language backgrounds who are beginning their college careers. It focuses on cross-cultural and interdisciplinary readings as models for writing. It also uses a process approach to writing—encouraging brainstorming, freewriting, multiple drafting, and self-evaluation. Discussion and regular writing assignments are important elements in building better writers. These activities go hand in hand with this text.

To the Teacher

STRUCTURE

The Newbury House Guide to Writing falls into three parts. The first three chapters present a brief overview of the writing process as explained by professional writers and writing teachers. It includes seven readings on writing and reading, as well as exercises and discussion to engage the student during the creation process. These chapters should be used as an introduction to a writing course. In these chapters readings are found both within the body of each chapter and in a section called "Additional Readings" at the end of each chapter. These additional readings are thematically related to those in the chapter. Depending on one's time frame, these readings can be used to augment the discussion and assignments, left out, or assigned as extra-curricular reading.

Chapters 4 through 7 constitute the heart of this book. They cover personal essays, literary analysis, persuasive writing, and research papers. This section has readings from different genres: memoirs, poetry, short stories, promotional literature, persuasive essays and letters, and non-fiction science writing. All of the major essay assignments are contained within this section, and most of the time using this book will be spent working with these four chapters.

The final three chapters can be used as a reference section. There is an editing guide with basic grammatical explanations, brief style guides for APA and MLA referencing formats, and a brief introduction to in-class writing, using computers, and preparing manuscripts.

Finally, there is a glossary of the grammatical terminology that is used in this text. This glossary is cross-referenced to *The Tapestry Grammar.*

STRATEGIES

As in all Tapestry textbooks, the students are given strategies to assist in their developing independent learning styles. In contrast to many other Tapestry texts, however, the strategies given here are typically "higher order" or metacognitive strategies. These are intended to prompt students to examine their own learning strategies and reflect on their successes. (See Welcome to Tapestry for further information about strategy use.)

MINOR ASSIGNMENTS

There are many short assignments and activities throughout the book. These are important elements in building up to the essay assignments. However, it is not necessary that they be graded assignments. Done collaboratively, or as "practice work," these exercises can help students to develop their own style and ideas in writing in a low-risk way. Occasional "low-stakes" work which allows students to extend their grasp is necessary for their development into confident writers.

ESSAY ASSIGNMENTS

Essay topics are suggested for Chapters 4 through 7. However, these assignments can easily be amended by either the student or teacher to suit individual or programmatic needs. I encourage the teacher and the student to explore topics that are meaningful and important to them.

To the Student

Too many students do not think of themselves as writers. But being a student means being a writer. This book builds on the fact that you are *already* a writer. These chapters merely provide you with additional tools to help you become a better writer.

Reading, writing, thinking, and observing are all parts of one whole: learning. Unless you participate in all of these activities, your potential as a student will never be fully realized. Read the cereal box, the school paper, or a book a friend recommends. As you read, think about the writing you find there. Does it excite you? Make you angry? Why?

This book will introduce you to a number of different themes and issues: writers talking about their own writing and reading; stories about families and childhood in different cultures; hunger and homelessness; civil rights; and the effect of disease on societies and individuals. React to these readings—they aren't "right" or "wrong" or "good" or "bad." But, at one point an author had something to say—an author wanted to connect with a reader. Did he or she succeed in making you think? Making you angry? Making you want to write?

I hope so.

You will become a better writer if you practice. A piano player practices, a football player practices, and a writer needs to practice, too. Keep a journal, write letters and postcards, take good notes in your classes; in other words, just keep writing. As you try the activities in this book, think of others you can do on your own.

Finally, this book will help you learn to find and correct your own mistakes. Use the charts at the ends of the chapters to keep track of errors in your writing. If you monitor your mistakes, you will really begin to see progress.

The goal of this book is to make you a better writer. Reading, practice, and attention will all help you, but *you* have to do it.

Acknowledgments

The danger in acknowledgments lies in failing to recall. Here is my best recollection of everyone who contributed to the making of this book in some way. Forgive my forgetting.

The first acknowledgment must always go to my students. They worked with this material, gave me feedback, suggested improvements, and most of all, displayed genuine good humor through it all. In particular, I would like to thank my 1994 Berkeley Summer Bridge class and my 1994 Fall College Writing 1A classes. Their comments were especially helpful.

Next, I need to thank my colleagues at UC Berkeley who gave me suggestions and lent me books. I received advice or suggestions from Stephanie Bobo, Melinda Erickson, Jane Jones, Gail Offen-Brown, and Steve Tollefson, all of College Writing Programs. My deepest thanks go to them. Additionally, Art Quinn, through example and support as the director of College Writing Programs, deserves heartfelt thanks.

Many other colleagues throughout the world contributed as well, either by suggesting readings and exercises or lending moral support (in no particular order): Peter Master, Sharon Hilles, Donna Lardiere, Yuet Sim Chiang, Margaret Perrow, Cheryl Chan, Eileen Prince, Margaret Van Naersson, Grace Low, Louise Hirasawa, Anthea Tillyer, Tracy Henninger-Chiang, Jim Swan, Echo Farrow, Theresa Ammirati, Judith Snoke, Gary James, Neil Anderson, Judee Reel, Joyce West, Susan Simon, and Sharona Levy.

I would also like to thank the following people for their assistance in reviewing manuscripts or responding to our request for information about their standards and practices in teaching writing; I hope I have fulfilled their criticisms, hopes, and dreams: Barbara Campbell, State University of New York at Buffalo; Julia Cayuso, University of Miami; Christopher Ely, Ball State University; Linda Robinson Fellag, Community College of Philadelphia; Robert Fox, St. Michael's College; Suzanne Koons, Boston University and Bentley College; Karl Krahnke, Colorado State University; Philip Less, University of Arkansas at Little Rock; Monica Maxwell-Paegle, Georgetown University; Maureen O'Brien, Cornell University; Teresa Pica, University of Pennsylvania; Melinda Reichelt, Purdue University; Barbara Reisman, Bellevue Community College; Janice Silva, State University of New York at Buffalo; Mara Thorson, University of Arizona; Bart Wayand, University of Southern Maine; and Dee A. Worman, Harvard University.

Special thanks go to those who keep my life running so smoothly: my R.A. extraordinaire, Abraham Lee, and the office staff of College Writing Programs, Natalie Kato and Medina Goertz.

Penultimately, a rather Uriah-Heepish thank you to Heinle & Heinle for continuing to support my work. I appreciate the faith they continue to show in my labors. Thanks go to Ken Mattsson and especially to David Lee, who has been with me through three books and three cities now. Also, Rebecca Oxford and Robin Scarcella deserve continuing credit for making the Tapestry series so wonderful to create materials for—their support and kind words are always appreciated.

And ultimately, thanks always to Michael Smith. Nothing more needs to be said.

M.E. Sokolik
University of California
Berkeley, California USA

CONTENTS

Getting Started

1

CHAPTER

*F*irst impressions are very important. That's why getting started in writing can seem so difficult—we want to make a good first impression. However, when the first words aren't perfect, it's easy to become frustrated and give up too early.

This chapter will provide you with some strategies and techniques for getting started. Not all of them may work for you, but don't dismiss any of these techniques and strategies until you've tried them at least twice.

> **Think about . . .**
> What strategies do you use when you write?
> How do you get started?
> Where do you do your best writing?

BRAINSTORMING

Brainstorming is an easy and popular technique for getting started. You can brainstorm alone, with a partner, or with a group of friends or classmates. You can brainstorm aloud, on paper, or in your head.

Brainstorming is what it sounds like—creating a "storm" of ideas in your head. Storms aren't slow, logical events that stop to think and correct themselves. They move quickly. You should, too.

Imagine you are assigned to write an essay that describes the effect an important historical event has had on your life. If you are working alone, start listing all your ideas. If you're working in a group, keep talking and asking questions, writing them down as you discuss them. Start by making a list of any important historical events that have occurred in your lifetime. Include elections, wars, discoveries, or anything else that became a news event. Then shorten your list by eliminating any selections that don't interest you much or that you don't remember clearly. Your list should now include a few potential writing topics. Keep your list for future reference.

LEARNING STRATEGY

Managing Your Learning: When freewriting, don't think about organization, spelling, or grammar—just keep writing.

FREEWRITING

Freewriting is another technique for generating writing ideas. This technique was developed by Peter Elbow, who explains this method in the following essay.

LEARNING STRATEGY

Forming Concepts: Gathering information from classmates can give you valuable ideas for your writing.

FREEWRITING

by Peter Elbow

The most effective way I know to improve your writing is to do freewriting exercises regularly. At least three times a week. They are sometimes called "automatic writing," "babbling," or "jabbering" exercises. The idea is simply to write for ten minutes (later on, perhaps fifteen or twenty). Don't stop for anything. Go quickly without rushing. Never stop to look back, to cross something out, to wonder how to spell something, to wonder what word or thought to use, or to think about what you are doing. If you can't think of a word or a spelling, just use a squiggle or else write, "I can't think of it." Just put down something. The easiest thing is just to put down whatever is in your mind. If you get stuck it's fine to write "I can't think what to say, I can't think what to say" as many times as you want, or repeat the last word you wrote over and over again; or anything else. The only requirement is that you *never* stop.

What happens to a freewriting exercise is important. It must be a piece of writing which, even if someone reads it, doesn't send any ripples back to you. It is like writing something and putting it in a bottle in the sea. The teacherless class helps your writing by providing maximum feedback. Freewritings help you by providing no feedback at all. When I assign one, I invite the writer to let me read it. But I also tell him to keep it if he prefers. I read it quickly and make no comments at all and I do not speak with him about it. The main thing is that a freewriting must never be evaluated in any way; in fact there must be no discussion or comment at all.

Here is an example of a fairly coherent exercise (sometimes they are very incoherent, which is fine):

> I think I'll write what's on my mind, but the only thing on my mind right now is what to write for ten minutes. I've never done this before and I'm not prepared in any way—the sky is cloudy today, how's that? now I'm afraid I won't be able to think of what to write when I get to the end of the sentence—well, here I am at the end of the sentence—here I am again, again, again, again, at least I'm still writing—Now I ask is there some reason to be happy that I'm still writing—ah yes! Here comes the question again—What am I getting out of this? What point is there in it? It's almost obscene to always ask it but I seem to question everything that way and I was gonna say something else pertaining to that but I got so busy writing down the first part that I forgot what I was leading into. This is kind of fun oh don't stop writing—cars and trucks speeding by somewhere out the window, pens clittering across people's papers. The sky is cloudy—is it symbolic that I should be mentioning it? Huh? I dunno. Maybe I should try colors, blue, red, dirty words— wait a minute—no can't do that, orange, yellow, arm tired, green pink violent magenta lavender red brown black green—now that I can't think of any more colors—just about done—relief? maybe.

Threads

Born in New York, Peter Elbow is a professor of English at the University of Massachusetts at Amherst. He has taught writing at a number of universities and is well-known for his expertise on writing.

Threads

This selection comes from a longer work called *The Teacherless Class*. This title refers to students' taking responsibility for their own learning.

Freewriting may seem crazy, but actually it makes simple sense. Think of the difference between speaking and writing. Writing has the advantage of permitting more editing. But that's its downfall, too. Almost everybody interposes a massive and complicated series of editings between the time words start to be born into consciousness and when they finally come off the end of the pencil or typewriter onto the page. This is partly because schooling makes us obsessed with the "mistakes" we make in writing. Many people are constantly thinking about spelling and grammar as they try to write. I am always thinking about the awkwardness, wordiness, and general mushiness of my natural verbal product as I try to write down words.

But it's not just "mistakes" or "bad writing" we edit as we write. We also edit unacceptable thoughts and feelings, as we do in speaking. In writing there is more time to do it so the editing is heavier: when speaking, there's someone right there waiting for a reply and he'll get bored or think we're crazy if we don't come out with *something.* Most of the time in speaking, we settle for the catch-as-catch-can way in which the words tumble out. In writing, however, there's a chance to try to get them right. But the opportunity to get them right is a terrible burden: you can work for two hours trying to get a paragraph "right" and discover it's not right at all. And then give up.

Editing, *in itself,* is not the problem. Editing is usually necessary if we want to end up with something satisfactory. The problem is that editing goes on *at the same time* as producing. The editor is, as it were, constantly looking over the shoulder of the producer and constantly fiddling with what he's doing while he's in the middle of trying to do it. No wonder the producer gets nervous, jumpy, inhibited, and finally can't be coherent. It's an unnecessary burden to try to think of words and also worry at the same time whether they're the right words.

The main thing about freewriting is that it is *nonediting.* It is an exercise in bringing together the process of producing words and putting them down on the page. Practiced regularly, it undoes the ingrained habit of editing at the same time you are trying to produce. It will make writing less blocked because words will come more easily. You will use up more paper, but chew up fewer pencils.

Next time you write, notice how often you stop yourself from writing down something you were going to write down. Or else cross it out after it's written. "Naturally," you say. "It wasn't any good." But think for a moment about the occasions when you spoke well. Seldom was it because you first got the beginning just right. Usually it was a matter of a halting or even garbled beginning, but you kept going and your speech finally became coherent and even powerful. There is a lesson here for writing: trying to get the beginning just right is a formula for failure—and probably a secret tactic to make yourself give up writing. Make some words, whatever they are, and then grab hold of that line and reel in as hard as you can. Afterwards you can throw away lousy beginnings and make new ones. This is the quickest way to get into good writing.

The habit of compulsive, premature editing doesn't just make writing hard. It also makes writing dead. Your voice is damped out by all the interruptions, changes, and hesitations between the consciousness and the page. In your natural way of producing words there is a sound, a texture, a rhythm—a voice—which is the main source of power in your writing. I don't know how it works, but this voice is the force that will make a reader listen to you, the energy that drives the meanings through his thick skull. Maybe you don't *like* your voice; maybe people have made fun of it. But it's the only voice you've got. It's your only source of power. You better get back into it, no matter what you think of it. If you keep writing in it, it may change into something you like better. But if you abandon it, you'll likely never have a voice and never be heard.

Freewritings are vacuums. Gradually you will begin to carry over into your regular writing some of the voice, force, and connectedness that creep into those vacuums.

Remembering New Material: Discussing your reading with classmates will help you understand and learn new ideas.

For Group Discussion

ABOUT THE CONTENT

1. Why is freewriting an important technique, according to Elbow?
2. Do you agree with Elbow that freewriting makes "simple sense"? What is your opinion of not getting feedback (teacher response) on your writing? Why do you think Elbow recommends no feedback on freewriting?
3. What are both the problems and advantages associated with editing?
4. What does Elbow mean by "nonediting" and "premature editing"? How can you avoid these problems?
5. What is "voice" in writing?

ABOUT THE WRITING

1. How would you describe Elbow's "voice" in this essay? What type of style does he use to convey his message?
2. Elbow uses the second person "you" in this writing. What effect does it have on the reader?

Ready to Write

Use Elbow's instructions and freewrite (*without stopping*) for 10 minutes, about any topic you want.

QUICKWRITING

Throughout this book, you will be asked to respond to reading or other ideas through a technique called "quickwriting." Quickwriting is similar to freewriting, except this book or your instructor will suggest a topic for quickwriting. All the other guidelines are the same as for freewriting: keep writing, don't worry about spelling, punctuation, or grammar. Continue to write and generate ideas. You can edit and revise later, if you want to develop your ideas further.

Ready to Write

Review the list you produced in the brainstorming activity on page 2 and choose one of the ideas you listed. Write about your memory of that event. Let your mind roam freely; write down any thought or reaction to that event.

Looping

Looping is a technique that uses the products of your freewriting or quickwriting. In looping, start with a piece of freewriting or quickwriting. Then, identify an idea or passage in the writing that interests you and start writing from that point. Just as you did in the first piece of writing, write nonstop for five or ten minutes again. Repeat this process as many times as you want, and gradually a more focused piece of writing will emerge.

EXAMPLE   The following quickwrite and looping exercises were written by student Vivien Tso. Tso chose the topic of the Tiananmen Square uprising of 1989 from her brainstorming list. First, she quickwrote for 10 minutes. Then, she selected the underlined phrase as a starting point for a second quickwrite, and wrote for another five minutes.

The Tiananmen Square event had a significant influence on my life. This event embarrassed not only China but also the Chinese who live in other countries. China is such a huge and rich country. It is full of valuable natural resources and lands. It is a shame that the Communists are not using this great advantage. <u>The people are so scattered, everyone thinks only for themselves, not caring for others</u>. I wish that one day Communism will let China become a strong country. I can't think of anything to write anymore. My dad always talks about politics, telling us about the Chinese government. He was astonished by the Tiananmen Square event. He had always thought that China was a hopeless country. But since the Tiananmen Square event, it changed his perspective toward China. His hopes are increasing every day.

<u>Looping:</u>

<u>The people are so scattered, everyone thinks only for themselves, not caring for others</u>. Rich people degrade the poor, while at the same time the rich are taking money from the poor. They do not value each other. What else is there to say? My mother went to China once. I grew up in Hong Kong.

Ready to Write

Reread the passage you wrote in the quickwrite exercise on this page. Choose one passage or phrase that contains an idea you would like to pursue. Underline it. Then, quickwrite for another five minutes, using that idea as your starting point. When you finish, repeat the process as many times as you need until you have a piece of writing that you are satisfied with—something that you could develop into an essay.

Word-Mapping

Another way to explore a topic is to start with a thought or word and produce a "word-map," which is a diagram that illustrates the relationships between ideas.

Take a large piece of unlined paper. Write your topic in the center, and then draw a circle or box around it. Write the major elements of the topic in the space around it, and circle or box each one. Draw arrows from your topic to each of the subtopics. Then, working outward from each subtopic, write the main points about each.

Feel free to "associate" any ideas you want; they don't have to be simple facts or information. Your feelings, reactions, and memories, are all parts of the map. Ms. Tso's wordmap is shown in the figure below.

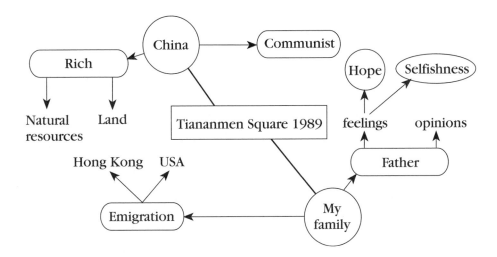

LEARNING STRATEGY

Remembering New Material: Reviewing helps you remember what you have learned.

For Discussion

You've now experimented with several invention techniques. Discuss or write about the following questions:

1. Which invention strategy worked best for you? Why?
2. Which was less effective? Explain.
3. Do you have your own invention technique that wasn't described in this chapter? Explain your technique to your classmates.

A journal, or any kind of notebook in which you keep your personal writing, is a good place to keep your different writing "experiments." In a writer's journal, you can jot down your thoughts on any subject matter, at any time. You can be creative, analytical, even angry, if you want. A writer's journal can help you develop ideas which you later turn into polished pieces of writing.

In the following article, Lois Rosenthal talks to writer May Sarton about Sarton's journals.

MAY SARTON
by Lois Rosenthal

This passage—the entry for one entire day in *Journal of a Solitude*—is an excellent example of the way May Sarton looks at life:

A gray day . . . but strangely enough, a gray day makes the bunches of daffodils in the house have a particular radiance, a kind of white light. From my bed this morning I could look through at a bunch in the big room, in that old Dutch blue-and-white drug jar, and they glowed. I went out before seven in my pajamas, because it looked like rain, and picked a sampler of twenty-five different varieties. It was worth getting up early, because the first thing I saw was a scarlet tanager a few feet away on a lilac bush—stupendous sight! There is no scarlet so vivid, no black so black.

The mystical quality Sarton gives to what she sees around her moves readers of her journals to deluge her with letters telling her how much they identify with her feelings. As Sarton stops to revel in the beauty of a sunrise, as she is comforted by the warmth of a cat nestled next to her in bed during a worrisome night, she is able to propel these feelings straight to the heart of people who read her work. Then readers see their worlds as May Sarton sees hers—as poetry. She writes:

Keeping a journal is much harder than it looks. I know that I have underrated its form compared to the novel and poetry and even the memoir, which is distilled, but there's no doubt it does have a discipline of its own. For any writer who wants to keep a journal, remember to be alive to everything, not just to what you're feeling, but also to your pets, to flowers, to what you are reading.

Remember to write about what you are seeing every day, and if you are going to hold the reader's interest, you must write very well. And what does writing well mean? It means seeing very well, seeing in a totally original way.

Look at the bowl of irises on the table in front of me. Five different people who are asked to draw them would produce five totally different works of art, which is good. In the same way, journal writers must be just as honest in what they see because it's freshness that matters. Keeping a journal is exciting because it gives a certain edge to the ordinary things in life.

Let's use another example. Say you've burned something in a pot, and you are standing at the sink scrubbing it. What comes to your mind as you are doing this? What does it mean to you in a funny way? Are you angry because you burn pots all too often? You can rage against the fact that it seems to be women who are mostly having to scrub pots, or you can ask yourself why you are bothering about this pot anyway. Why not throw it away if you can afford to get another? Is there something wrong with you that you are so compulsive you must try to clean something that is really beyond repair?

Keeping a journal helps you get in touch with your own feelings. I think that's why I started the first one. I was in a depression when I began *Journal of a Solitude;* I was in the middle of a very unhappy love affair, and writing was my way of handling things.

But a writer must always be perfectly honest. That's the key to people wanting to read a journal and that ingredient always astonishes me. When I've written things I felt were awfully weird and that no one would agree with, those are the very things that have made people say, 'you know, that's just how I feel.'

My advice to any writer is never think of the effect of what you are doing while you are doing it. Don't project to a possible audience while you are writing. Hold on to your idea and get it down, and then maybe there'll be an audience, and maybe there won't. But have the courage to write whatever your dream is for yourself.

For Group Discussion

ABOUT THE CONTENT

1. Why does Sarton say that writing in a journal is much harder than one might think?
2. Why does Sarton think that journal writing is exciting?
3. Summarize Sarton's advice for journal writers. Do you think it is good advice? Why or why not?

ABOUT THE WRITING

Since this is part of an interview, rather than a written essay, what differences do you see between this and the Elbow essay?

Quickwrite

Take Sarton's advice. Write what you see right now. Look around the room, and write about it in meaningful detail. Paint a picture for your audience. Write this in your journal if you are keeping one.

Each chapter ends with an "Additional Reading." These readings expand upon the issues raised in each chapter. Some of the discussion questions that follow each additional reading will ask you to relate the ideas in the new reading to those found in the chapter.

ACCEPT OURSELVES

by Natalie Goldberg

I tell students, "Don't throw out your writing. Keep it in a notebook." High-school students especially seem to ball up sheets of paper on their desks as they write. Sometimes I stop and unball one of the papers. Bill's had a date, then his full name scrawled in the upper left-hand corner, then "I remember my mother's"—and that was it. A whole white page with blue lines wasted. I looked down at his notebook, at the page he was working on: Date and name in the upper left-hand corner, then "I remember my mother's hat." Nothing different but the word *hat*. The crumpled paper was his hesitation. My guess is if I hadn't walked by and bent low and whispered in his ear, "Keep going. You're doing fine. Don't cross out. Don't think," another sheet of paper—the one he was working on—would also be crumpled.

I say keep your writing in notebooks rather than on separate sheets of paper or in looseleaf binders because you are less likely to tear out, throw out, or lose those written pages. I say this not so much because I am concerned about the loss of a particular writing—we are all capable of lots of writing—but because it is another practice in accepting the whole mind. Keeping in one notebook the good and bad writing—no, don't even think *good* and *bad;* think instead of writing where you were present or not, present and connected to your words and thoughts—is another chance to allow all kinds of writing to exist side by side, as though your notebook were Big Mind accepting it all. When you reread a notebook and if it has all of your writing, then you have a better chance to study your mind, to observe its ups and downs, as if the notebook were a graph.

We need to learn to accept our minds. Believe me, for writing, it is all we have. It would be nice if I could have Mark Twain's mind, but I don't. Mark Twain is Mark Twain. Natalie Goldberg is Natalie Goldberg. What does Natalie Goldberg think? The truth is I'm boring some of the time. I even think about rulers, wood desks, algebra problems. I wonder why the hell my mother gave me tuna fish every day for lunch in high school. Then zoom, like a bright cardinal on a gray day, something brilliant flashes through my mind, and for a moment I'm turned upside down. Just for a moment, then the sky is gray again for another half hour or a day or eight pages of writing in my notebook. In rereading your notebook and keeping all your writing in it, you get an opportunity to study your mind. Somehow in seeing the movement of your mind through writing, you become less attached to your thoughts, less critical of them.

We have to accept ourselves in order to write. Now none of us does that fully; few of us do it even halfway. Don't wait for one hundred percent acceptance of yourself before you write, or even eight percent acceptance. Just write. The process of writing is an activity that teaches us about acceptance.

"What did you do for your summer vacation?" That one September long ago my eighth-grade teacher asked my English class to write about this. I began with "I went." Then I thought, "Oh, Nat, can't you think of a better word than *I* to begin with and *went!* Write a better verb." I crossed out "I went." I wrote "She rode." I crossed it out. I began again. "The family visited," then "This summer," then "This past summer," then "Thinking back." Each one was crossed out. What did the first two words matter? I could have rewritten them later anyway, but I should have gotten on with it.

Next I wrote that I played softball all summer. Well, that was a lie. Not once all summer did I play softball, but I thought that was what normal kids did in the summer, so that's what I wrote. I thought it was what the teacher wanted to hear. I also managed to add, "It was fun. I had an interesting summer. It was nice."

Right off, first rule: Don't use *nice, interesting, fun* in your writing. It doesn't say anything.

The truth is, "What I did last summer" could be an interesting topic. (Uh-oh! I just used *interesting* in the last sentence after saying not to. We can also break all rules. It's good to know them, but do what you want with them. After all, who made up the rule anyway? I did in the last paragraph a moment ago as I wrote.) The problem is no one in school ever taught us how to enter a topic or gave us permission to write what really happened. "My father sat at the dinner table in his underwear, drinking beer and swatting mosquitoes, while I sat on the kitchen floor trying to put together a two-thousand-piece jigsaw puzzle of the island of Hawaii. I mostly ate Oreos. My brother had a splinter in his thumb that he got from the back screen door. No one could get it out and it became infected, swelled like an elephant. And my mother dyed her hair red and snuck out each night with a man named Charlie after my father got so drunk he couldn't see."

Write the truth. And remember what I whispered in that kid's ear at the beginning of the chapter: "Keep going. You're doing fine. Don't think. Don't cross out." Develop a "sweetheart" inside yourself who whispers in your ear to encourage you. Let's face it. You who have created the editor are also capable of creating the sweetheart, that kind coach who thinks what you do is fine. "But what I do isn't fine." Says who? the editor? Have you murdered anyone in the last day, week, month, year, decade? Probably not. Then don't worry about it. Give yourself a break. You're probably a really fine person. Call up the sweetheart and let him or her give you some compliments.

For Group Discussion

ABOUT THE CONTENT

1. What does Goldberg mean when she says "think . . . of writing where you were present or not"?
2. Goldberg says twice, "Don't think." How do you interpret this advice?
3. Summarize Goldberg's attitude toward rules. Do you agree?
4. What is the relationship between Goldberg's "sweetheart" and Elbow's "editor"?

ABOUT THE WRITING

1. How would you describe Goldberg's writing style? What phrases or sentences show examples of this style?
2. Why does Goldberg include stories from her own childhood? How might different examples affect this essay? For example, what if she had written about being a graduate student? Or climbing a mountain?

Quickwrite

Goldberg claims that the topic "What did you do for your summer vacation?" could be an interesting one. Accept her challenge—write an interesting story about what you did during your last vacation. Be honest, don't use words like "nice" or "interesting," and don't cross out.

Reading for
Writing

2

CHAPTER

When you read as a writer, you are taking a more active role in the reading process. Instead of sitting back, relaxing, and letting a story unfold, you are thinking, questioning, and challenging the author. You are also considering how the author uses language—what words did she or he choose, and why?

Threads

'Tis the good reader that makes the good book.

Ralph Waldo Emerson

Think about . . .

What do you like to read?
Where is your favorite place to read?
When is the best time of day for you to read?

LEARNING STRATEGY

Remembering New Material: Using mnemonic (memory) devices, such as initials of words, helps you remember lists of material.

Before you begin a reading assignment, use the following READ-IT checklist to prepare to get the most out of your reading.

TABLE 2.1 READ-IT CHECKLIST
Résumé: What do you know about the author? Are you familiar with his or her work? What expertise does this writer have to write about the topic?
Experience: What do you know about the topic? What would you like to learn?
Appearance: How is the writing organized? Look at subheadings, figures, tables, or other important features.
Decision: Why are you reading this piece of writing? Is it for discussion? For a writing assignment? To study for an examination? Just for fun?
Intention: What will the main point of the text be? How can you tell?
Title: What does the title mean, in your opinion?

Underlining, highlighting, and notetaking can aid your understanding of a text. But remember, the main activity is *reading;* other activities should be secondary.

Here are some techniques to try while you are reading:

- Put a ✓ in the margin near any word you don't understand. Don't stop and look it up yet; keep reading.
- Put a ? in the margin near passages that are confusing or that you want to read again.
- Put a ! in the margin next to any idea you react strongly to—either by agreeing or disagreeing with it.
- Highlight or underline only key words or main points.
- After you complete your reading, review your marks and write a paragraph that summarizes the main points, interesting ideas, and your reactions. Look up words now if you need to.

The following paragraph, taken from the reading at the end of Chapter 1 (page 10), shows a sample of this technique.

> ✓ I say keep your writing in notebooks rather than on separate sheets of paper or in looseleaf binders because you are less likely to tear out, throw out, or lose those written pages. I say this not so much because I am concerned about the loss of a particular writing—we are all capable of lots of writing—but because it is another practice in <u>accepting the whole mind</u>. Keeping in one notebook the good and bad writing—no, don't even think *good* and *bad;* think instead of writing where you were present or not, ! present and connected to your words and thoughts—is another chance to allow all kinds of writing to exist side by side, as though your notebook were
> ? Big Mind accepting it all. When you reread a notebook and if it has all of your writing, then you have a better chance to study your mind, to observe its ups and downs, as if the notebook were a graph.

—Natalie Goldberg, "Accept Ourselves"

In the following reading, Lin Yu-T'ang, a Chinese scholar, expresses his opinion about reading. As you read this essay, use the READ-IT checklist as well as the highlighting and notetaking system to help you read actively.

LEARNING STRATEGY

Forming Concepts: Reading without looking up each new word helps you to concentrate on the main ideas.

Threads

Lin Yu-T'ang was born in 1895 in China. He was educated at Harvard University in the United States and at the University of Leipzig in Germany. He wrote novels as well as nonfiction, and he is well known for his writing, which explains China to readers from other countries. He was a professor at Peking National University as well as the chancellor of Nanyang University in Singapore. He died in 1976.

THE ART OF READING

by Lin Yu-T'ang

Reading or the enjoyment of books has always been regarded among the charms of a cultured life and is respected and envied by those who rarely give themselves that privilege. This is easy to understand when we compare the difference between the life of a man who does no reading and that of a man who does. The man who has not the habit of reading is imprisoned in his immediate world, in respect to time and space. His life falls into a set routine; he is limited to contact and conversation with a few friends and acquaintances, and he sees only what happens in his immediate neighborhood. From this prison there is no escape. But the moment he takes up a book, he immediately enters a different world, and if it is a good book, he is immediately put in touch with one of the best talkers of the world. This talker leads him on and carries him into a different country or a different age, or unburdens to him some of his personal regrets, or discusses with him some special line or aspect of life that the reader knows nothing about. An ancient author puts him in communion with a dead spirit of long ago, and as he reads along, he begins to imagine what that ancient author looked like and what type of person he was. Both Mencius and Ssema Ch'ien, China's greatest historian, have expressed the same idea. Now to be able to live two hours out of twelve in a different world and take one's thoughts off the claims of the immediate present is, of course, a privilege to be envied by people shut up in their bodily prison. Such a change of environment is really similar to travel in its psychological effect.

The best formula for the object of reading, in my opinion, was stated by Huang Shanku, a Sung poet and friend of Su Tungp'o. He said, "A scholar who hasn't read anything for three days feels that *his talk has no flavor* (becomes insipid), *and his own face becomes hateful to look at* (in the mirror)." What he means, of course, is that reading gives a man a certain charm and flavor, which is the entire object of reading, and only reading with this object can be called an art. One doesn't read to "improve one's mind," because when one begins to think of improving his mind, all the pleasure of reading is gone. He is the type of person who says to himself: "I must read Shakespeare, and I must read Sophocles, and I must read the entire Five-foot Shelf of Dr. Eliot, so I can become an educated man." I'm sure that man will never become educated. He will force himself one evening to read Shakespeare's *Hamlet* and come away, as if from a bad dream, with no greater benefit than that he is able to say that he had "read" *Hamlet.* Anyone who reads a book with a sense of obligation does not understand the art of reading. This type of reading with a business purpose is in no way different from a senator's reading up on files and reports before he makes a speech. It is asking for business advice and information, and not reading at all.

Reading for the cultivation of personal charm and appearance and flavor in speech is then, according to Huang, the only admissible kind of reading. This charm of appearance must evidently be interpreted as something other than physical beauty. What Huang means by "hateful to look at" is not physical ugliness. There are ugly faces that have a fascinating charm and beautiful faces that are insipid to look at. I have among my Chinese friends one whose head is shaped like a bomb and yet who is nevertheless always a pleasure to see. The most beautiful face among Western authors, so far as I have seen them in pictures, was that of G. K. Chesterton. There was such a diabolical conglomeration of mustache, glasses, fairly bushy eyebrows, and knitted lines where the eyebrows met. One felt there were a vast number of ideas playing about inside that forehead, ready at any time to burst out from those quizzically penetrating eyes. That is what Huang would call a beautiful face, a face not made up by powder and rouge, but by the sheer force of thinking. As for flavor of speech, it all depends on one's way of reading. Whether one has "flavor" or not in his talk, depends on his method of reading. If a reader gets the flavor of books, he will show that flavor in his conversations, and if he has flavor in his conversations, he cannot help also having a flavor in his writing.

Hence I consider flavor or taste as the key to all reading. It necessarily follows that taste is selective and individual, like the taste for food. The most hygienic way of eating is, after all, eating what one likes, for then one is sure of his digestion. In reading as in eating, what is one man's meat may be another's poison. A teacher cannot force his pupils to like what he likes in reading, and a parent cannot expect his children to have the same tastes as himself. And if the reader has no taste for what he reads, all the time is wasted. As Yüan Chunglang says, "You can leave the books that you don't like alone, *and let other people read them.*"

There can be, therefore, no books that one absolutely must read. For our intellectual interests grow like a tree or flow like a river. So long as there is proper sap, the tree will grow anyhow, and so long as there is fresh current from the spring, the water will flow. When water strikes a granite cliff, it just goes around it; when it finds itself in a pleasant low valley, it stops and meanders there a while; when it finds itself in a deep mountain pond, it is content to stay there; when it finds itself traveling over rapids, it hurries forward. Thus, without any effort or determined aim, it is sure of reaching the sea some day. There are no books in this world that everybody must read, but only books that a person must read at a certain time in a given place under given circumstances and at a given period of his life. I rather think that reading, like matrimony, is determined by fate or *yinyüan.* Even if there is a certain book that everyone must read, like the Bible, there is a time for it. When one's thoughts and experience have not reached a certain point for reading a masterpiece, the masterpiece will leave only a bad flavor on his palate. Confucius said, "When one is fifty, one may read *The Book of Changes,*" which means that one should not read it at forty-five. The extremely mild flavor of Confucius' own sayings in the *Analects* and his mature wisdom cannot be appreciated until one becomes mature himself.

I regard the discovery of one's favorite author as the most critical event in one's intellectual development. There is such a thing as the affinity of spirits, and among the authors of ancient and modern times, one must try to find an author whose spirit is akin with his own. Only in this way can one get any real good out of reading. One has to be independent and search out his masters. Who is one's favorite author, no one can tell, probably not even the man himself. It is like love at first sight. The reader cannot be told to love this one or that one, but when he has found the author he loves, he knows it himself by a kind of instinct. We have such famous cases of discoveries of authors. Scholars seem to have lived in different ages, separated by centuries, and yet their modes of thinking and feeling were so akin that their coming together across the pages of a book was like a person finding his own image. In Chinese phraseology, we speak of these kindred spirits as reincarnations of the same soul, as Su Tungp'o was said to be a reincarnation of Chuangtse or T'ao Yüanming, and Yüan Chunglang was said to be the reincarnation of Su Tungp'o. Su Tungp'o said that when he first read Chuangtse, he felt as if all the time since his childhood he had been thinking the same things and taking the same views himself. When Yüan Chunglang discovered one night Hsü Wench'ang, a contemporary unknown to him, in a small book of poems, he jumped out of bed and shouted to his friend, and his friend began to read it and shout in turn, and then they both read and shouted again until their servant was completely puzzled. George Eliot described her first reading of Rousseau as an electric shock. Nietzsche felt the same thing about Schopenhauer, but Schopenhauer was a peevish master and Nietzsche was a violent-tempered pupil, and it was natural that the pupil later rebelled against the teacher.

It is only this kind of reading, this discovery of one's favorite author, that will do one any good at all. Like a man falling in love with his sweetheart at first sight, everything is right. She is of the right height, has the right face, the right color of hair, the right quality of voice, and the right way of speaking and smiling. This author is not something that a young man needs to be told about by his teacher. The author is just right for him; his style, his taste, his point of view, his mode of thinking, are all right. And then the reader proceeds to devour every word and every line that the author writes, and because there is a spiritual affinity, he absorbs and readily digests everything. The author has cast a spell over him, and he is glad to be under the spell, and in time his own voice and manner and way of smiling and way of talking become like the author's own. Thus he truly steeps himself in his literary lover and derives from these books sustenance for his soul. After a few years, the spell is over and he grows a little tired of this lover and seeks for new literary lovers, and after he has had three or four lovers and completely eaten them up, he emerges as an author himself. There are many readers who never fall in love, like many young men and women who flirt around and are incapable of forming a deep attachment to a particular person. They can read any and all authors, and they never amount to anything.

Such a conception of the art of reading completely precludes the idea of reading as a duty or an obligation. In China, one often encourages students to "study bitterly." There was a famous scholar who studied bitterly and who stuck an awl in his calf when he fell asleep while studying at night. There was another scholar who had a maid stand by his side as he was studying at night, to wake him up every time he fell asleep. This was nonsensical. If one has a book lying before him and falls asleep while some wise ancient author is talking to him, he should just go to bed. No amount of sticking an awl in his calf or of shaking him up by a maid will do him any good. Such a man has lost all sense of pleasure of reading. Scholars who are worth anything at all never know what is called "a hard grind" or what "bitter study" means. They merely love books and read on because they cannot help themselves.

What, then, is the true art of reading? The simple answer is to just take up a book and read when the mood comes. To be thoroughly enjoyed, reading must be entirely spontaneous.

LEARNING STRATEGY

Personalizing: Review learning tasks, and make them fit your own style when possible.

For Group Discussion

Before discussing the following questions, discuss with your classmates or write about the results of using the READ-IT checklist and notetaking system on page 14.

- Which techniques worked best for you?
- Which didn't you find useful? How would you improve them?
- Which passages were confusing or interesting?
- What techniques have you used in the past? What advantages or disadvantages do they have?

ABOUT THE CONTENT

1. What, according to the author, should be the main reason for reading? If you agree with him, how can you justify doing reading assignments for your courses?
2. According to the author, what is an important advantage that a reader has, compared to a nonreader?

3. Do you agree that reading newspapers is not really reading? Why or why not?

4. Why is it important for readers to discover their favorite authors? How can this discovery help you?

5. What is the meaning of the phrase "bitter study"? What does it reveal about cultural values?

ABOUT THE WRITING

1. Identify at least two metaphors or similes used by the author. Why does he use these devices?

2. The author alludes (or refers) to several other authors. What effect does this have on you as a reader? Why do writers use other writers' words?

Quickwrite

Have you had a favorite author at any time (in any language)? Describe that author's writing and explain why it was so important to you.

 **RESPONDING TO READING**

Responding to reading not only helps you think about an author's ideas, it also helps you formulate ideas for your own writing. You can take different approaches to response—for example, you can *analyze* a reading or you can *react* to it. When you *analyze* a text, you try to explain its meaning. When you *react* to a text, you describe how it made you feel. However, in both cases, asking yourself questions will help you to respond. Here is a list of questions you *might* ask. (But don't respond just by answering these questions. Use them only as a starting point).

Analyzing
- What was the author's main point? Was it proven? How?
- Was the author biased in her or his presentation? Find an example in the text that shows this bias.
- Was the author well-informed? How do you know this?
- Why did the author write the article or story?

Reacting
- Did you enjoy the reading? Why or why not?
- Were you confused by any part of the essay or story? Identify the source of your confusion.
- What did you learn? What would you still like to learn?
- Would you recommend this reading to your friends? Why or why not?

Keep your responses in either your writer's journal or in a separate "reader's journal," which is described in the next section.

As you read in Chapter 1, you can monitor your progress and thoughts about reading by keeping a journal. Your journal can be in any form—in a notebook, on a computer diskette, in a folder—whatever you or your teacher may decide. A reader's journal contains your responses to the reading you do. You can keep a reader's journal for your writing class alone, or for everything you read. Remember, the entries in your journal are important for their *ideas,* not their grammar or organization. Write your ideas down; if the time comes to complete a more formal piece of writing, you can edit it then. Part of the writing process is "thinking on paper."

Quickwrite

For your first entry in your reader's journal, respond to one of the essays you have read in this book (or anything else you've read recently). Write without stopping for 10 minutes. You may want to use the questions in the preceding section to help you get started.

ADDITIONAL READING

FOUR KINDS OF READING
by Donald Hall

Everywhere one meets the idea that reading is an activity desirable in itself. It is understandable that publishers and librarians—and even writers—should promote this assumption, but is strange that the idea should have general currency. People surround the idea of reading with piety and do not take into account the purpose of reading or the value of what is being read. Teachers and parents praise the child who reads, and praise themselves, whether the text be *The Reader's Digest* or *Moby Dick.* The advent of TV has increased the false values ascribed to reading, since TV provides a vulgar alternative. But this piety is silly; and most reading is no more cultural nor intellectual nor imaginative than shooting pool or watching *What's My Line.*

It is worth asking how the act of reading became something to value in itself, as opposed for instance to the act of conversation or the act of taking a walk. Mass literacy is a recent phenomenon, and I suggest that the aura which decorates reading is a relic of the importance of reading to our great-great-grandparents. Literacy used to be a mark of social distinction, separating a small portion of humanity from the rest. The farm laborer who was ambitious for his children did not daydream that they would become schoolteachers or doctors; he daydreamed that they would learn to read, and that a world would therefore open up to them in which they did not have to labor in the fields fourteen hours a day for six days a week in order to buy salt and cotton. On the next rank of society, ample time for reading meant that the reader was free from the necessity to spend most of his waking hours making a living. This sort of attitude shades into the contemporary man's boast of his wife's cultural activities. When he says that his wife is interested in books and music and pictures, he is not only enclosing the arts in a female world, he is saying that he is rich enough to provide her with the leisure to do nothing. Reading is an inactivity, and therefore a badge of social class. Of course, these reasons for the piety attached to reading are never acknowledged. They show themselves in the shape of our attitudes towards books; reading gives off an air of gentility.

It seems to me possible to name four kinds of reading, each with a characteristic manner and purpose. The first is reading for information—reading to learn about a trade, or politics, or how to accomplish something. We read a newspaper this way, or most textbooks, or directions on how to assemble a bicycle. With most of this material, the reader can learn to scan the page quickly, coming up with what he needs and ignoring what is irrelevant to him, like the rhythm of the sentence, or the play of metaphor. Courses in speed reading can help us read for this purpose, training the eye to jump quickly across the page. If we read the *New York Times* with the attention we should give a novel or a poem, we will have time for nothing else, and our mind will be cluttered with clichés and dead metaphor. Quick eye-reading is a necessity to anyone who wants to keep up with what's happening, or learn much of what has happened in the past. The amount of reflection, which interrupts and slows down the reading, depends on the material.

But it is not the same activity as reading literature. There ought to be another word. If we read a work of literature properly, we read slowly, and we *hear* all the words. If our lips do not actually move, it's only laziness. The muscles in our throat move, and come together when we see the word "squeeze." We hear the sounds so accurately that if a syllable is missing from a line of poetry we hear the lack, though we may not know what we are lacking. In prose we accept the rhythms, and hear the adjacent sounds. We also register a track of feeling through the metaphors and associations of words. Careless writing prevents this sort of attention, and becomes offensive. But the great writers reward it. Only by the full exercise of our powers to receive language can we absorb their intelligence and their imagination. This kind of reading goes through the ear—though the eye takes in the print, and decodes it into sound—to the throat and the understanding, and it can never be quick. It is slow and sensual, a deep pleasure that begins with touch and ends with the sort of comprehension that we associate with dream.

Too many intellectuals read in order to reduce images to abstractions. One reads philosophy slowly, as if it were literature, but much time must be spent with the eyes turned away from the page, reflecting on the text. To read literature this way is to turn it into something it is not—to concepts clothed in character, or philosophy sugar-coated. I think that most literary intellectuals read this way, including brighter professors of English, with the result that they miss literature completely, and concern themselves with a minor discipline called the history of ideas. I remember a course in Chaucer at my University in which the final exam required the identification of a hundred or more fragments of Chaucer, none as long as a line. If you like poetry, and read Chaucer through a couple of times slowly, you found yourself knowing them all. If you were a literary intellectual, well-informed about the great chain of being, chances are you had a difficult time. To read literature is to be intimately involved with the words on the page, and never to think of them as the embodiments of ideas which can be expressed in other terms. On the other

Threads

Moby Dick was written by Herman Melville in 1851. It is considered an American classic.

Threads

Geoffrey Chaucer (c. 1340–1400) wrote the *Canterbury Tales* sometime after 1387. These poems are considered to be among the most important writings in early English.

Threads

Johnny Carson was a popular late-night-television talk-show host from 1963 to 1993 in the United States.

Threads

The Valley of the Dolls was a popular novel in the 1960s, often criticized as being an example of a shallow, "soap-opera" type of writing. *Anna Karenina* was written by Leo Tolstoy between 1875 and 1877. It is considered a Russian classic and has been translated into many languages.

Threads

Virginia Woolf (1882–1941) was one of the first influential women writers in English. Her books include *To the Lighthouse* (1927) and *A Room of One's Own* (1929).

hand, intellectual writing—closer to mathematics on a continuum that has at its opposite pole lyric poetry—requires intellectual reading, which is slow because it is reflective and because the reader must pause to evaluate concepts.

But most of the reading which is praised for itself is neither literary nor intellectual. It is narcotic. Novels, stories, and biographies—historical sagas, monthly regurgitations of book clubs, four- and five-thousand word daydreams of magazines—these are the opium of the suburbs. The drug is not harmful except to the addict himself, and is no more injurious to him than Johnny Carson or a bridge club, but it is nothing to be proud of. This reading is the automated daydream, the mild trip of the housewife and the tired businessman, interested not in experience and feeling but in turning off the possibilities of experience and feeling. Great literature, if we read it well, opens us up to the world, and makes us more sensitive to it, as if we acquired eyes that could see through walls and ears that could hear the smallest sounds. But by narcotic reading, one can reduce great literature to the level of *The Valley of the Dolls*. One can read *Anna Karenina* passively and inattentively, and float down the river of lethargy as if one were reading a confession magazine: "I Spurned My Husband for a Count."

I think that everyone reads for narcosis occasionally, and perhaps most consistently in late adolescence, when great readers are born. I remember reading to shut the world out, away at school where I did not want to be; I invented a word for my disease: "bibliolepsy," on the analogy of narcolepsy. But after a while the books became a window on the world, and not a screen against it. This change doesn't always happen. I think that late adolescent narcotic reading accounts for some of the badness of English departments. As a college student, the boy loves reading and majors in English because he would be reading anyway. Deciding on a career, he takes up English teaching for the same reason. Then in graduate school he is trained to be a scholar, which is painful and irrelevant, and finds he must write papers and publish them to be a Professor—and at about this time he no longer requires reading for narcosis, and he is left with nothing but a Ph.D. and the prospect of fifty years of teaching literature; and he does not even like literature.

Narcotic reading survives the impact of television, because this type of reading has even less reality than melodrama; that is, the reader is in control: once the characters reach into the reader's feelings, he is able to stop reading, or glance away, or superimpose his own daydream. The trouble with television is that it embodies its own daydream. Literature is often valued precisely because of its distance from the tangible. Some readers prefer looking into the text of a play to seeing it performed. Reading a play, it is possible to stage it oneself by an imaginative act; but it is also possible to remove it from real people. Here is Virginia Woolf, who was lavish in her praise of the act of reading, talking about reading a play rather than seeing it: "Certainly there is a good deal to be said for reading *Twelfth Night* in the book if the book can be read in a garden, with no sound but the thud of an apple falling to the earth, or of the wind ruffling the branches of the trees." She sets her own stage; the play is called *Virginia Woolf Reads Twelfth Night in a Garden*. Piety moves into narcissism, and the high metaphors of Shakespeare's lines dwindle into the flowers of an English garden; actors in ruffles wither, while the wind ruffles branches.

For Group Discussion

ABOUT THE CONTENT

1. Why does Hall think leisure reading is a mark of a social class?
2. What are the four types of reading Hall describes? What are the characteristics of each type?
3. What is the meaning of the word Hall invented—"bibliolepsy"? How does this word fit into his philosophy of reading?
4. In what ways do you think Hall and Yu-T'ang would agree in their views of reading? In what ways would they disagree? Find examples in each of the readings to defend your answers.
5. Summarize Hall's attitude toward television.

ABOUT THE WRITING

1. Who is Hall addressing, in your opinion? What parts of this essay indicate who that audience is?
2. Both Hall and Yu-T'ang use many allusions to other authors. Is this effective? Is one more effective than the other?
3. Do you find any stereotypes of gender roles in this essay? Explain how Hall or Yu-T'ang might revise their language if they were to rewrite these essays today.

Quickwrite

What kind of writing do you do most? Do you have a feeling about reading like Hall's or Yu-T'ang's points of view? Explain.

The Writer's Intentions

You may already consider yourself a writer, or, you may believe that you will never be considered a writer. Perhaps you would like to be, but you think your English language skills are too weak. Whatever category you fall into, to write effectively you must first define the *purpose* behind your writing.

> **Think about ...**
>
> Why do you write?
> For whom do you like to write?
> What types of writing do you enjoy doing?

Think about the following list of possible purposes for writing.

- to share your special knowledge or experience with your readers
- to convince your readers to change their minds about a controversial topic
- to entertain your readers with humor or elegant writing
- to show what you've learned from your reading

What other purposes can you add to this list? Is it necessary to combine purposes sometimes?

In the following excerpt, Joan Didion explores some of her reasons for writing. As you read, remember to use the active reading techniques you learned in Chapter 2.

Threads

Joan Didion was born in Sacramento, California, in 1934. She received a B.A. in English from the University of California at Berkeley in 1956. She won a Vogue magazine's essay contest for young writers. She has written several books and screenplays, both on her own and with her husband.

LEARNING STRATEGY

Forming Concepts: Asking yourself questions before reading helps you to understand the material better. (Recall the READ-IT checklist on page 14.)

WHY I WRITE

by Joan Didion

Of course I stole the title for this talk, from George Orwell. One reason I stole it was that I like the sound of the words: Why I Write. There you have three short unambiguous words that share a sound, and the sound they share is this:

I
I
I

In many ways writing is the act of saying *I*, of imposing oneself upon other people, of saying *listen to me, see it my way, change your mind.* It's an aggressive, even a hostile act. You can disguise its aggressiveness all you want with veils of subordinate clauses and qualifiers and tentative subjunctives, with ellipses and evasions—with the whole manner of intimating rather than claiming, of alluding rather than stating—but there's no getting around the fact that setting words on paper is the tactic of a secret bully, an invasion, an imposition of the writer's sensibility on the reader's most private space.

Threads

George Orwell, author of *1984* and *Animal Farm* wrote an essay entitled "Why I Write" in 1946.

I stole the title not only because the words sounded right but they seem to sum up, in a no-nonsense way, all I have to tell you. Like many writers I have only this one "subject," this one "area": the act of writing. I can bring you no reports from any other front. I may have other interests: I am "interested," for example, in marine biology, but I don't flatter myself that you would come out to hear me talk about it. I am not a scholar. I am not in the least an intellectual, which is not to say that when I hear the word "intellectual" I reach for my gun, but only to say that I do not think in abstracts. During the years when I was an undergraduate at Berkeley I tried, with a kind of hopeless late-adolescent energy, to buy some temporary visa into the world of ideas, to forge for myself a mind that could deal with the abstract.

In short I tried to think. I failed. My attention veered inexorably back to the specific, to the tangible, to what was generally considered, by everyone I knew then and for that matter have known since, the peripheral. I would try to contemplate the Hegelian dialectic and would find myself concentrating instead on a flowering pear tree outside my window and the particular way the petals fell on my floor. I would try to read linguistic theory and would find myself wondering instead if the lights were on in the bevatron up the hill. When I say that I was wondering if the lights were on in the bevatron you might immediately suspect, if you deal in ideas at all, that I was registering the bevatron as a political symbol, thinking in shorthand about the military-industrial complex and its role in the university community, but you would be wrong. I was only wondering if the lights were on in the bevatron, and how they looked. A physical fact.

I had trouble graduating from Berkeley, not because of this inability to deal with ideas—I was majoring in English, and I could locate the house-and-garden imagery in *The Portrait of a Lady* as well as the next person, "imagery" being by definition the kind of specific that got my attention—but simply because I had neglected to take a course in Milton. For reasons which now sound baroque I needed a degree by the end of that summer, and the English department finally agreed, if I would come down from Sacramento every Friday and talk about the cosmology of *Paradise Lost,* to certify me proficient in Milton. I did this. Some Fridays I took the Greyhound bus, other Fridays I caught the Southern Pacific's City of San Francisco on the last leg of its intercontinental trip. I can no longer tell you whether Milton put the sun or the earth at the center of his universe in *Paradise Lost,* the central question of at least one century and a topic about which I wrote 10,000 words that summer, but I can still recall the exact rancidity of the butter in the City of San Francisco's dining car, and the way the tinted windows on the Greyhound bus cast the oil refineries around Carquinez Straits into a grayed and obscurely sinister light. In short my attention was always on the periphery, on what I could see and taste and touch, on the butter, and the Greyhound bus. During those years I was traveling on what I knew to be a very shaky passport, forged papers: I knew that I was no legitimate resident in any world of ideas. I knew I couldn't think. All I knew then was what I couldn't do. All I knew then was what I wasn't, and it took me some years to discover what I was.

Which was a writer.

By which I mean not a "good" writer or a "bad" writer but simply a writer, a person whose most absorbed and passionate hours are spent arranging words on pieces of paper. Had my credentials been in order I would never have become a writer. Had I been blessed with even limited access to my own mind there would have been no reason to write. I write entirely to find out what I'm thinking, what I'm looking at, what I see and what it means. What I want and what I fear. Why did the oil refineries around Carquinez Straits

Threads

Definition: A *bevatron* is a large accelerator used in physics research. It comes from the initials of the words <u>B</u>illion <u>E</u>lectron <u>V</u>olts Elec<u>tron</u>.

Threads

Georg Hegel (1770–1831) was a German philosopher.

John Milton (1608–1674) was an English writer who wrote *Paradise Lost* and *Paradise Regained.*

Threads

The Portrait of a Lady is a novel by author Henry James.

seems sinister to me in the summer of 1956? Why have the night lights in the bevatron burned in my mind for twenty years? *What is going on in these pictures in my mind?*

When I talk about pictures in my mind I am talking, quite specifically, about images that shimmer around the edges. There used to be an illustration in every elementary psychology book showing a cat drawn by a patient in varying stages of schizophrenia. This cat had a shimmer around it. You could see the molecular structure breaking down at the very edges of the cat: The cat became the background and the background the cat, everything interacting, exchanging ions. People on hallucinogens describe the same perception of objects. I'm not a schizophrenic, nor do I take hallucinogens, but certain images do shimmer for me. Look hard enough, and you can't miss the shimmer. It's there. You can't think too much about these pictures that shimmer. You just lie low and let them develop. You stay quiet. You don't talk to many people and you keep your nervous system from shorting out and you try to locate the cat in the shimmer, the grammar in the picture.

Just as I meant "shimmer" literally I mean "grammar" literally. Grammar is a piano I play by ear, since I seem to have been out of school the year the rules were mentioned. All I know about grammar is its infinite power. To shift the structure of a sentence alters the meaning of that sentence, as definitely and inflexibly as the position of a camera alters the meaning of the object photographed. Many people know about camera angles now, but not so many know about sentences. The arrangement of the words matters, and the arrangement you want can be found in the picture in your mind. The picture dictates the arrangement. The picture dictates whether this will be a sentence with or without clauses, a sentence that ends hard or a dying-fall sentence, long or short, active or passive. The picture tells you how to arrange the words and the arrangement of the words tells you, or tells me, what's going on in the picture. *Nota bene.*

It tells you.

You don't tell it.

Threads

Nota bene is an Italian phrase meaning "Note well."

For Group Discussion

ABOUT THE CONTENT

1. Why does Didion consider writing "an aggressive, even a hostile act"? Do you agree or disagree? Why?
2. What is the difference, according to the author, between a writer and an intellectual? Do you agree with her?
3. Is there a contradiction in Didion saying that "writing is a way of imposing oneself on other people" and her claim that she writes to find out what she means? Explain your answer.
4. Why does Didion write?

ABOUT THE WRITING

1. The first paragraph has a different tone from the rest of the excerpt. Can you identify it?

2. Didion states that she prefers "specifics," or concrete details. Can you find examples in this essay? What does concrete language do for a piece of writing?

3. Didion states that "To shift the structure of a sentence alters the meaning of that sentence, as definitely and inflexibly as the position of a camera alters the meaning of the object photographed." Can you give an example of how using two different grammatical structures to say the same thing alters the meaning?

Quickwrite

Choose one of the following topics:

a. Why do you write? Explain your reasons for writing—what you like about it, what you hate about it.

b. Respond to Didion's essay.

IDENTIFYING YOUR AUDIENCE

Who are you writing for?

Answering this question isn't as easy as it seems. Imagine you need $1,000 for tuition. You have three choices of people to borrow it from: your parents, your best friend (who has lots of money!), or the bank. If you wrote a letter to each of these people asking for the money, each letter would be different. In writing for this loan, you have considered your *audience.* If you wrote a letter to the bank that sounded like the letter to your best friend, it might receive a very negative reception. Similarly, your best friend might feel offended if you wrote in the official, formal style you would use when corresponding with a bank.

Consider the following three situations:

Situation A	Situation B	Situation C
Your history examination asks for a short essay in which you explain the effects of Christopher Columbus's voyage to the New World on the native Americans.	You disagree with the decision to shorten the hours at the school basketball court as a cost-cutting measure. You write two letters: one to the school newspaper and the other to the director of the recreation program.	You enter an essay contest sponsored by the Alumni Association. The topic of the essay is "The Most Influential Person in My Life." You will receive a scholarship if you win.

Who is your audience for each case? What is your purpose in writing in each situation?

Once you decide who your audience is, you must make some stylistic choices that will determine how to appeal to that audience. One of those choices (there are many, of course) is which *point of view* you are going to use. Your choice of point of view will affect your choice of pronouns. Table 4.1 shows the options in pronoun use and the effects each choice may have on your reader. It also suggests questions you should ask yourself when you make a choice.

TABLE 4.1 PRONOUN CHOICE

IF YOU CHOOSE . . .	YOUR READER MAY THINK:	YOU SHOULD ASK YOURSELF:
First person "I" *Example:* I believe the effect was negative.	The writer relies on his or her own experience and opinions.	Have I offered appropriate evidence? Do my own opinions and experiences matter to this piece of writing?
First person "We" *Example:* We must protest the new hours.	The writer is including the reader in the narrative.	Am I sure that the reader shares my feelings and opinions on this subject?
Second person "You" *Example:* You must protest the new hours.	The writer is addressing the reader directly, who may feel the writer is "commanding" or "instructing" him or her.	Will the reader feel insulted by my commands and instructions?
Third person "One" *Example:* One will be impressed by my friend Albert.	The writer has chosen an impersonal, formal pronoun.	Does the style of my writing match this impersonal and formal pronoun choice?
Third person "He" (his) *Example:* The Native American respected his land.	The writer has chosen to refer to all individuals as "he" whether they are men or women.	Will readers be offended by referring to all people as "he"? Do I care if they are?
Third person "He or she" (his or her) *Example:* Each student, whether he or she plays basketball or not, should write a letter to the director.	The writer has chosen to use this construction to include both genders.	Is this structure overused and awkward in my writing?
Third person plural "People . . . they" (their) *Example:* People should contact their local representatives.	The writer has chosen plural pronouns to avoid the "he/she" problem.	Is the plural appropriate in the context of my writing?
Third person plural "Someone (Everyone) . . . they" *Example:* Everyone should contact their local representatives.	The writer has chosen a form some may consider ungrammatical (singular subject, plural pronoun) in order to avoid the "he/she" problem.	Will my readers think I don't understand English grammar? Do I care?

Examine any of the essays you've read in this book so far. Identify the pronoun choices the authors made. With your classmates, discuss the effects those pronoun choices have on you as a reader.

In an ideal world, we would all write only when we wanted. But the demands of education and employment require us to write at times we don't feel like it, or about subjects we don't want to write about. This section discusses writing for such assignments.

When you are given a writing assignment in any course, you can use the following RAPPORT checklist to determine your strategies for completing an assignment.

Threads

Definition: "Rapport" means a relationship of harmony.

TABLE 4.2 RAPPORT CHECKLIST

Requirements: What are the specifications for the assignment? How long should it be? Should it be handwritten or typed? Do you need a bibliography? What is the due date?

Audience: Who are you writing for? Your instructor? Your classmates? A publication? Yourself?

Purpose: What are you trying to accomplish? Will you demonstrate what you've learned, defend your opinion, or entertain your readers?

Personalization: Can you adapt the topic to make it more interesting or relevant? Have you asked your instructor?

Orientation: What attitude will you adopt in your writing? Humorous? Serious? Ironic? Angry? Objective?

Research: What background information do you need to complete the task? Is your own experience enough, or do you need to do more reading?

Task: What exactly are you required to do? Explain a concept? Describe a process? Persuade your readers? If you aren't sure, check with classmates and/or your instructor.

Keep this checklist in mind as you start your first essay assignment in Chapter 4.

Theme for English B
by Langston Hughes

The instructor said,
    Go home and write
    a page tonight.
    And let that page come out of you—
    Then, it will be true.
I wonder if it's that simple?
I am twenty-two, colored, born in Winston-Salem.
I went to school there, then Durham, then here
to this college on the hill above Harlem.
I am the only colored student in my class.

The steps from the hill lead down into Harlem,
through a park, then I cross St. Nicholas,
Eighth Avenue, Seventh, and then I come to the Y,
the Harlem Branch Y, where I take the elevator
up to my room, sit down, and write this page:

It's not easy to know what is true for you or me
at twenty-two, my age. But I guess I'm what
I feel and see and hear, Harlem, I hear you:
hear you, hear me—we two—you, me, talk on this page.
(I hear New York, too.) Me—who?
Well, I like to eat, sleep, drink, and be in love.
I like to work, read, learn, and understand life.

I like a pipe for a Christmas present,
or records—Bessie, bop, or Bach.
I guess being colored doesn't make me not like
the same things other folks like who are other races.
So will my page be colored that I write?
Being me, it will not be white.
But it will be
a part of you, instructor.
You are white—
yet a part of me, as I am a part of you.
That's American.
Sometimes perhaps you don't want to be a part of me.
Nor do I often want to be a part of you.
But we are, that's true!
As I learn from you,
I guess you learn from me—
although you're older—and white—
and somewhat more free.

This is my page for English B.

Threads

Langston Hughes was born in Joplin, Missouri in 1902. He wrote poetry, fiction, and drama, and wrote regularly for the *New York Post.* He was an important figure in the Harlem Renaissance, a period of artistic growth centered around Harlem, a primarily African-American section of New York City.

Threads

"This college on the hill" refers to Columbia University, which is near Harlem.

For Group Discussion

ABOUT THE CONTENT

1. What is the assignment and the instructions the student has been given? Do you think this is a good assignment?
2. What does the instructor mean by the writing should "come out of you"?
3. In the lines that say the student is part of the instructor, and the instructor part of the student, what is the narrator trying to say?
4. The narrator also says the teacher might learn from him as much as he learns from the teacher. Do you agree?

ABOUT THE WRITING

1. What are some of the *images* (descriptions of things you can see or feel; for example, the fact that the university is on the hill above Harlem) of this poem? Explain their importance to the poem's meaning.
2. Do you think Hughes is the narrator (that is, the student who is speaking) of the poem? Why or why not?
3. The narrator uses the word "colored" to refer to himself. How might the language of the poem change if it were written today?
4. Compare this poem to Didion's essay. How do you think Hughes would answer the question "Why do I write?"

Quickwrite

Write your own "Theme for English B." What do you want the teacher to know about you? This need not be a poem, but you can try one if you like.

Threads

The "Y" refers to the YMCA, a club that offers recreational activities and inexpensive rooms.

Threads

Bessie Smith (1898?–1937) was an American blues singer, considered to be the greatest jazz singer of her time.

Writing to Express Yourself: Personal Essays

CHAPTER 4

Since most writing is meant to be shared, writing about your own experience presents a special challenge. In personal essays, you must have a **point** or **idea** to share as well as an interesting way to convey that idea. For example, if you wrote about an experience of

being wrongly accused of stealing when you were a child, you might be making a point about justice. Perhaps you want to show how you feel about people who jump to conclusions. These kinds of stories are called *personal narratives*.

When you write a personal narrative, you tell what happened. Newspaper stories, fairy tales, and chemistry lab reports are all types of narratives. They share an important feature: they have a beginning, middle, and end. The following two selections are examples of writing about personal experience. Both of these selections address a common theme and a memory from childhood.

SHAME

by Dick Gregory

I never learned hate at home, or shame. I had to go to school for that. I was about seven years old when I got my first big lesson. I was in love with a little girl named Helene Tucker, a light-complexioned little girl with pigtails and nice manners. She was always clean and she was smart in school. I think I went to school then mostly to look at her. I brushed my hair and even got me a little old handkerchief. It was a lady's handkerchief, but I didn't want Helene to see me wipe my nose on my hand. The pipes were frozen again, there was no water in the house, but I washed my socks and shirt every night. I'd get a pot and go over to Mister Ben's grocery store, and stick my pot down into his soda machine. Scoop out some chopped ice. By evening the ice melted to water for washing. I got sick a lot that winter because the fire would go out at night before the clothes were dry. In the morning I'd put them on, wet or dry, because they were the only clothes I had.

Everybody's got a Helene Tucker, a symbol of everything you want. I loved her for her goodness, her cleanness, her popularity. She'd walk down my street and my brothers and sisters would yell, "Here comes Helene," and I'd rub my tennis sneakers on the back of my pants and wish my hair wasn't so nappy and the white folks' shirt fit me better. I'd run out on the street. If I knew my place and didn't come too close, she'd wink at me and say hello. That was a good feeling. Sometimes I'd follow her all the way home, and shovel the snow off her walk and try to make friends with her Momma and her aunts. I'd drop money on her stoop late at night on my way back from shining shoes in the taverns. And she had a Daddy, and he had a good job. He was a paper hanger.

I guess I would have gotten over Helene by summertime, but something happened in that classroom that made her face hang in front of me for the next twenty-two years. When I played the drums in high school it was for Helene and when I broke track records in college it was for Helene and when I started standing behind microphones and heard applause I wished Helene could hear it, too. It wasn't until I was twenty-nine years old and married and making money that I finally got her out of my system. Helene was sitting in that classroom when I learned to be ashamed of myself.

It was on a Thursday. I was sitting in the back of the room, in a seat with a chalk circle drawn around it. The idiot's seat, the troublemaker's seat.

The teacher thought I was stupid. Couldn't spell, couldn't read, couldn't do arithmetic. Just stupid. Teachers were never interested in finding out that you couldn't concentrate because you were so hungry, because you hadn't had any breakfast. All you could think about was noontime, would it ever come? Maybe you could sneak into the cloakroom and steal a bite of some kid's lunch out of a coat pocket. A bit of something. Paste. You can't really make a meal of paste, or put it on bread for a sandwich, but sometimes I'd scoop a few spoonfuls out of the paste jar in the back of the room. Pregnant people get strange tastes. I was pregnant with poverty. Pregnant with dirt and pregnant with smells that made people turn away, pregnant with cold and pregnant with shoes that were never bought for me, pregnant with five other people in my bed and no Daddy in the next room, and pregnant with hunger. Paste doesn't taste too bad when you're hungry.

The teacher thought I was a troublemaker. All she saw from the front of the room was a little black boy who squirmed in his idiot's seat and made noises and poked the kids around him. I guess she couldn't see a kid who made noises because he wanted someone to know he was there.

It was on a Thursday, the day before the Negro payday. The eagle always flew on Friday. The teacher was asking each student how much his father would give to the Community Chest. On Friday night, each kid would get money from his father, and on Monday he would bring it to school. I decided I was going to buy me a Daddy right then. I had money in my pocket from shining shoes and selling papers, and whatever Helene Tucker pledged for her Daddy I was going to top it. And I'd hand the money right in. I wasn't going to wait until Monday to buy me a Daddy.

I was shaking, scared to death. The teacher opened her book and started calling out names alphabetically.

"Helene Tucker?"

"My Daddy said he'd give two dollars and fifty cents."

"That's very nice, Helene. Very, very nice indeed."

That made me feel pretty good. It wouldn't take too much to top that. I had almost three dollars in dimes and quarters in my pocket. I stuck my hand in my pocket and held onto the money, waiting for her to call my name. But the teacher closed her book after she called everybody else in the class.

I stood up and raised my hand.

"What is it now?"

"You forgot me."

She turned toward the blackboard. "I don't have time to be playing with you, Richard."

"My Daddy said he'd . . ."

"Sit down, Richard, you're disturbing the class."

"My Daddy said he'd give . . . fifteen dollars."

She turned around and looked mad. "We are collecting this money for you and your kind, Richard Gregory. If your Daddy can give fifteen dollars you have no business being on relief."

"I got it right now, I got it right now, my Daddy gave it to me to turn in today, my Daddy said . . ."

"And furthermore," she said, looking right at me, her nostrils getting big and her lips getting thin and her eyes opening wide, "we know you don't have a Daddy."

Helene Tucker turned around, her eyes full of tears. She felt sorry for me. Then I couldn't see her too well because I was crying, too.

"Sit down, Richard."

And I always thought the teacher kind of liked me. She always picked me to wash the blackboard on Friday, after school. That was a big thrill, it made me feel important. If I didn't wash it, come Monday the school might not function right.

"Where are you going, Richard?"

I walked out of school that day, and for a long time I didn't go back very often. There was shame there.

Now there was shame everywhere. It seemed like the whole world had been inside that classroom, everyone had heard what the teacher had said, everyone had turned around and felt sorry for me. There was shame in going to the Worthy Boys Annual Christmas Dinner for you and your kind, because everybody knew what a worthy boy was. Why couldn't they just call it the Boys Annual Dinner, why'd they have to give it a name? There was shame in wearing the brown and orange and white plaid mackinaw the welfare gave to three thousand boys. Why'd it have to be the same for everybody so when you walked down the street the people could see you were on relief? It was a nice warm mackinaw and it had a hood, and my Momma beat me and called me a little rat when she found out I stuffed it in the bottom of a pail full of garbage way over on Cottage Street. There was shame in running over to Mister Ben's at the end of the day and asking for his rotten peaches, there was shame in asking Mrs. Simmons for a spoonful of sugar, there was shame in running out to meet the relief truck. I hated that truck, full of food for you and your kind. I ran into the house and hid when it came. And then I started to sneak through alleys, to take the long way home so the people going into White's Eat Shop wouldn't see me. Yeah, the whole world heard the teacher that day, we all know you don't have a Daddy.

For Group Discussion

ABOUT THE CONTENT

1. Is Gregory talking only about shame? Find other ideas that he examines in this passage.

2. What does Gregory mean by "Everybody's got a Helene Tucker"? Why would her face "hang in front of [him] for the next twenty-two years"?

3. Why did Gregory throw out his jacket, even though it was "a nice warm mackinaw and it had a hood"?

4. Explain the last paragraph of this reading. Why has Gregory found shame?

ABOUT THE WRITING

1. Gregory uses the repetition of words and phrases to emphasize his ideas. Can you find examples of this? What effect does it have on the reader?

2. How does Gregory use concrete details to make the story come alive? (Recall that a concrete detail is a description of something you can touch, see, smell, hear, or taste.)

3. Gregory uses fragment sentences in this excerpt. What effect do they have?

ELEVEN

by Sandra Cisneros

What they don't understand about birthdays and what they never tell you is when you're eleven, you're also ten, and nine, and eight, and seven, and six, and five, and four, and three, and two, and one. And when you wake up on your eleventh birthday you expect to feel eleven, but you don't. You open your eyes and everything's just like yesterday, only it's today. And you don't feel eleven at all. You feel like you're still ten. And you are—underneath the year that makes you eleven.

Like some days you might say something stupid, and that's the part of you that's still ten. Or maybe some days you might need to sit on your mama's lap because you're scared, and that's the part of you that's five. And maybe one day when you're all grown up maybe you will need to cry like if you're three, and that's okay. That's what I tell Mama when she's sad and needs to cry. Maybe she's feeling three.

Because the way you grow old is kind of like an onion or like the rings inside a tree trunk or like my little wooden dolls that fit one inside the other, each year inside the next one. That's how being eleven years old is.

You don't feel eleven. Not right away. It takes a few days, weeks even, sometimes even months before you say Eleven when they ask you. And you don't feel smart eleven, not until you're almost twelve. That's the way it is.

Only today I wish I didn't have only eleven years rattling inside 'me like pennies in a tin Band-Aid box. Today I wish I was one hundred and two instead of eleven because if I was one hundred and two I'd have known what to say when Mrs. Price put the red sweater on my desk. I would've known how to tell her it wasn't mine instead of just sitting there with that look on my face and nothing coming out of my mouth.

"Whose is this?" Mrs. Price says, and she holds the red sweater up in the air for all the class to see. "Whose? It's been sitting in the coatroom for a month."

"Not mine," says everybody. "Not me."

"It has to belong to somebody," Mrs. Price keeps saying, but nobody can remember. It's an ugly sweater with red plastic buttons and a collar and sleeves all stretched out like you could use it for a jump rope. It's maybe a thousand years old and even if it belonged to me I wouldn't say so.

Maybe because I'm skinny, maybe because she doesn't like me, that stupid Sylvia Saldívar says, "I think it belongs to Rachel." An ugly sweater like that, all raggedy and old, but Mrs. Price believes her. Mrs. Price takes the sweater and puts it right on my desk, but when I open my mouth nothing comes out.

"That's not, I don't, you're not . . . Not mine," I finally say in a little voice that was maybe me when I was four.

"Of course it's yours," Mrs. Price says. "I remember you wearing it once." Because she's older and the teacher, she's right and I'm not.

Not mine, not mine, not mine, but Mrs. Price is already turning to page thirty-two, and math problem number four. I don't know why but all of a sudden I'm feeling sick inside, like the part of me that's three wants to come out of my eyes, only I squeeze them shut tight and bite down on my teeth real hard and try to remember today I am eleven, eleven. Mama is making a cake for me tonight, and when Papa comes home everybody will sing Happy birthday, happy birthday to you.

But when the sick feeling goes away and I open my eyes, the red sweater's still sitting there like a big red mountain. I move the red sweater to the corner of my desk with my ruler. I move my pencil and books and eraser as far from it as possible. I even move my chair a little to the right. Not mine, not mine, not mine.

In my head I'm thinking how long till lunchtime, how long till I can take the red sweater and throw it over the schoolyard fence, or leave it hanging on a parking meter, or bunch it up into a little ball and toss it in the alley. Except when math period ends Mrs. Price says loud and in front of everybody, "Now, Rachel, that's enough," because she sees I've shoved the red sweater to the

Threads

Sandra Cisneros lives in California, and has taught writing at different schools and universities. She was born in Chicago.

tippy-tip corner of my desk and it's hanging all over the edge like a waterfall, but I don't care.

"Rachel," Mrs. Price says. She says it like she's getting mad. "You put that sweater on right now and no more nonsense."

"But it's not—"

"Now!" Mrs. Price says.

This is when I wish I wasn't eleven, because all the years inside of me—ten, nine, eight, seven, six, five, four, three, two, and one—are pushing at the back of my eyes when I put one arm through one sleeve of the sweater that smells like cottage cheese, and then the other arm through the other and stand there with my arms apart like if the sweater hurts me and it does, all itchy and full of germs that aren't even mine.

That's when everything I've been holding in since this morning, since when Mrs. Price put the sweater on my desk, finally lets go, and all of a sudden I'm crying in front of everybody. I wish I was invisible but I'm not. I'm eleven and it's my birthday today and I'm crying like I'm three in front of everybody. I put my head down on the desk and bury my face in my stupid clown-sweater arms. My face all hot and spit coming out of my mouth because I can't stop the little animal noises from coming out of me, until there aren't any more tears left in my eyes, and it's just my body shaking like when you have the hiccups, and my whole head hurts like when you drink milk too fast.

But the worst part is right before the bell rings for lunch. That stupid Phyllis Lopez, who is even dumber than Sylvia Saldívar, says she remembers the red sweater is hers! I take it off right away and give it to her, only Mrs. Price pretends like everything's okay.

Today I'm eleven. There's a cake Mama's making for me tonight, and when Papa comes home from work we'll eat it. There'll be candles and presents and everybody will sing Happy birthday, happy birthday to you, Rachel, only it's too late.

I'm eleven today. I'm eleven, ten, nine, eight, seven, six, five, four, three, two, and one, but I wish I was one hundred and two. I wish I was anything but eleven, because I want today to be far away already, far away like a runaway balloon, like a tiny *o* in the sky, so tiny-tiny you have to close your eyes to see it.

For Group Discussion

ABOUT THE CONTENT

1. Why is the sweater a **symbol** of Rachel's shame?
2. Why do you think Rachel wishes she were "one hundred and two" instead of eleven?

ABOUT THE WRITING

1. What words or phrases in the story tell you that the narrator is a child?
2. How does Cisneros use concrete details to make the story come alive?

Now, compare the two stories in the following discussion questions.

ABOUT THE CONTENT

1. Compare the actions of the teachers in each of these stories. Why do you think Gregory's teacher does not have a name, but Cisneros calls hers "Mrs. Price"?
2. List all the similarities you can think of between these two selections. What differences are there?

ABOUT THE WRITING

1. Look at the way each author uses dialogue. Why didn't the authors just summarize what the characters said? Do you think the writing is improved by the use of dialogue? Why or why not?
2. How is the point of view different in each of the stories? What is the age of each of the narrators? What effect does this have on the stories?
3. Compare the use of clothing as a symbol of shame in both stories. What are the similarities and differences?

Quickwrite

Have you ever felt publicly ashamed of yourself? Who made you feel that way? What happened? Explain the experience.

USING VIVID LANGUAGE

In these two reading passages, the authors "paint a picture" with words. Dick Gregory didn't say he wore "a coat," he had a "brown and orange and white plaid mackinaw . . . [that] had a hood." In a personal narrative, it is important to let the reader "see" your story by selecting details that are important to the narration. On the other hand, if you spend a lot of time describing unimportant details, the reader might become bored or frustrated.

When you include details, try to appeal to all of the reader's senses: touch, taste, smell, hearing, seeing. This helps your reader to experience your story more fully. Examine Cisneros's description of the red sweater. Find details about the sweater that appeal to the following three senses:

SENSE	DETAIL
Sight	_____
	_____
Smell	_____
	_____
Touch	_____
	_____

One key to vivid writing is vocabulary use. This isn't simply a matter of using "big words," but instead, *specific* words or comparisons to help your reader.

Ready to Write

Use your imagination and expand on the following phrases by making them more *concrete.*

> *EXAMPLE* An ugly dress
> *REVISION* An old green striped dress with coffee stains on the front, and two buttons missing.

1. A beautiful tree
2. A good book
3. A big building
4. A small dog
5. An interesting movie

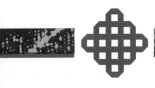

DEVELOPING YOUR OWN STYLE

What is "style"? Many students complain that their writing lacks "style," and they don't know how to repair it. You can learn a lot about style by examining the style of other writers.

Brainstorm

Choose either the Gregory or Cisneros selection, and list all the features of the author's style that you can.

Surprisingly, one way that writers develop their own styles is by imitating other writers. This works because it helps the writer think about the elements of style and what gives a piece of writing its unique characteristics. Even copying sentences you like from stories into your journal will help you get the "feel" of the word choice and structure the author chose.

Ready to Write

Read each of the sentences. Then, as closely as possible, imitate that style, writing about the subject given in the second column.

ORIGINAL SENTENCE	WRITE ABOUT . . .
<u>Uncle Willie</u> was making his way down the long shadowed aisle between the shelves and the counter—hand over hand, like a man climbing out of a dream. —Maya Angelou, *I Know Why the Caged Bird Sings*	An animal The Siamese cat was creeping down the dark narrow hallway, past the bedroom and bathroom—step by quiet step, like a burglar seeking out jewelry.
<u>He</u> was a little, fat man, with a big red nose and rat's eyes, but dressed expensive, and carrying a hand-satchel careful, as if it had eggs or railroad bonds in it. —O. Henry, "The Man Higher Up"	An automobile
<u>Mashenka Pavletsky, a young girl</u> who had only just finished her studies at a boarding school, returning from a walk to the house of the Kushkins, with whom she was living as a governess, found the household in terrible turmoil. —Anton Chekhov, "The Lady and the Dog"	A teacher
<u>The girls</u> sat side by side at their desks, they lunched together every noon, together they set out for home at the end of the day's work. —Dorothy Parker, "Standard of Living"	Boats

WRITING THE FIRST ESSAY

Topic: Write a narrative essay about an event in your life from which you learned an important lesson.

Choose an event that your readers will be able to identify with. Tell your story vividly, using concrete language and appealing to the senses. (Remember, you'll be sharing your story with an audience; don't write about an event you are uncomfortable talking about.)

LEARNING STRATEGY

Understanding and Using Emotions: Choosing an interesting topic will increase your interest in a writing assignment.

Preparation: Use one or more of the invention strategies outlined in Chapter 1 to explore ideas for your essay. Freewriting may help you recall details about the event and the people and places that were important to it.

LEARNING STRATEGY

Forming Concepts: When you discuss your writing with classmates, it helps you clarify your ideas.

Peer Response: Tell a partner or a small group of classmates the details of your story. After each group member tells his or her story, the group should interview the storyteller about that event. Here are a few questions you might ask, although you should add your own questions to this list:

- Why is this event significant to you?
- How did the event make you feel at that time?
- How did you react to this event (that is, what did you do)?
- How do you feel about the event now? Is it different from how you felt then?
- Why is this event so memorable?

After all the stories are told and the group members interviewed, you should take five to ten minutes to write any new thoughts or ideas that might be added to your essay.

LEARNING STRATEGY

Forming Concepts: Hearing what you have written gives you a new way of thinking about your word choices.

Ready to Write

Write a piece of **dialogue** that is part of your story. Ask classmates to read the parts of the dialogue, as in a play. Listen carefully to their reading. Does the dialogue sound authentic? Make changes if necessary.

Drafting: You now have several pieces of writing and notes for your essay. Review what you have (take an inventory) to see if you are ready to start writing your draft. Answer the following questions about your preparation so far:

- Will I be able to supply enough details about the event?
- Do I know what point I want to make?
- Will my story be interesting to my audience?

If you aren't sure about any of these questions, use freewriting or other techniques to fill in any gaps in your story.

LEARNING STRATEGY

Managing Your Learning: Taking an inventory of your preparation for writing will help you avoid "writer's block."

When you are satisfied that you have gathered enough information to begin writing, you can start to plan the structure of your essay. Here is what should be contained in your narrative:

Beginning: Intriguing opening sentences that capture the reader's interest.
Middle: A point at which there is a problem or conflict to overcome.
End: A resolution of your problem or a reflection on the meaning of your experience.

You may want to outline your story in order to remind yourself of your organizational plan.

LEARNING STRATEGY

Managing Your Learning: Organizing your ideas before you write will help you to write more efficiently.

Ready to Write

Write your first draft.

Feedback

Effective writers get others' opinions about their writing. Exchange your draft with a classmate, and use Part I of the following review chart to comment on your classmate's story. When your classmate returns your essay and his or her comments, respond to the review by completing the questions in Part II of the review sheet.

LEARNING STRATEGY

Managing Your Learning: Getting feedback from a classmate helps you learn more about your writing.

REVIEW CHART: PART I

> *NOTE* The reviewer should write this part, answering all questions completely and specifically.

Writer's Name _____

Reviewer's Name _____

Title of Essay _____

1. Is this an interesting and appropriate title? Explain.
2. Reread the first sentence of the essay. Is it intriguing? boring? Explain. If you don't like it, how would you rewrite it?
3. Find the most effective sentence in the essay and put a star by it. What makes it effective?
4. Find a weak sentence and put an "x" by it. How could it be improved?
5. Locate three words or phrases that should be made more concrete. Circle them. Can you suggest better choices?
6. Are the details of the narrative clear? Summarize the main event. If anything is confusing, point it out.
7. How does the essay end? What impression does it leave you with? If it needs improvement, explain.
8. What is your overall impression of the essay? What did you learn? What would you still like to know?

LEARNING STRATEGY

Managing Your Learning: Evaluating your own writing helps you to improve.

REVIEW CHART: PART II

NOTE The author of the essay should write this part after reading the reviewer's comments.

1. Do you think you need to change your title? If so, how will you do so?
2. Will you change the opening of your essay? How?
3. Do you agree that the sentence chosen as weak by your reviewer needs changing? If not, why not? If so, how will you change it?
4. How will you make the three weak words more concrete? Is it necessary?
5. Will you make any changes to the ending? Why or why not?
6. Do you agree with your reviewer's overall comments about your paper?

LEARNING STRATEGY

Managing Your Learning: Creating a plan for revision helps you develop better writing skills.

Revision

Revision doesn't mean merely correcting your spelling and grammar and inserting a few commas. In the revision phase of the writing process, you should reorganize, cut, add detail, and improve your choices. Looking at the review you received from your partner and your response to it, formulate a revision plan. You may use the following chart to help you identify the areas that need the most improvement.

REVISION PLAN

FEATURE	PROBLEM	POSSIBLE SOLUTION
Title		
Opening paragraph		
Storytelling style		
Organization		
Word choice		
Conclusion		
Other		

Use your revision plan to guide your rewriting.

Final Version

After you have solved the problems identified in your revision plan, you can focus on editing and proofreading your paper. The editing phase includes double-checking your grammar, spelling, punctuation, and so forth. Use Chapter 8 to guide you. Your problems are unique, so it will be helpful to take an inventory of your own problem spots, based on your past experience as a writer. You can change this inventory as you progress.

LEARNING STRATEGY

Managing Your Learning: Focusing on only a few areas of grammar at once will help you to edit more effectively.

Which of the following items are a problem for you? Check the appropriate column; then find the section of this book that addresses that problem.

PROBLEM CHECKLIST

PROBLEM	Minor Problem	Major Problem	No Problem	Don't Know	Section
Spelling					
Punctuation					
Subject-verb agreement					
Verb tenses					
Articles and prepositions					
Plurals					
Sentence fragments					
Run-on sentences					
Wordiness					
Transitions					
Relative clauses					

If you have checked more than three as a "major problem," decide which three you would like to work on first. It's easier to concentrate on a few problem areas at a time.

The last step should be proofreading—that is, looking for careless mistakes: misspellings, leaving out words, typing the same word twice in a row, and so forth. Before you turn your paper in, proofread it carefully.

A Writer's Memo

A memo is a short piece of correspondence that addresses a specific topic. In your writer's memo you should write to your instructor, explaining the following about your essay:

- What is the main point you wanted to make in this paper?
- What did you have problems with during its writing?
- What are you proud of?
- What did you learn from writing this essay?
- What do you want your instructor to comment upon specifically?

You may add any other remarks you want to your memo. Clip it to your paper before turning it in.

Figure 4.1 Memo format

Business memos usually have the following heading. "Re:" indicates the subject matter of the memo.

Memo	
To:	From:
Re:	Date:

ADDITIONAL READING

SCENES FROM TWO CHILDHOODS

by Margaret Atwood

My mother's family lived in a large white house near an apple orchard, in Nova Scotia. There was a barn and a carriage-house, in the kitchen there was a pantry. My mother can remember the days before commercial bakeries, when flour came in barrels and all the bread was made at home. She can remember the first radio broadcast she ever heard, which was a singing commercial about socks.

In this house there were many rooms. Although I have been there, although I have seen the house with my own eyes, I still don't know how many. Parts of it were closed off, or so it seemed; there were back staircases. Passages led elsewhere. Five children lived in it, two parents, a hired man and a hired girl,

Threads

Margaret Atwood is one of Canada's most famous and important writers. She was born in Ottawa, Ontario, in 1939 and attended Victoria College, the University of Toronto, Radcliffe College, and Harvard University. Her most recent work is *The Robber Bride*, published in 1993.

Threads

Nova Scotia is an eastern province of Canada. Its current population is approximately 900,000.

Threads

Tarnation is an interjection which is a more polite form of the word "damnation." It has been in use in the United States since colonial times.

whose names and faces kept changing. The structure of the house was hierarchical, with my grandfather at the top, but its secret life—the life of pie crusts, clean sheets, the box of rags in the linen closet, the loaves in the oven—was female. The house, and all the objects in it, crackled with static electricity; undertow washed through it, the air was heavy with things that were known but not spoken. Like a hollow log, a drum, a church, it amplified, so that conversations whispered in it sixty years ago can be half-heard even today.

In this house you had to stay at the table until you had eaten everything on your plate. "'Think of the starving Armenians,' mother used to say," says my mother. "I didn't see how eating my bread crusts was going to help them out one jot."

It was in this house that I first saw a stalk of oats in a vase, each oat wrapped in the precious silver paper which had been carefully saved from a chocolate box. I thought it was the most wonderful thing I had ever seen, and began saving silver paper myself. But I never got around to wrapping the oats, and in any case I didn't know how. Like many other art forms of vanished civilizations, the techniques for this one have been lost and cannot quite be duplicated.

"We had oranges at Christmas," says my mother. "They came all the way from Florida; they were very expensive. That was the big treat; to find an orange in the toe of your stocking. It's funny to remember how good they tasted, now."

When she was sixteen, my mother had hair so long she could sit on it. Women were bobbing their hair by then; it was getting to be the twenties. My mother's hair was giving her headaches, she says, but my grandfather, who was very strict, forbade her to cut it. She waited until one Saturday when she knew he had an appointment with the dentist.

"In those days there was no freezing," says my mother. "The drill was worked with a foot pedal, and it went *grind, grind, grind.* The dentist himself had brown teeth: he chewed tobacco, and he would spit the tobacco juice into a spittoon while he was working on your teeth."

Here my mother, who is a good mimic, imitates the sounds of the drill and the tobacco juice: "*Rrrrr! Rrrrr! Rrrrr! Phtt! Rrrrr! Rrrrr! Rrrrr! Phtt!* It was always sheer agony. It was a heaven-sent salvation when gas came in."

My mother went into the dentist's office, where my grandfather was sitting in the chair, white with pain. She asked him if she could have her hair cut. He said she could do anything in tarnation as long as she would get out of there and stop pestering him.

"So I went out straight away and had it all chopped off," says my mother jauntily. "He was furious afterwards, but what could he do? He'd given his word."

My own hair reposes in a cardboard box in a steamer trunk in my mother's cellar, where I picture it becoming duller and more brittle with each passing year, and possibly moth-eaten; by now it will look like the faded wreaths of hair in Victorian funeral jewelry. Or it may have developed a dry mildew; inside its tissue-paper wrappings it glows faintly, in the darkness of the trunk. I suspect my mother has forgotten it's in there. It was cut off, much to my relief, when I was twelve and my sister was born. Before that it was in long curls: "Otherwise," says my mother, "it would have been just one big snarl." My mother combed it by winding it around her index finger every morning, but when she was in the hospital my father couldn't cope. "He couldn't get it around his stubby fingers," says my mother. My father looks down at his fingers. They are indeed broad compared with my mother's long elegant ones, which she calls bony. He smiles a pussy-cat smile.

So it was that my hair was sheared off. I sat in the chair in my first beauty parlor and watched it falling, like handfuls of cobwebs, down over my shoulders. From within my head began to emerge, smaller, denser, my face more angular. I aged five years in fifteen minutes. I knew I could go home now and try out lipstick.

"Your father was upset about it," says my mother, with an air of collusion. She doesn't say this when my father is present. We smile, over the odd reactions of men to hair.

"You had such an acute sense of smell when you were younger," says my mother.

Now we are on more dangerous ground: my mother's childhood is one thing, my own quite another. This is the moment at which I start rattling the silverware, or ask for another cup of tea. "You used to march into houses that were strange to you, and you would say in a loud voice, 'What's that funny smell?'" If there are guests present, they shift a little away from me, conscious of their own emanations, trying not to look at my nose.

"I used to be so embarrassed," says my mother absentmindedly. Then she shifts gears. "You were such an easy child. You used to get up at six in the morning and play by yourself in the playroom, singing away. . . ." There is a pause. A distant voice, mine, high and silvery, drifts over the space between us. "You used to talk a blue streak. Chatter, chatter, chatter, from morning to night." My mother sighs imperceptibly, as if wondering why I have become so silent, and gets up to poke the fire.

Hoping to change the subject, I ask whether or not the crocuses have come up yet, but she is not to be diverted. "I never had to spank you," she says. "A harsh word, and you would be completely reduced." She looks at me sideways; she isn't sure what I have turned into, or how. "There were just one or two times. Once, when I had to go out and I left your father in charge." (This may be the real point of the story: the inability of one to second-guess small children.) "I came back along the street, and there were you and your brother, throwing mud balls at an old man out of the upstairs window."

We both know whose idea this was. For my mother, the proper construction to be put on this event is that my brother was a hell-raiser and I was his shadow, "easily influenced," as my mother puts it. "You were just putty in his hands."

"Of course, I had to punish both of you equally," she says. Of course. I smile a forgiving smile. The real truth is that I was sneakier than my brother, and got caught less often. No front-line charges into enemy machine-gun nests for me, if they could be at all avoided. My own solitary acts of wickedness were devious and well concealed; it was only in partnership with my brother that I would throw caution to the winds.

"He could wind you around his little finger," says my mother. "Your father made each of you a toy box, and the rule was—" (my mother is good at the devising of rules) "—the rule was that neither of you could take the toys out of the other one's toy box without permission. Otherwise he would have got all your toys away from you. But he got them anyway, mind you. He used to talk you into playing house, and he would pretend to be the baby. Then he would pretend to cry, and when you asked what he wanted, he'd demand whatever it was out of your toy box that he wanted to play with at that moment. You always gave it to him."

I don't remember this, though I do remember staging World War Two on the living-room floor, with armies of stuffed bears and rabbits, but surely some primal patterns were laid down. Have these early toy-box experiences—and "toy box" itself, as a concept, reeks with implications—have they made me suspicious of men who wish to be mothered, yet susceptible to them at the same time? Have I been conditioned to believe that if I am not solicitous, if I am not forthcoming, if I am not a never-ending cornucopia of entertaining delights, they will take their collections of milk-bottle tops and their mangy one-eared teddy bears and go away into the woods by themselves to play snipers? Probably. What my mother thinks was merely cute may have been lethal.

But this is not her only story about my suckiness and gullibility. She follows up with the *coup de grace,* the tale of the bunny-rabbit cookies.

"It was in Ottawa. I was invited to a government tea," says my mother, and this fact alone should signal an element of horror: My mother hated official functions, to which however she was obliged to go because she was the wife of a civil servant. "I had to drag you kids along; we couldn't afford a lot of babysitters in those days." The hostess had made a whole plateful of decorated cookies for whatever children might be present, and my mother proceeds to describe these: wonderful cookies shaped like bunny rabbits, with faces and clothes of colored icing, little skirts for the little girl bunny rabbits, little pants for the little boy bunny rabbits.

"You chose one," says my mother. "You went off to a corner with it, by yourself. Mrs. X noticed you and went over. 'Aren't you going to eat your cookie?' she said. 'Oh, no,' you said. 'I'll just sit here and talk to it.' And there you sat, as happy as a clam. But someone had made the mistake of leaving the plate near your brother. When they looked again, there wasn't a single cookie left. He'd eaten every one. He was very sick that night, I can tell you."

Some of my mother's stories defy analysis. What is the moral of this one? That I was a simp is clear enough, but on the other hand it was my brother who got the stomach ache. Is it better to eat your food, in a straightforward materialistic way, and as much of it as possible, or go off into the corner and talk to it? This used to be a favorite of my mother's before I was married, when I would bring what my father referred to as "swains" home for dinner. Along with the dessert, out would come the bunny-rabbit cookie story, and I would cringe and twiddle my spoon while my mother forged blithely on with it. What were the swains supposed to make of it? Were my kindliness and essential femininity being trotted out for their inspection? Were they being told in a roundabout way that I was harmless, that they could expect to be talked to by me, but not devoured? Or was she, in some way, warning them off? Because there is something faintly crazed about my behavior, some tinge of the kind of person who might be expected to leap up suddenly from the dinner table and shout, "Don't eat that! It's alive!"

"In my next incarnation," my mother said once, "I'm going to be an archaeologist and go around digging things up." We were sitting on the bed that had once been my brother's, then mine, then my sister's; we were sorting out things from one of the trunks, deciding what could now be given away or thrown out. My mother believes that what you save from the past is mostly a matter of choice.

At the same time something wasn't right in the family; someone wasn't happy. My mother was angry; her good cheer was not paying off.

This statement of hers startled me. It was the first time I'd ever heard my mother say that she might have wanted to be something other than what she was. I must have been thirty-five at the time, but it was still shocking and slightly offensive to me to learn that my mother might not have been totally contented fulfilling the role in which fate had cast her: that of being my mother. What thumb-suckers we all are, I thought, when it comes to mothers.

Shortly after this I became a mother myself, and this moment altered for me.

While she was combing my next-to-impossible hair, winding it around her long index finger, yanking out the snarls, my mother used to read me stories. Most of them are still in the house somewhere, but one has vanished. It may have been a library book. It was about a little girl who was so poor she had only one potato left for her supper, and while she was roasting it the potato got up and ran away. There was the usual chase, but I can't remember the ending: a significant lapse.

"That story was one of your favorites," says my mother. She is probably still under the impression that I identified with the little girl, with her hunger and her sense of loss; whereas in reality I identified with the potato.

Early influences are important. It took that one a while to come out; probably until after I went to university and started wearing black stockings and pulling my hair back into a bun, and having pretensions. Gloom set in. Our next-door neighbor, who was interested in wardrobes, tackled my mother: "'If she would only *do* something about herself,'" my mother quotes, "'she could be *quite attractive.*'"

"You always kept yourself busy," my mother says charitably, referring to this time. "You always had something cooking. Some project or other."

It is part of my mother's mythology that I am as cheerful and productive as she is, though she admits that these qualities may be occasionally and temporarily concealed. I wasn't allowed much angst around the house. I had to indulge it in the cellar, where my mother wouldn't come upon me brooding and suggest I should go out for a walk, to improve my circulation. This was her answer to any sign, however slight, of creeping despondency. There wasn't a lot that a brisk sprint through dead leaves, howling winds, or sleet couldn't cure.

It was, I knew the *zeitgeist* that was afflicting me, and against it such simple remedies were powerless. Like smog I wafted through her days, dankness spreading out from around me. I read modern poetry and histories of Nazi atrocities, and took to drinking coffee. Off in the distance, my mother vacuumed around my feet while I sat in chairs, studying, with car rugs tucked around me, for suddenly I was always cold.

My mother has few stories to tell about these times. What I remember from them is the odd look I would sometimes catch in her eyes. It struck me, for the first time in my life, that my mother might be afraid of me. I could not even reassure her, because I was only dimly aware of the nature of her distress, but there must have been something going on in me that was beyond her: At any time I might open my mouth and out would come a language she had never heard before. I had become a visitant from outer space, a time-traveler come back from the future, bearing news of a great disaster.

For Discussion

ABOUT THE CONTENT

1. Who are the main characters of this selection? Describe their relationships with each other.
2. What time periods occur in this story? How do these eras play a role?
3. Atwood wonders what point her mother was trying to make when telling Atwood stories. What point do you think Atwood is trying to make in this narrative?

ABOUT THE WRITING

1. Why doesn't the author use names in referring to the main characters? What effect does this have on her story?
2. How does Atwood show the reader that different time periods are being referred to?
3. How does Atwood make the reader feel "part of the story"?

Quickwrite

Do any family members tell stories about you as a child? How do you feel about these stories? Are they told in the way you recall them?

GIRLHOOD AMONG GHOSTS

by Maxine Hong Kingston

Threads

Maxine Hong Kingston was born in 1940 in Stockton, California. Like Joan Didion, she graduated from the University of California, Berkeley. Her parents came to the United States from China in the 1930s. She has written several books about her own life, as well as a novel, *Tripmaster Monkey*, (1988).

Long ago in China, knot-makers tied string into buttons and frogs, and rope into bell pulls. There was one knot so complicated that it blinded the knot-maker. Finally an emperor outlawed this cruel knot, and the nobles could not order it anymore. If I had lived in China, I would have been an outlaw knot-maker.

Maybe that's why my mother cut my tongue. She pushed my tongue up and sliced the frenum. Or maybe she snipped it with a pair of nail scissors. I don't remember her doing it, only her telling me about it, but all during childhood I felt sorry for the baby whose mother waited with scissors or knife in hand for it to cry—and then, when its mouth was wide open like a baby bird's, cut. The Chinese say "a ready tongue is an evil."

I used to curl up my tongue in front of the mirror and tauten my frenum into a white line, itself as thin as a razor blade. I saw no scars in my mouth. I thought perhaps I had had two frena, and she had cut one. I made other children open their mouths so I could compare theirs to mine. I saw perfect pink membranes stretching into precise edges that looked easy enough to cut. Sometimes I felt very proud that my mother committed such a powerful act upon me. At other times I was terrified—the first thing my mother did when she saw me was to cut my tongue.

"Why did you do that to me, Mother?"

"I told you."

"Tell me again."

"I cut it so that you would not be tongue-tied. Your tongue would be able to move in any language. You'll be able to speak languages that are completely different from one another. You'll be able to pronounce anything. Your frenum looked too tight to do those things, so I cut it."

"But isn't 'a ready tongue an evil'?"

"Things are different in this ghost country."

"Did it hurt me? Did I cry and bleed?"

"I don't remember. Probably."

She didn't cut the other children's. When I asked cousins and other Chinese children whether their mothers had cut their tongues loose, they said, "What?"

"Why didn't you cut my brothers' and sisters' tongues?"

"They didn't need it."

"Why not? Were theirs longer than mine?"

"Why don't you quit blabbering and get to work?"

If my mother was not lying she should have cut more, scraped away the rest of the frenum skin, because I have a terrible time talking. Or she should not have cut at all, tampering with my speech. When I went to kindergarten and had to speak English for the first time, I became silent. A dumbness—a shame— still cracks my voice in two, even when I want to say "hello" casually, or ask an easy question in front of the checkout counter, or ask directions of a bus driver. I stand frozen, or I hold up the line with the complete, grammatical sentence that comes squeaking out at impossible length. "What did you say?" says the cab driver, or "Speak up," so I have to perform again, only weaker the second time. A telephone call makes my throat bleed and takes up that day's courage. It spoils my day with self-disgust when I hear my broken voice come skittering out into the open. It makes people wince to hear it. I'm getting better, though. Recently I asked the postman for special-issue stamps; I've waited since childhood for postmen to give me some of their own accord. I am making progress a little every day.

My silence was thickest—total—during the three years that I covered my school paintings with black paint. I painted layers of black over houses and flowers and suns, and when I drew on the blackboard, I put a layer of chalk on top. I was making a stage curtain, and it was the moment before the curtain parted or rose. The teachers called my parents to school, and I saw they had been saving my pictures, curling and cracking, all alike and black. The teachers pointed to the pictures and looked serious, talked seriously too, but my parents did not understand English. ("The parents and teachers of criminals were executed," said my father.) My parents took the pictures home. I spread them out (so black and full of possibilities) and pretended the curtains were swinging open, flying up, one after another, sunlight underneath, mighty operas.

During the first silent year I spoke to no one at school, did not ask before going to the lavatory, and flunked kindergarten. My sister also said nothing for three years, silent in the playground and silent at lunch. There were other Chinese girls not of our family, but most of them got over it sooner than we did. I enjoyed the silence. At first it did not occur to me I was supposed to talk or to pass kindergarten. I talked at home and to one or two of the Chinese kids in class. I made motions and even made some jokes. I drank out of a toy saucer when the water spilled out of the cup, and everybody laughed, pointing at me, so I did it some more. I didn't know that Americans don't drink out of saucers.

I liked the Negro students (Black Ghosts) best because they laughed the loudest and talked to me as if I were a daring talker too. One of the Negro girls had her mother coil braids over her ears Shanghai-style like mine; we were Shanghai twins except that she was covered with black like my paintings. Two Negro kids enrolled in Chinese school, and the teachers gave them Chinese names. Some Negro kids walked me to school and home, protecting me from the Japanese kids, who hit me and chased me and stuck gum in my ears. The Japanese kids were noisy and tough. They appeared one day in kindergarten, released from concentration camp, which was a tic-tac-toe mark, like barbed wire, on the map.

It was when I found out I had to talk that school became a misery, that the silence became a misery. I did not speak and felt bad each time that I did not speak. I read aloud in first grade, though, and heard the barest whisper with little squeaks come out of my throat. "Louder," said the teacher, who scared the voice away again. The other Chinese girls did not talk either, so I knew the silence had to do with being a Chinese girl.

Reading out loud was easier than speaking because we did not have to make up what to say, but I stopped often, and the teacher would think I'd gone quiet again. I could not understand "I." The Chinese "I" had seven strokes, intricacies. How could the American "I," assuredly wearing a hat like the Chinese, have only three strokes, the middle so straight? Was it out of politeness that this writer left off strokes the way a Chinese has to write her own name small and crooked? No, it was not politeness; "I" is a capital and "you" is lowercase. I stared at the middle line and waited so long for its black center to resolve into tight strokes and dots that I forgot to pronounce it. The other troublesome word was "here," no strong consonant to hang on to, and so flat, when "here" is two mountainous ideographs. The teacher, who had already told me every day how to read "I" and "here" put me in the low corner under the stairs again, where the noisy boys usually sat.

When my second grade class did a play, the whole class went to the auditorium except the Chinese girls. The teacher, lovely and Hawaiian, should have understood about us, but instead left us behind in the classroom. Our voices were too soft or nonexistent, and our parents never signed the permission slips anyway. They never signed anything unnecessary. We opened the door a crack and peeked out, but closed it again quickly. One of us (not me) won every spelling bee, though.

I remember telling the Hawaiian teacher, "We Chinese can't sing 'land where our fathers died.'" She argued with me about politics, while I meant because of curses. But how can I have that memory when I couldn't talk? My mother says that we, like the ghosts, have no memories.

After American school, we picked up our cigar boxes, in which we had arranged books, brushes, and an inkbox neatly, and went to Chinese school, from 5:00 to 7:30 P.M. There we changed together, voices rising and falling, loud and soft, some boys shouting, everybody reading together, reciting together and not alone with one voice. When we had a memorization test, the teacher let each of us come to his desk and say the lesson to him privately, while the rest of the class practiced copying or tracing. Most of the teachers were men. The boys who were so well behaved in the American school played tricks on them and talked back to them. The girls were not mute. They screamed and yelled during recess, when there were no rules; they had fistfights. Nobody was afraid of children hurting themselves or of children hurting school property. The glass doors to the red and green balconies with the gold joy symbols were left wide open so that we could run out and climb the fire escapes. We played capture-the-flag in the auditorium, where Sun Yat-sen and Chiang Kai-shek's pictures hung at the back of the stage, the Chinese flag on their left and the American flag on their right. We climbed the teak ceremonial chairs and made flying leaps off the stage. One flag headquarters was behind the glass door and the other on stage right. Our feet drummed on the hollow stage. During recess the teachers locked themselves up in their office with the shelves of books, copybooks, inks from China. They drank tea and warmed their hands at a stove. There was no play supervision. At recess we had the school to ourselves, and also we could roam as far as we could go—downtown, Chinatown stores, home—as long as we returned before the bell rang.

At exactly 7:30 the teacher again picked up the brass bell that sat on his desk and swung it over our heads, while we charged down the stairs, our cheering magnified in the stairwell. Nobody had to line up.

Not all of the children who were silent at American school found voice at Chinese school. One new teacher said each of us had to get up and recite in front of the class, who was to listen. My sister and I had memorized the lesson perfectly. We said it to each other at home, one chanting, one listening. The teacher called on my sister to recite first. It was the first time a teacher had called on the second-born to go first. My sister was scared. She glanced at me and looked away; I looked down at my desk. I hoped that she could do it because if she could, then I would have to. She opened her mouth and a voice came out that wasn't a whisper, but it wasn't a proper voice either. I hoped that she would not cry, fear breaking up her voice like twigs underfoot. She sounded as if she were trying to sing though weeping and strangling. She did not pause or stop to end the embarrassment. She kept going until she said the last word, and then sat down. When it was my turn, the same voice came out, a crippled animal running on broken legs. You could hear splinters in my voice, bones rubbing jagged against one another. I was loud, though. I was glad I didn't whisper. There was one little girl who whispered.

Threads

Sun Yat-sen was an important Chinese leader in the early 1900s. Chiang Kai-shek was a military leader who fled to Taiwan in 1949, because of China's Communist Revolution.

For Discussion

ABOUT THE CONTENT

1. In the first paragraph, Kingston says she would have been an "outlaw knot-maker." Why would she have been a knot-maker? Why an "outlaw"?
2. What is the significance of the "cutting" of her tongue? Do you think her mother really did this? Provide evidence for your opinion from the story.
3. What does the difference between Chinese and English "I" symbolize, in your opinion?
4. What situations seem to cause Kingston to remain silent? When is she more comfortable with her voice?
5. Compare and contrast the Chinese and American schools.
6. What is meant by "Black Ghosts"?
7. Why does Kingston think that the Hawaiian teacher "should have understood" the Chinese girls?

ABOUT THE WRITING

1. In what order is the plot told? Why does Kingston use this narrative technique?
2. What effect do the references to "ghosts" have on the narrative?
3. How do the physical descriptions of the different schools contribute to your understanding of them?

Quickwrite

Has there been a time when speaking was difficult for you? What were the circumstances? How did it make you feel?

Writing About Literature: Family and Tradition

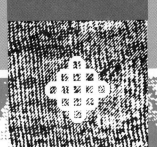

Discussing and writing about literature are important parts of an education in English. This chapter provides you with the tools you need to discuss and write about literature. In order to discuss a

story effectively, you typically have to do a *close* reading—reading it once for the overall ideas and plot, then rereading it to focus on specific features of the writing itself.

As you read a work of fiction, it is important to ask questions about the story:

- How does it make you feel?
- Why do the main characters behave the way they do?
- What changes take place during the story?
- Why are these changes important?
- What is the main problem of the story?
- How is the main problem resolved?

Threads

Definition: Jargon is the specialized vocabulary of a field of study or profession.

By thinking about these questions, as well as any others that occur to you, you will be able to solve some of the mysteries of understanding fiction.

Although it is not *necessary* to have a specialized vocabulary in order to discuss literature, it is helpful. Just as doctors or engineers have specialized vocabulary for discussing their work, writers who analyze literature use a "jargon" of their own. This makes talking about literature easier, because you can use precise vocabulary rather than long descriptions.

LITERARY TERMINOLOGY

Here are some common literary terms and their definitions. Important vocabulary items are printed in bold type.

1. **Plot** is the order of events in a story. Traditional plots are usually told in chronological order, that is, according to a time sequence. But **flashbacks,** (the memories of a character or the narrator of scenes that preceded the main story) may also be used. The plot depends on some sort of **conflict,** and as the plot develops, this conflict usually develops into a **crisis,** a major event in which the main character must take some action or make a decision. This decision leads to the story's **resolution,** or conclusion. The plots of short stories might seem less dramatic or conclusive than those of novels. Therefore, you may have to read shorter works more closely for a clear understanding.
2. The **characters** are the people in a story. The description of a character's personality, appearance, and actions are called the **development** of that

character. Characters are either "major" or "minor": major characters have complex personalities and undergo changes and crises; minor characters support the plot and actions of the main characters, but usually we learn less about them, and they don't change significantly.

The main character is called the **protagonist,** and the person or force who acts against this character is called the **antagonist.** A protagonist isn't necessarily a "positive" or "good" character, just the *main* character; similarly, the antagonist isn't necessarily negative or evil.

3. When you read a story, a **narrator** tells the story from a particular **point of view.** (The author of the story typically is *not* the narrator.) Following are the most popular choices for point of view.

First person: First person point of view is that of the narrator, who uses the pronoun "I" and plays a part in the story. The first person narrator can be either a major or a minor character. If a first person point of view is used, then the narrator's involvement in the story affects the reporting of the events, and the potential bias of the narrator is an important part of an analysis.

Third person: Third person point of view is that of a narrator who is not directly involved in the story. There are two kinds of third person narrators: **omniscient** and **limited omniscient.** The omniscient narrator can see into the thoughts and motivations of all the characters and can tell the story from every perspective. The limited omniscient narrator can usually see into only the thoughts of the major characters.

4. The **setting** is the time, place, and context in which a story takes place. The setting informs us of the history and environment in which the characters act. Elements of the setting, such as the seasons of the year, or natural phenomena, such as an ocean or thunderstorm, may act as a force of action in the story just as a character does.

5. A **symbol** is an object or an action that represents something else, typically a more complicated or abstract concept. For example, in the story "Eleven" in Chapter 4, the red sweater symbolizes Rachel's shame—it is a complex symbol because red also represents embarrassment. Symbols are important to a story because they increase its depth and complexity. It helps to understand symbols, but it is equally important not to see everything as a potential symbol or to "read meaning into" things that may not be symbols.

6. **Style** refers to the language that a writer chooses and the way that a story is constructed. For example, a writer might write in a dialect to show the regional origins of the characters. Or the writer may compose a highly symbolic and abstract story, or one that is heavily plotted—that is, having a lot of action. Style has many different elements, but two of the major elements are **tone** and **irony:**

   a. **Tone** relates to the mood of the story. Think of tone as a story's "personality": Is it serious? Depressing? Tragic? Joyful? Optimistic? Some mixture of these? To understand tone, look at the word choice, imagery—such as colors or sounds, and the symbols that the author uses.

Threads

A second person point of view, that is, one that uses "you" in its narration, is also possible but is rarely used.

From this cartoon, can you guess what the word "oxymoron" means? How many oxymorons can you find in this cartoon?

GARY KELL

    b. Irony occurs when the actions don't match either the intentions of the characters or the reader's predictions. For example, in "Shame" in Chapter 4, the fact that Dick Gregory throws out his nice, warm coat because it is a source of shame presents a sad irony in the story. Individual words or phrases can also be used ironically, when a character says the opposite of what he or she really means.

7. The **theme** is a main point of a story. It is difficult sometimes to define a theme, however, because a complex work of fiction may have more than one or because different readers may interpret a single theme differently; there's no one absolute, "correct" theme. That's why literature is analyzed—each reader may have a slightly different understanding of what is important and interesting in a work of fiction.

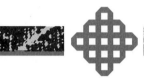

READING SHORT STORIES

We will first examine the story "Crickets," by Robert Olen Butler. Read it once from start to finish. Then reread it, and take notes identifying the elements in the preceding definitions. Use the chart on page 65 to help you.

CRICKETS

by Robert Olen Butler

    They call me Ted where I work and they've called me that for over a decade now and it still bothers me, though I'm not very happy about my real name being the same as the former President of the former Republic of Vietnam. Thiêu is not an uncommon name in my homeland and my mother had nothing more in mind than a long-dead uncle when she gave it to me. But in Lake Charles, Louisiana, I am Ted. I guess the other Mr. Thiêu has enough of my former country's former gold bullion tucked away so that in London, where he probably wears a bowler and carries a rolled umbrella, nobody's calling him anything but Mr. Thiêu.

    I hear myself sometimes and I sound pretty bitter, I guess. But I don't let that out at the refinery, where I'm the best chemical engineer they've got and they even admit it once in a while. They're good-hearted people, really. I've done enough fighting in my life. I was eighteen when Saigon fell and I was only recently mustered into the Army, and when my unit dissolved and everybody ran, I stripped off my uniform and put on my civilian clothes again and I threw rocks at the North's tanks when they rolled through the streets. Very few of my people did likewise. I stayed in the mouths of alleys so I could run and then return and throw more rocks, but because what I did seemed so isolated and so pathetic a gesture, the gunners in the tanks didn't even take notice. But I didn't care about their scorn. At least my right arm had said no to them.

    And then there were Thai Pirates in the South China Sea and idiots running the refugee centers and more idiots running the agencies in the U.S. to find a place for me and my new bride, who braved with me the midnight escape by boat and the terrible sea and all the rest. We ended up here in the flat bayou land of Louisiana, where there are rice paddies and where the water and the land are in the most delicate balance with each other, very much like the Mekong Delta, where I grew up. These people who work around me are good people and maybe they call me Ted because they want to think of me as one of them, though sometimes it bothers me that these men are so much bigger than me. I am the size of a woman in this country and these American men are all massive and they speak so slowly, even to one another, even though English is their native language. I've heard New Yorkers on television and I speak as fast as they do.

My son is beginning to speak like the others here in Louisiana. He is ten, the product of the first night my wife and I spent in Lake Charles, in a cheap motel with the sky outside red from the refineries. He is proud to have been born in America, and when he leaves us in the morning to walk to the Catholic school, he says, "Have a good day, y'all." Sometimes I say good-bye to him in Vietnamese and he wrinkles his nose at me and says, "Aw, Pop," like I'd just cracked a corny joke. He doesn't speak Vietnamese at all and my wife says not to worry about that. He's an American.

But I do worry about that, though I understand why I should be content. I even understood ten years ago, so much so that I agreed with my wife and gave my son an American name. Bill. Bill and his father Ted. But this past summer I found my son hanging around the house bored in the middle of vacation and I was suddenly his father Thiêu with a wonderful idea for him. It was an idea that had come to me in the first week of every February we'd been in Lake Charles, because that's when the crickets always begin to crow here. This place is rich in crickets, which always make me think of my own childhood in Vietnam. But I never said anything to my son until last summer.

I came to him after watching him slouch around the yard one Sunday pulling the Spanish moss off the lowest branches of our big oak tree and then throwing rocks against the stop sign on our corner. "Do you want to do something fun?" I said to him.

"Sure, Pop," he said, though there was a certain suspicion in his voice, like he didn't trust me on the subject of fun. He threw all the rocks at once that were left in his hand and the stop sign shivered at their impact.

I said, "If you keep that up, they will arrest me for the destruction of city property and then they will deport us all."

My son laughed at this. I, of course, knew that he would know I was bluffing. I didn't want to be too hard on him for the boyish impulses that I myself had found to be so satisfying when I was young, especially since I was about to share something of my own childhood with him.

"So what've you got, Pop?" my son asked me.

"Fighting crickets," I said.

"What?"

Now, my son was like any of his fellow ten-year-olds, devoted to superheroes and the mighty clash of good and evil in all of its high-tech forms in the Saturday-morning cartoons. Just to make sure he was in the right frame of mind, I explained it to him with one word, "Cricketmen," and I thought this was a pretty good ploy. He cocked his head in interest at this and I took him to the side porch and sat him down and I explained.

I told him how, when I was a boy, my friends and I would prowl the undergrowth and capture crickets and keep them in matchboxes. We would feed them leaves and bits of watermelon and bean sprouts, and we'd train them to fight by keeping them in a constant state of agitation by blowing on them and gently flicking the ends of their antennas with a sliver of wood. So each of us would have a stable of fighting crickets, and there were two kinds.

At this point my son was squirming a little bit and his eyes were shifting away into the yard and I knew that my Cricketman trick had run its course. I fought back the urge to challenge his set of interests. Why should the stiff and foolish fights of his cartoon characters absorb him and the real clash—real life and death—that went on in the natural world bore him? But I realized that I hadn't cut to the chase yet, as they say on the TV. "They fight to the death," I said with as much gravity as I could put into my voice, like I was James Earl Jones.

The announcement won me a glance and a brief lift of his eyebrows. This gave me a little scrabble of panic, because I still hadn't told him about the two types of crickets and I suddenly knew that was a real important part for me. I tried not to despair at his understanding and I put my hands on his shoulders and turned him around to face me. "Listen," I said. "You need to understand this if you are to have fighting crickets. There are two types, and all of us had some of each. One type we called the charcoal crickets. These were very large and strong, but they were slow and they could become confused. The other type was small and brown and we called them fire crickets. They weren't as strong, but they were very smart and quick."

"So who would win?" my son said.

"Sometimes one and sometimes the other. The fights were very long and full of hard struggle. We'd have a little tunnel made of paper and we'd slip a sliver of wood under the cowling of our cricket's head to make him mad and we'd twirl him by his antenna, and then we'd each put our cricket into the tunnel at opposite ends. Inside, they'd approach each other and begin to fight and then we'd lift the paper tunnel and watch."

"Sounds neat," my son said, though his enthusiasm was at best moderate, and I knew I had to act quickly.

So we got a shoe box and we started looking for crickets. It's better at night, but I knew for sure his interest wouldn't last that long. Our house is up on blocks because of the high water table in town and we crawled along the edge, pulling back the bigger tufts of grass and turning over rocks. It was one of the rocks that gave us our first crickets, and my son saw them and cried in my ear, "There, there," but he waited for me to grab them. I cupped first one and then the other and dropped them into the shoe box and I felt a vague disappointment, not so much because it was clear that my boy did not want to touch the insects, but that they were both the big black ones, the charcoal crickets. We crawled on and we found another one in the grass and another sitting in the muddy shadow of the house behind the hose faucet and then we caught two more under an azalea bush.

"Isn't that enough?" my son demanded. "How many do we need?"

I sat with my back against the house and put the shoe box in my lap and my boy sat beside me, his head stretching this way so he could look into the box. There was no more vagueness to my feeling. I was actually weak with disappointment because all six of these were charcoal crickets, big and inert and just looking around like they didn't even know anything was wrong.

"Oh, no," my son said with real force, and for a second I thought he had read my mind and shared my feeling, but I looked at him and he was pointing at the toes of his white sneakers. "My Reeboks are ruined!" he cried, and on the toe of each sneaker was a smudge of grass.

I glanced back into the box and the crickets had not moved and I looked at my son and he was still staring at his sneakers. "Listen," I said, "this was a big mistake. You can go on and do something else."

He jumped up at once. "Do you think Mom can clean these?" he said.

"Sure," I said. "Sure."

He was gone at once and the side door slammed and I put the box on the grass. But I didn't go in. I got back on my hands and knees and I circled the entire house and then I turned over every stone in the yard and dug around all the trees. I found probably two dozen more crickets, but they were all the same. In Louisiana there are rice paddies and some of the bayous look like the Delta, but many of the birds are different, and why shouldn't the insects be different, too? This is another country, after all. It was just funny about the fire crickets. All of us kids rooted for them, even if we were fighting with one of our own charcoal crickets. A fire cricket was a very precious and admirable thing.

The next morning my son stood before me as I finished my breakfast and once he had my attention, he looked down at his feet, drawing my eyes down as well. "See?" he said. "Mom got them clean."

Then he was out the door and I called after him, "See you later, Bill."

For Discussion

Before answering the discussion questions, complete the following chart, identifying the important elements of this short story. Then compare and discuss your answers with your classmates. You may want to make several photocopies of this table or use a separate piece of paper, because you will use this table for other stories as well.

STORY CHART

STORY ELEMENT	DESCRIPTION
Characters: Major:	
Protagonist:	
Minor:	
Setting:	
Point of View:	
Plot Summary (brief):	
Style: Tone:	
Irony:	
Conflict:	
Theme:	
Symbolism:	

ABOUT THE CONTENT

1. What is the primary conflict in this story? Are there other conflicts? How are the conflicts resolved?
2. What do you think the crickets symbolize? Why does Butler distinguish between charcoal crickets and fire crickets?
3. Identify an important theme in this story. What other themes can you identify?
4. What is your reaction to this story? With whom do you sympathize?
5. How does Ted change?

ABOUT THE WRITING

1. Identify at least one example where the author uses irony.
2. Describe the tone of "Crickets." What words or phrases illustrate this tone?
3. What is the significance of the last paragraph of this story? Is it an effective way to end?

Quickwrite

Can you recall a time when you had a conflict in philosophy with a family member? Describe what happened.

The next selection addresses a similar theme as the previous story, but with different characters and setting. Again, make notes regarding the important elements of this story.

EVERYDAY USE
by Alice Walker

I will wait for her in the yard that Maggie and I made so clean and wavy yesterday afternoon. A yard like this is more comfortable than most people know. It is not just a yard. It is like an extended living room. When the hard clay is swept clean as a floor and the fine sand around the edges lined with tiny, irregular grooves, anyone can come and sit and look up into the elm tree and wait for the breezes that never come inside the house.

Maggie will be nervous until after her sister goes: she will stand hopelessly in corners homely and ashamed of the burn scars down her arms and legs, eyeing her sister with a mixture of envy and awe. She thinks her sister has held life always in the palm of one hand, that "no" is a word the world never learned to say to her.

You've no doubt seen those TV shows where the child who has "made it" is confronted, as a surprise, by her own mother and father, tottering in weakly from backstage. (A pleasant surprise, of course: What would they do if parent and child came on the show only to curse out and insult each other?) On TV mother and child embrace and smile into each other's faces. Sometimes the mother and father weep, the child wraps them in arms and leans across the table to tell how she would not have made it without their help. I have seen these programs.

Sometimes I dream a dream in which Dee and I are suddenly brought together on a TV program of this sort. Out of a dark and soft-seated limousine, I am ushered into a bright room filled with many people. There I met a smiling, gray, sporty man like Johnny Carson who shakes my hand and tells me what a fine girl I have. Then we are on the stage and Dee is embracing me with tears in her eyes. She pins on my dress a large orchid, even though she told me once that she thinks orchids are tacky flowers.

In real life I am a large, big-boned woman with rough, man-working hands. In the winter I wear flannel nightgowns to bed and overalls during the day. I can kill and clean a hog as mercilessly as a man. My fat keeps me hot in zero weather. I can work all day, breaking ice to get water for washing. I can eat pork liver cooked over the open fire minutes after it comes steaming from the hog. One winter I knocked a bull calf straight in the brain between the eyes with a sledge hammer and had the meat hung up to chill before nightfall. But of course all this does not show on television. I am the way my daughter would want me to be: a hundred pounds lighter, my skin like an uncooked barley pancake. My hair glistens in the hot bright lights. Johnny Carson has much to do to keep up with my quick and witty tongue.

But that is a mistake. I know even before I wake up. Who ever knew a Johnson with a quick tongue? Who can even imagine me looking a strange white man in the eye? It seems to me I have talked to them always with one foot raised in flight, with my head turned in whichever way is farthest from them. Dee, though. She would always look anyone in the eye. Hesitation was not part of her nature.

"How do I look, Mama?" Maggie says, showing just enough of her thin body enveloped in pink skirt and red blouse for me to know she's there, almost hidden by the door.

"Come out into the yard," I say.

Have you ever seen a lame animal, perhaps a dog run over by some careless person rich enough to own a car, sidle up to someone who is ignorant enough to be kind to him? That is the way my Maggie walks. She has been like this, chin on chest, eyes on ground, feet in shuffle, ever since the fire that burned the other house to the ground.

Dee is lighter than Maggie, with nicer hair and a fuller figure. She's a woman now, though sometimes I forget. How long ago was it that the other house burned? Ten, twelve years? Sometimes I can still hear the flames and feel Maggie's arm sticking to me, her hair smoking and her dress falling off her in little black papery flakes. Her eyes seemed stretched open, blazed open by the flames reflected in them. And Dee. I see her standing off under the sweet gum tree she used to dig gum out of; a look of concentration on her face as she watched the last dingy gray board of the house fall in toward the red-hot brick chimney. Why don't you do a dance around the ashes? I'd wanted to ask her. She had hated the house that much.

I used to think she hated Maggie, too. But that was before we raised the money, the church and me, to send her to Augusta to school. She used to read to us without pity; forcing words, lies, and other folks' habits, whole lives upon us two, sitting trapped and ignorant underneath her voice. She washed us in a river of make-believe, burned us with a lot of knowledge we didn't necessarily need to know. Pressed us to her with the serious way she read, to shove us away at just the moment, like dimwits, we seemed about to understand.

Dee wanted nice things. A yellow organdy dress to wear to her graduation from high school; black pumps to match a green suit she'd made from an old suit somebody gave me. She was determined to stare down any disaster in her efforts. Her eyelids would not flicker for minutes at a time. Often I fought off the temptation to shake her. At sixteen she had a style of her own: and knew what style was.

I never had an education myself. After second grade the school was closed down. Don't ask me why: in 1927 colored asked fewer questions than they do now. Sometimes Maggie reads to me. She stumbles along good-naturedly but can't see well. She knows she is not bright. Like good looks and money, quickness passed her by. She will marry John Thomas (who has mossy teeth in an earnest face) and then I'll be free to sit here and I guess just sing church songs to myself. Although I never was a good singer. Never could carry a tune. I was always better at a man's job. I used to love to milk till I was hoofed in the side in '49. Cows are soothing and slow and don't bother you, unless you try to milk them the wrong way.

I have deliberately turned my back on the house. It is three rooms, just like the one that burned, except the roof is tin; they don't make shingle roofs any more. There are no real windows, just some holes cut in the sides, like the portholes in a ship, but not round and not square, with rawhide holding the shutters up on the outside. The house is in a pasture, too, like the other one. No doubt when Dee sees it she will want to tear it down. She wrote me once that no matter where we "choose" to live, she will manage to come see us. But she will never bring her friends. Maggie and I thought about this and Maggie asked me, "Mama, when did Dee ever *have* any friends?"

She had a few. Furtive boys in pink shirts hanging about on washday after school. Nervous girls who never laughed. Impressed with her they worshiped the well-turned phrase, the cute shape, the scalding humor that erupted like bubbles in lye. She read to them.

When she was courting Jimmy T. she didn't have much time to pay to us, but turned all her faultfinding power on him. He *flew* to marry a cheap gal from a family of ignorant flashy people. She hardly had time to recompose herself.

When she comes I will meet—but there they are!

Maggie attempts to make a dash for the house, in her shuffling way, but I stay her with my hand. "Come back here," I say. And she stops and tries to dig a well in the sand with her toe.

It is hard to see them clearly through the strong sun. But even the first glimpse of leg out of the car tells me it is Dee. Her feet were always neat-looking, as if God himself had shaped them with a certain style. From the other side of the car comes a short, stocky man. Hair is all over his head a foot long and hanging from his chin like a kinky mule tail. I hear Maggie suck in her breath, "Uhnnnh," is what it sounds like. Like when you see the wriggling end of a snake just in front of your foot on the road. "Uhnnnh."

Dee next. A dress down to the ground, in this hot weather. A dress so loud it hurts my eyes. There are yellows and oranges enough to throw back the light of the sun. I feel my whole face warming from the heat waves it throws out. Earrings, too, gold and hanging down to her shoulders. Bracelets dangling and making noises when she moves her arm up to shake the folds of the dress out of her armpits. The dress is loose and flows, and as she walks closer, I like it. I hear Maggie go "Uhnnnh" again. It is her sister's hair. It stands straight up like the wool on a sheep. It is black as night and around the edges are two long pigtails that rope about like small lizards disappearing behind her ears.

"Wa-su-zo-Tean-o!" she says, coming on in that gliding way the dress makes her move. The short stocky fellow with the hair to his navel is all grinning and he follows up with "Asalamalakim, my mother and sister!" He moves to hug Maggie but she falls back, right up against the back of my chair. I feel her trembling there and when I look up I see the perspiration falling off her chin.

"Don't get up," says Dee. Since I am stout it takes something of a push. You can see me trying to move a second or two before I make it. She turns, showing white heels through her sandals, and goes back to the car. Out she peeks next with a Polaroid. She stoops down quickly and lines up picture after picture of me sitting there in front of the house with Maggie cowering behind me. She never takes a shot without making sure the house is included. When a cow comes nibbling around the edge of the yard she snaps it and me and Maggie *and* the house. Then she puts the Polaroid in the back seat of the car, and comes up and kisses me on the forehead.

Meanwhile Asalamalakim is going through the motions with Maggie's hand. Maggie's hand is as limp as a fish, and probably as cold, despite the sweat, and she keeps trying to pull it back. It looks like Asalamalakim wants to shake hands but wants to do it fancy. Or maybe he don't know how people shake hands. Anyhow, he soon gives up on Maggie.

"Well," I say. "Dee."

"No, Mama," she says. "Not 'Dee.' Wangero Leewanika Kemanjo!"

"What happened to 'Dee'?" I wanted to know.

"She's dead." Wangero said. "I couldn't bear it any longer being named after the people who oppress me."

"You know as well as me you was named after your aunt Dicie." I said. Dicie is my sister. She named Dee. We called her "Big Dee" after Dee was born.

"But who was *she* named after?" asked Wangero.

"I guess after Grandma Dee," I said.

"And who was she named after?" asked Wangero.

"Her mother," I said, and saw Wangero was getting tired. "That's about as far back as I can trace it," I said. Though, in fact, I probably could have carried it back beyond the Civil War through the branches.

"Well," said Asalamalakim, "there you are."

"Uhnnnh," I heard Maggie say.

"There I was not," I said, "before 'Dicie' cropped up in our family, so why should I try to trace it that far back?"

He just stood there grinning looking down on me like somebody inspecting a Model A car. Every once in a while he and Wangero sent eye signals over my head.

"How do you pronounce this name?" I asked.

"You don't have to call me by it if you don't want to," said Wangero.

"Why shouldn't I?" I asked. "If that's what you want us to call you, we'll call you."

"I know it might sound awkward at first," said Wangero.

"I'll get used to it," I said. "Ream it out again."

Well, soon we got the name out of the way. Asalamalakim had a name twice as long and three times as hard. After I tripped over it two or three times he told me to just call him Hakim-a-barber. I wanted to ask him was he a barber, but I didn't really think he was, so I didn't ask.

"You must belong to those beef-cattle peoples down the road," I said. They said "Asalamalakim" when they met you, too, but they didn't shake hands. Always too busy: feeding the cattle, fixing the fences, putting up salt-lick shelters, throwing down hay. When the white folks poisoned some of the herd the men stayed up all night with rifles in their hands. I walked a mile and a half just to see the sight.

Hakim-a-barber said, "I accept some of their doctrines, but farming and raising cattle is not my style." (They didn't tell me, and I didn't ask, whether Wangero [Dee] had really gone and married him.)

We sat down to eat and right away he said he didn't eat collards and pork was unclean. Wangero, though, went on through the chitlins and corn bread, the greens and everything else. She talked a blue streak over the sweet potatoes. Everything delighted her. Even the fact that we still used the benches her daddy made for the table when we couldn't afford to buy chairs.

"Oh, Mama!" she cried. Then turned to Hakim-a-barber. "I never knew how lovely these benches are. You can feel the rump prints," she said, running her hands underneath her and along the bench. Then she gave a sigh and her hand closed over Grandma Dee's butter dish. "That's it!" she said. "I knew there was something I wanted to ask you if I could have." She jumped up from the table and went over in the corner where the churn stood, the milk in its clabber by now. She looked at the churn and looked at it.

"This churn top is what I need," she said. "Didn't Uncle Buddy whittle it out of a tree you all used to have?"

"Yes," I said.

"Uh huh," she said happily. "And I want the dasher, too."

"Uncle Buddy whittle that, too?" asked the barber.

Dee (Wangero) looked up at me.

"Aunt Dee's first husband whittled the dash," said Maggie so low you almost couldn't hear her. "His name was Henry, but they called him Stash."

"Maggie's brain is like an elephant's," Wangero said, laughing. "I can use the churn top as a centerpiece for the alcove table," she said, sliding a plate over the churn, "and I'll think of something artistic to do with the dasher."

When she finished wrapping the dasher the handle stuck out. I took it for a moment in my hands. You didn't even have to look close to see where hands pushing the dasher up and down to make butter had left a kind of sink in the wood. In fact, there were a lot of small sinks; you could see where thumbs and fingers had sunk into the wood. It was beautiful light yellow wood, from a tree that grew in the yard where Big Dee and Stash had lived.

After dinner Dee (Wangero) went to the trunk at the foot of my bed and started rifling through it. Maggie hung back in the kitchen over the dishpan. Out came Wangero with two quilts. They had been pieced by Grandma Dee and then Big Dee and me had hung them on the quilt frames on the front porch and quilted them. One was in the Lone Star pattern. The other was Walk Around the Mountain. In both of them were scraps of dresses Grandma Dee had worn fifty and more years ago. Bits and pieces of Grandpa Jarrell's paisley shirts. And one teeny faded blue piece, about the size of a penny matchbox, that was from Great Grandpa Ezra's uniform that he wore in the Civil War.

"Mama," Wangero said sweet as a bird. "Can I have these old quilts?"

I heard something fall in the kitchen, and a minute later the kitchen door slammed.

"Why don't you take one or two of the others?" I asked "These old things were just done by me and Big Dee from some tops your grandma pieced before she died."

"No," said Wangero. "I don't want those. They are stitched around the borders by machine."

"That's to make them last better," I said.

"That's not the point," said Wangero. "These are all pieces of dresses Grandma used to wear. She did all this stitching by hand. Imagine!" she held the quilts securely in her arms, stroking them.

"Some of the pieces, like those lavender ones, come from old clothes her mother handed down to her," I said, moving up to touch the quilts. Dee (Wangero) moved back just enough so that I couldn't reach the quilts. They already belonged to her.

"Imagine!" she breathed again, clutching them closely to her bosom.

"The truth is," I said, "I promised to give them quilts to Maggie, for when she marries John Thomas."

She gasped like a bee had stung her.

"Maggie can't appreciate these quilts!" she said. "She'd probably be backward enough to put them to everyday use."

"I reckon she would," I said. "God knows I have been saving 'em for long enough with nobody using 'em. I hope she will!" I didn't want to bring up how I had offered Dee (Wangero) a quilt when she went away to college. Then she had told me they were old-fashioned, out of style.

"But they're *priceless!*" she was saying now, furiously, for she has a temper. "Maggie would put them on the bed and in five years they'd be in rags. Less than that!"

"She can always make some more," I said. "Maggie knows how to quilt."

Dee (Wangero) looked at me with hatred. "You just will not understand. The point is these quilts, *these* quilts!"

"Well, I said, stumped. "What would *you* do with them?"

"Hang them," she said. As if that was the only thing you *could* do with quilts.

Maggie by now was standing in the door. I could hear the sound her feet made as they scraped over each other.

"She can have them, Mama," she said, like somebody used to never winning anything, or having anything reserved for her. "I can 'member Grandma Dee without the quilts."

I looked at her hard. She had filled her bottom lip with checkerberry snuff and it gave her face a kind of dopey, hangdog look. It was Grandma Dee and Big Dee who taught her how to quilt herself. She stood there with her scarred hands hidden in the folds of her skirt. She looked at her sister with something like fear but she wasn't mad at her. This was Maggie's portion. This was the way she knew God to work.

When I looked at her like that something hit me in the top of my head and ran down to the soles of my feet. Just like when I'm in church and the spirit of God touches me and I get happy and shout. I did something I never had done before: hugged Maggie to me, then dragged her on into the room, snatched the quilts out of Miss Wangero's hands and dumped them into Maggie's lap. Maggie just sat there on my bed with her mouth open.

"Take one or two of the others," I said to Dee.

But she turned without a word and went out to Hakim-a-barber.

"You just don't understand," she said, as Maggie and I came out to the car.

"What don't I understand?" I wanted to know.

"Your heritage," she said. And then she turned to Maggie, kissed her, and said, "You ought to try to make something of yourself, too, Maggie. It's really a new day for us. But from the way you and Mama still live you'd never know it."

She put on some sunglasses that hid everything above the tip of her nose and her chin.

Maggie smiled; maybe at the sunglasses. But a real smile, not scared. After we watched the car dust settle I asked Maggie to bring me a dip of snuff. And then the two of us sat there just enjoying, until it was time to go in the house and go to bed.

For Discussion

Before the discussion questions, you will find a short quiz. Answer the questions in the quiz; then compare and discuss your answers with your classmates.

72

LEARNING STRATEGY

Remembering New Material: Discussing new concepts and vocabulary with your classmates will help you remember them.

QUIZ

Answer the following questions without consulting the first part of this chapter. You may consult the story, however.

1. Name and describe the **protagonist** of the story.

2. Name and describe the **antagonist** of the story.

3. Who are the **minor characters?** Describe each of them.

4. Briefly describe the **setting** of this story.

5. Who is the **narrator** and what **point of view** is the story written from?

6. What is the major **conflict?**

7. What do you think the quilts **symbol**ize?

8. Identify one major element of **style** in the story.

9. What do you think the **theme** of this story is?

10. Briefly summarize the **plot.**

ABOUT THE CONTENT

1. What is the significance of Mama's "dream" about appearing on the television show?
2. What importance does the setting of this story have in relationship to one of its major themes?
3. What is Mama's attitude toward reading?
4. Why did Dee (Wangero) change her name? What is the cause of her mother's misunderstanding about her name?
5. What change does the narrator, Mama, undergo? What does she realize?
6. What does the title mean, in your opinion?

ABOUT THE WRITING

1. How does Walker use dialogue to emphasize the conflict between Dee and her mother?
2. How does Walker use concrete descriptions to show the difference between the characters? Give examples.
3. Can you find examples of irony in this story?
4. How does Walker use humor?
5. What vocabulary items give this story a "regional" flavor?

Quickwrite

Who deserves the quilts, in your opinion? Why? How would you resolve this conflict?

WRITING THE SECOND ESSAY

LEARNING STRATEGY

Personalizing: Shaping your writing topic to your own interests helps you to communicate more effectively and become more interested in your writing.

For this essay, you will develop your own writing topic. The subject for the paper is <u>the role of traditions in family life</u>. You will write an essay on this subject using the two stories found in this chapter as well as your own experience. (You may also use the additional reading on families and traditions at the end of this chapter.)

PREPARATION

A. Selecting a Topic

The preceding assignment gives you the **subject** matter for the essay. You need to decide on how you will narrow that subject area to a workable topic, and then a thesis statement. A good way to visualize this distinction is by imagining a triangle:

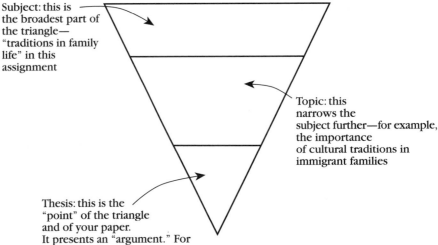

Subject: this is the broadest part of the triangle—"traditions in family life" in this assignment

Topic: this narrows the subject further—for example, the importance of cultural traditions in immigrant families

Thesis: this is the "point" of the triangle and of your paper. It presents an "argument." For example, a possible thesis might be "Even though it is frustrating, it is important for immigrant parents to pass their cultural traditions on to their children."

B. Developing a Thesis

For most types of college (or expository) writing, the success of your essay depends on a strong **thesis** statement. A thesis presents a specific argument or point you want to make.

Thesis statements are composed of two major elements: a **topic** and a **comment.** The topic is the part of the thesis that states generally what subject matter is discussed, and the comment specifies one important point relating to the topic. For example:

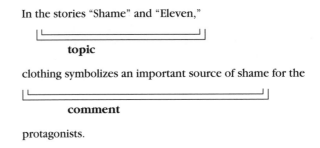

In the stories "Shame" and "Eleven,"

topic

clothing symbolizes an important source of shame for the

comment

protagonists.

The thesis statement represents the writer's interpretation of a topic; for that reason, it should make an interesting and arguable claim. In order to be arguable, it must try to convince the readers of something that they may disagree with or may not have considered previously.

Typical Thesis Statement Problems

OBSERVATIONS

The following statement is an **observation**—that is, it states a fact with which no one could disagree. Thesis statements that offer observations lead to overly descriptive essays.

> ***EXAMPLE*** "Crickets" tells the story of a Vietnamese immigrant and his American-born son.

TOO MANY IDEAS

A thesis statement should focus on one idea, and not try to argue for several issues at once. Both parts of the following statement make good points, but they are two separate ideas and therefore deserve two separate essays.

> ***EXAMPLE*** Reading literature provides an important way of understanding a culture; furthermore, it is a relaxing hobby.

Thesis statements that try to cover more than one main point lead to essays that are difficult to organize.

ARGUING BOTH SIDES

A thesis statement should focus on one side of the issue. The following thesis statement tries to argue both sides.

> ***EXAMPLE*** Some readers believe Wangero deserves the family quilts while others do not.

This thesis could lead to an unsatisfying essay—one that leaves the reader wanting to know not what "some readers believe," but what the *writer* believes.

Thesis Statement Exercise:

Part I. With a group of classmates, discuss which of the following statements are good thesis statements and which are not. Identify the problems in those that are not good theses. Be prepared to explain your decisions to your class.

1. Prejudice in the educational systems is to blame for the protagonists' problems in the stories "Shame" and "Eleven."
2. The main characters of "Shame" and "Eleven" are poor.
3. In order to be a good writer, you must also read a lot of literature.
4. Many writers record their ideas in journals.
5. Some people enjoy literature while others do not; it's a matter of taste.
6. Even though the main characters of "Shame" and "Eleven" are very different, their problems are similar.
7. It is important to build a book collection of works you enjoy; in addition, you should read magazines often.
8. The plot of "Eleven" involves a young girl, Rachel, being embarrassed on her birthday by her teacher.

Part II. Now, write a **draft thesis statement** (it doesn't have to be perfect). Put your thesis statement on the board in your classroom for analysis by your classmates. When you look at your own and your classmates' thesis statements, discuss the following questions for each:

- Is it a single sentence?
- Is it arguable?
- Is there enough information to support it?
- Is it grammatical?
- Is it specific (that is, does it make only one point)?
- Is it interesting?

After your discussion, make any changes to your thesis statement that you think are necessary.

DRAFTING

When you have formulated a good thesis, assemble the materials you will need to begin the drafting process.

- Notes from your reading and class discussion
- Relevant quickwrite topics
- Notes on personal experience that you want to include
- Quotations from your reading that support your thesis

If you don't have enough information to get started, review your reading and find quotations, freewrite on your thesis, and review your notes and memories of class discussions. Once you have your materials assembled, begin by writing an outline of your paper. An outline can be in any form you are familiar or comfortable with—a list, a formal outline (with Roman numerals and letters), or any other format that works for you.

You are now ready to write your first draft.

PEER RESPONSE

After you have completed your draft, fill out the following information and include it with a copy of your essay. Bring your paper and this topsheet to class and exchange them with a classmate. Read your partner's paper, answer his or her questions, and add any ideas you have.

DRAFT TOPSHEET

1. Please tell me . . .

2. The part of my paper. I am most concerned about is . . .

3. Other questions I have are . . .

Revision

Remember that revision is not merely correcting your spelling and grammar and inserting a few commas. In the revision phase of the writing process, you are reorganizing, cutting, adding detail, and improving your choices. Looking at the review you received from your partner and your response to it, formulate a **revision plan.** Use the following chart to help you identify the areas that need the most improvement.

REVISION PLAN

FEATURE	PROBLEM	POSSIBLE SOLUTION
Title		
Thesis		
Opening paragraph		
Examples		
Organization		
Word choice		
Conclusion		
Other		

Use your revision plan and the following section to guide your rewriting.

PARAGRAPH UNITY AND COHERENCE

This section will help you revise your essay by taking a closer look at its paragraphs. If you examine different types of writing, you will notice that paragraph lengths and structures vary a great deal. However, in expository writing, each paragraph typically requires the following elements:

- **A topic sentence** that states the main idea
- **Development** of the main idea through examples or explanation

The **topic sentence** states what the paragraph is about; unity is achieved when all the sentences in the paragraph relate to that idea. A topic sentence can be placed anywhere in the paragraph. In your draft, underline the topic sentence in each paragraph. Then reread the paragraph sentence by sentence. Does each sentence relate to your topic? If not, put an **X** by it, and consider eliminating or moving it.

In addition to your main idea, each paragraph needs **development** of that idea—that is, an example or explanation. Reread each paragraph in your draft and make a note in the margin showing what kind of development you use:

- Example from your own experience
- Example or quotation from your reading
- Personal opinion
- Definition of a word
- Explanation of an event
- Other (label it with a name)

Now look at your margin notes: how balanced is your development? Do you have a variety of types of support, or do you tend to use only your own opinion? If necessary, make notes about any changes you should make to balance your examples.

Coherence in a paragraph (and in an essay) means that the word choices and sequence of ideas fit together in a logical way and draw attention to the most important concepts. Coherence can be achieved in many ways. Three major techniques are:

1. Using transitions
2. Repeating key words and ideas
3. Using parallel structures

Look at the following passage:

> Macaws nest in cozy tree cavities a hundred feet or more off the ground. Two questions loomed as I set out to investigate macaw reproduction. *How would I get up there, and how would the birds react once I did?*
>
> I **start** with a giant slingshot, launching a weight on a thin line over *a branch* near the nest. **Then** I tie *a climbing rope* to the unweighted end and pull the weighted end by hand **until** *the rope* is hanging over *the branch*.
>
> "Macaws: Winged Rainbows," by Charles A. Munn. *National Geographic 185*(1): 131, January 1994.

In the first paragraph, the single underlined phrases refer to the same things, the macaws. The double-underlined phrases refer to the position of the climber ("up there"). The italicized last sentence shows a parallel structure—two questions formed in the same way, making up part of a complex sentence.

The second paragraph shows the author's use of transitions, shown in bold type, as well as more use of repeated phrases to obtain coherence. These techniques help the reader keep track of the order of the story and the main ideas.

Finally, examine your own writing again. In each of your paragraphs, identify your use of transitions, the repetition of key words and phrases, and parallel structures; then ask yourself the following questions:

Transitions: Do I supply enough guidance for my reader? Is the sequence of events or ideas made clearer through my use of transitions?

Keywords: Do I highlight the main ideas in my writing by repeating keywords and concepts? Do I repeat the same word *too* frequently? (If so, use synonyms or rewrite in a way to avoid unnecessary repetition.)

Parallel Structures: Is each part of a parallel structure in the same grammatical form as the other? For example,

> Parallel: I enjoy *reading, cooking, and watching TV.*
> Not Parallel: I like *swimming, fishing, and to hike.*

Final Version

Once again, your last steps before turning in your paper should include editing and proofreading your paper. Use the information found in Chapter 8 of this book to guide you. You may want to look at the results of your last paper and your recent assignments to make changes to your inventory of problem spots. Include a writer's memo (see page 49) with your paper.

PROBLEM CHECKLIST

PROBLEM	Minor Problem	Major Problem	No Problem	Don't Know	Section
Spelling					
Punctuation					
Subject-verb agreement					
Verb tenses					
Articles and prepositions					
Plurals					
Sentence fragments					
Run-on sentences					
Wordiness					
Transitions					
Relative clauses					

GRANDMA'S WAKE

by Emilio Díaz Valcárcel

We welcomed Uncle Segundo this morning. We sat waiting on one of the benches at the airport for four hours while mobs of people came and went. The people were looking at us and saying things and I was thinking how it would be to ride in an airplane and leave behind the *barrio,* my friends in school, Mamá moaning about the bad times and the cafés that don't let anybody sleep. And then to live talking other words, far from the river where we bathe every afternoon. That's what I was thinking about this morning, dead tired because we'd gotten up at five. A few planes arrived but Uncle Segundo wasn't to be seen anywhere. Mamá was saying that he hadn't changed a bit, that he was the same old Segundo, arriving late at places, and probably mixed up with the police. That he'd probably got in some kind of a jam up there in the North and they'd arrested him, that he hadn't paid the store and was in court. That's what Mamá was saying, looking all around her, asking people, cursing every time they stepped on her new slippers.

I'd never met Uncle Segundo. They said that he had my face and that if I had a moustache we'd be like made to order. That's what the big people argued about on Sunday afternoon when Aunt Altagracia came from San Juan with her bag full of smells and sweets, and told us to ask her for a blessing and then talked with Mamá about how drawn and skinny I was, and whether I attended Sunday school and whether I studied, after which they would almost come to blows because Aunt Altagracia would say that I was Segundo through and through. Mamá didn't like it at first, but later she would say yes, that I was really another Segundo in the flesh, except without the moustache. But one thing, my aunt would snap, let's hope he doesn't have his fiendish nature, for one time someone called him "one ear" and he slashed the man's back and he also castrated the dog that ripped up the pants he wore for calling on his women. And Mamá would say no, I wouldn't have her brother's high-flown disposition, 'cause I was more like a sick little mouse if you were to judge by the way I sneaked around. Then Mamá would send me for a nickel's worth of cigarettes or to milk the goat, so that I wouldn't hear when she began to talk of Papá, and of the nights she couldn't sleep waiting for him while he played dominoes in Eufrasio's, and my aunt would turn all red and say she had it coming to her and that they'd warned her plenty and told her don't be crazy that man's a barfly don't be crazy watch what you're doing.

That was every Sunday, the only day that Aunt Altagracia could come from San Juan and visit this *barrio,* which she says she hates because the people don't have manners. But today is Tuesday and she came to see Grandma and to wait for her brother, because they wrote him that Grandma was on her last legs and he said all right if that's the way it is I'm coming but I've got to leave right away. And we were waiting four hours at the airport, dead tired, while all the people looked at us and said things.

Neither Mamá nor Aunt Altagracia recognized the man who came up dressed in white, looking plenty smooth and fat. He threw himself into their arms and nearly squeezed them both dry at the same time. As for me, he gave a tug at my sideburns and then stared at me awhile, then he picked me up and told me I was a real he-man and asked if I had a girlfriend. Mamá said that I'd been born a bit sickly and that from what I'd shown so far I'd turn out to be a sick little mouse. Aunt Altagracia said that they should take a good look, a real good look, for if I had a moustache I'd be the double in miniature of my uncle.

During the trip Uncle Segundo talked about his business in the North. My mother and my aunt both agreed that someday they would go up there, because here the sun makes one age ahead of time, and the work, the heat, the few opportunities to improve one's life. . . . We reached home without my being aware of it. Uncle Segundo woke me up tugging hard at my ear and asking if I could see God and saying straighten up 'cause nobody pays attention to people who hang their heads.

Uncle Segundo found Grandma a bit pale, but not as bad as they'd told him. He put his hand on her chest and told her to breathe, to come on and breathe, and he nearly turned the bed over and threw Grandma on the floor. He patted her on the face and then claimed she was all right, and that he'd come from so far away and that he'd left his business all alone and this was the only—listen, you—the *only* chance right now. Because after all he'd come to a funeral, and nothing else. My mother and my aunt opened their mouths to yell and they said it was true, he hadn't changed a bit. But my uncle said the old woman was fine, look at her, and what would people say if he couldn't come back from the North for the funeral next time? And he said it plenty clear: it had to happen in the three days he was going to spend in the *barrio* and if not they'd have to give him back the money he'd spent on the trip. My mamá and my aunt had their hands to their heads yelling barbarian, you're nothing but a heretic barbarian. Uncle Segundo's neck swelled up, he started saying things I didn't understand and he took Grandma's measurements. He measured her with his hands from head to foot and side to side. Grandma was smiling and it looked like she wanted to talk to him. Uncle made a face and went looking for Santo, the carpenter, and told him to make a coffin of the best wood there was, that his family wasn't cheap. They spoke about the price for a while and then Uncle left to see the four women he's got in the *barrio*. He gave each one six bits and brought them over to our house. They lit a few candles and put Grandma in the coffin where she could've danced, she was so skinny. My uncle complained and said the coffin was too wide, that Santo had made it like that just to charge more, and that he wouldn't pay a cent over three fifty. Grandma kept on laughing there, inside the coffin, and moved her lips like she wanted to say something. Uncle's women hadn't begun to cry when two of their dogs started to fight beneath the coffin. Uncle Segundo was furious and he kicked them until they peed and came out from under and left, their tails between their legs, yelping. Then Uncle moved his hand up and down and the women began to cry and shout. Uncle pinched them so they'd make more noise. Mamá was stretched out on the floor, howling just like the dogs; Aunt Altagracia was fanning her and sprinkling her with *alcoholado*. Papá was there, lying down at her side, saying that these things do happen and that it was all their fault, 'cause if they hadn't said anything to his brother-in-law nothing would have happened.

All that yelling began to draw people to the wake. Papá wasn't too happy about Eufrasio coming because he was always trying to collect debts with those hard looks of his. The twins, Serafin and Evaristo, arrived, and they tossed a coin heads or tails to see who would lead the rosary. Chalí came up with his eight children and sat them down on the floor and searched them for bugs while he mumbled his prayers. The Cané sisters came in through the kitchen looking at the cupboard, fanning themselves with a newspaper and saying things in each other's ears. The dogs were fighting outside. Cañón came up to Mamá and said he congratulated her, 'cause these things, well, they have to happen and that God Almighty would fix things up so as to find a little corner on his throne for the poor old woman. Aunt Altagracia was saying that the wake would have been more proper in San Juan and not in this damned *barrio*, which she unfortunately had to visit. Uncle Segundo was telling Grandma to shut her damned mouth, not to laugh, for this was no joke but a wake where she, though it might not seem so, was the most important thing.

Threads

Definition: "Six bits" is an old-fashioned way of saying 75 cents. Two bits is a quarter, or 25 cents.

Mamá got up and took Grandma out of the coffin. She was carrying her toward the room when Uncle, drunk and saying bad words, grabbed Grandma by the head and began to pull her back toward the coffin. Mamá kept pulling her by the ankles and then the dogs came in and started to bark. Uncle Segundo threw them a kick. The dogs left, but my uncle went sideways and fell on the floor with Mamá and Grandma. Papá squatted down next to Mamá and told her that this was incredible, that they should please their brother after all the years he'd been away. But Mamá didn't give in and then Uncle began to stamp his feet and Aunt Altagracia said, see, this boy hasn't changed a bit.

But my uncle still got things his way. Cañón was stretching out in a corner crying. The Cané sisters came up to my grandma and said how pretty the old woman looks, still smiling as in life, how pretty, eh?

I felt sort of shrunk. My uncle was a big strong man. I, Mamá herself said it, will turn out to be just a sick little mouse, the way I'm going. I would like to be strong, like my uncle, and fight anyone who gets in my way. I felt tiny whenever my uncle looked at me and said that I wouldn't look like him even with a moustache, that they'd fooled him so many times, and what was this? He would end up telling me that I'd become the spitting image of my father, and that one couldn't expect much from someone with my looks.

Cañón began to talk with Rosita Cané and after a while they went into the kitchen, acting as if they weren't up to something. The other Cané was fanning herself with a paper and looking enviously toward the kitchen and also looking at Eufrasio who, they say, bought off Melina's parents with a refrigerator. Melina had left to give birth someplace else and since then Eufrasio just drinks and fights with customers. But now Eufrasio was nice and calm and he was looking at the Cané girl and talking sign-language. He came up with a bottle and offered her a drink and she said heavens how dare you, but then she hid behind the curtain and if Eufrasio hadn't taken the bottle away she wouldn't have left a drop.

The wake was now going full-steam ahead and the twins kept leading the rosary, looking toward the room where Aunt Altagracia was lying down. I was nearly asleep when the beating Uncle Segundo gave Cañón shook me up. My uncle was shouting and demanding to know what kind of things were going on and that they should all leave if each and every one of them didn't want to get their share. Rosita Cané was crying. My uncle grabbed his suitcase and said that all in all he was satisfied because he'd come to his mother's wake and that now he didn't have to go through it again. He went out saying that he didn't mind paying for the fare, or the box, or the mourners, and that in the whole *barrio* they wouldn't find such a sacrificing son. There's the coffin, he said, for whoever's turn it is. And he left, almost running.

When I went up to the coffin and looked at Grandma she wasn't laughing anymore. But I noticed a tiny bit of brightness flowing from her eyes and wetting her tightly closed lips.

For Discussion

ABOUT THE CONTENT

1. Why are people at the airport "saying things" about the narrator and his family?
2. What kind of person is Uncle Segundo? What physical characteristics does he have that emphasize his personality traits?
3. What are the people of the *barrio* like?
4. What is the typical meaning of holding a wake? In what way is this a different sort of wake?
5. Why do you think Papá felt it important to please their brother Segundo?
6. What is the symbolism of "the North" in this story? (see page 61 for a definition of symbolism)

ABOUT THE WRITING

1. From whose point of view is this story told? Why did the author choose this narrator, in your opinion? How would the story change if Uncle Segundo told it? or if Grandma told it?
2. How is speech represented? Why did the author choose this method rather than standard dialogue, in your opinion?
3. Why did the translator choose to leave Spanish words in this story? What effect does it have?

Quickwrite

Imagine you are the grandmother in this story. Write your feelings about what has taken place.

Writing to Persuade: Public Debate

6

PERSUASIVE WRITING

Whether you're writing for work or for school, almost every type of writing involves an element of persuasion—trying to convince your reader to agree with you. However, there are types of writing strongly associated with persuasion: editorials and letters to the editor, advertising

Think about . . .

Do you enjoy reading letters to the editor of your newspaper?
Have you ever written one yourself?
Do you enjoy reading about political debates?
Why or why not?

and letters of appeal, and essays arguing for political, religious, or economic causes.

In this chapter, we will discover some of the elements that make persuasive writing effective.

ELEMENTS OF PERSUASION

Many different methods can be used to persuade an audience. The following list explains some of the more common ones.

1. **Appeal to values.** Persuasive writing often appeals to an audience's sense of justice, fairness, and its attitudes towards the community or world. When a large corporation is accused of polluting the environment, it might design an advertisement showing how the company has actually contributed to better ecological conditions. In this way it appeals to the audience's belief in the protection of the ecosystem.

2. **Dramatize the issue.** Persuasive writing captures the audience's attention quickly. If you are writing a fund-raising brochure for a homeless family shelter, you might start by listing the statistics on homelessness in your community. Unfortunately, the facts alone may not attract your reader's attention. Instead, a more effective opening paragraph might tell the story of one homeless family. This would dramatically illustrate the problem and draw the reader into your argument.

3. **Establish authority.** The effectiveness of an argument often depends on the expertise or credibility of the writer. For example, if you are a nuclear physicist, you may be able to convince your readers of the dangers of nuclear power more effectively than can a local merchant who is worried about a new power plant. If you don't have the expertise or experience, you need to show your readers that you are knowledgeable. To do this, you can quote experts, and/or show that you have read widely about your subject by referring to information you have gotten from books and articles.

4. **Use effective language.** The most effective persuasion uses words that are neither too strong nor too weak to convey the urgency of the situation. If you are trying to convince your readers not to support a certain political candidate, you will probably use strong language that warns of the consequences of voting for that candidate. On the other hand, if you are advertising a new toy, you probably won't try to convince your readers that the world will end if they don't buy the toy for their children.

LEARNING STRATEGY

Managing Your Learning: Examining writing for features you have just learned about will help you to remember those features.

ACTIVITY 1: LOCATING PERSUASIVE WRITING

Bring a recent copy of a local or school newspaper to class. Read the editorials and letters to the editor. Underline or highlight uses of effective persuasion. Put a "1" next to passages that appeal to the reader's values, a "2" next to passages that dramatize an issue, a "3" by passages that establish authority, and a "4" next to effective phrases or sentences. Can you identify places where the writer could have been more persuasive? Discuss your findings with your classmates.

Fallacies and Weaknesses in Persuasive Writing

Failing to capture your audience's attention and sympathy makes for weak persuasive writing. You can also make your argument ineffective by going too far—overstepping the bounds of logic and appropriateness. The following table presents some of the fallacies and weaknesses of persuasive writing—techniques that may make your audience feel unfairly manipulated and thus react negatively to your argument.

TABLE 6.1 LOGICAL FALLACIES AND WEAKNESSES IN PERSUASIVE WRITING

FALLACY OR WEAKNESS	EXAMPLE
Ad Hominem Arguments Arguing against a person instead of against his or her beliefs or actions	"My opponent is not a college graduate, thus he should not be allowed to speak publicly."
Bandwagon Appeals Claiming that "everyone" believes a certain idea, or does a certain thing; therefore, the reader is not "part of the crowd" if he or she believes otherwise.	"All good patriots fly their flags on Independence Day; you don't want to be unpatriotic, do you?"
Exaggerated Claims Overstating the causes or effects of an event or situation	"If we don't stop the excessive bridge tolls, our entire economy will collapse."
False Analogies Comparing two things that aren't similar enough to compare	"People in cars don't have to wear helmets, why should motorcycle riders?"
Misrepresentation Purposely leaving out facts in order to slant an argument	"Excessive television-watching is no longer a major problem. Recent statistics show that network audiences have shrunk 54 percent." (This leaves out the fact that cable television audiences have grown 175 percent.)
Oversimplification Reducing complex problems into simple ones, or offering simplistic solutions to complicated problems	"The drug problem can be solved if we build more prisons."
Either-Or Thinking Arguing falsely that there are only two possible outcomes to a situation	"Either we require immigrants to learn English, or people won't be able to understand each other any longer."
Post Hoc (ergo Propter Hoc)* Relationships Arguing that because an event happened before another one it caused that event to happen *This phrase is Latin for "After the fact, therefore because of the fact."	"Ever since Ms. Blum was elected, unemployment has increased 5 percent. (In fact, perhaps the closing of a major factory contributed to the rise.)

LEARNING STRATEGY

Forming Concepts: Reading a variety of materials, including letters and advertising, helps you understand the styles of English better.

ACTIVITY 2: LOCATING LOGICAL FALLACIES

Advertising frequently uses logical fallacies in order to convince consumers to buy a product. Look through a recent national magazine, and identify an advertisement that uses one or more of the techniques from Table 6.1 in order to persuade you to buy a product. Bring your ad to class and explain how it uses fallacies to persuade consumers.

PERSUASION IN THE WORKPLACE

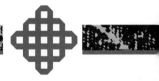

Employees in corporations need to persuade customers to buy their products. Similarly, nonprofit organizations need to convince the public to give them money or volunteer time. Therefore, every day, millions of pieces of mail sell products or ask for donations for worthwhile organizations.

The following promotional material was sent by Project Open Hand, a nonprofit organization in California benefiting AIDS patients.

Project Open Hand Kitchen

This Week's Shopping List

1,750 lbs   CHICKEN
1,500 lbs   BEEF
1,500 lbs   other meats such as TURKEY
$4,000   FRESH VEGETABLES, FRUITS & HERBS
360 lbs   BEANS
250 lbs   RICE
400 lbs   PASTA
150   ½ GALLONS OF MILK
400 lbs   HARD CHEESES AND TOFU
200 DOZEN EGGS
$8,000   VARIOUS GROCERIES

Clients can request regular meals,
vegetarian meals or culturally specific.

PROJECT OPEN HAND

Dear Friend,

Hello. I'm Martin Yan of Public Television's "Yan Can Cook" on KQED.

I've been actively involved with Project Open Hand for several years now. In fact, on a recent show I featured a recipe for "Rainbow chicken salad with glazed pecans" that's included in *The Open Hand Celebration Cookbook*.

But I'm not here to talk about myself. I'm going to talk about something more important: <u>Food.</u>

Ever since Ruth Brinker started Open Hand in 1985 by delivering meals she cooked herself to seven people with AIDS, Open Hand's mission has been to prepare meals using the freshest vegetables, fruit and meat.

Back then, no one could have foreseen how devastating the AIDS epidemic would become, or how many other people with AIDS would join those first seven clients in their need for home-delivered meals.

Today, over 10,000 people have died of AIDS in San Francisco alone. Currently, 28,000 are estimated to be infected with AIDS and HIV. Yet, despite these devastating statistics, <u>Project Open has never had to turn down a request for help from a person with AIDS</u>. That, I think you will agree, is nothing short of miraculous. And it's because of the caring and commitment of people from all over the Bay Area and beyond.

I'm asking you to join many of these wonderful, caring people.

As you can imagine, coming up with enough food is a daily battle. In fact, <u>it's the single biggest challenge facing Project Open Hand today</u>.

To meet the urgent need for food -- and to make sure there is a regular supply of it on a daily basis -- Open Hand has set

(over please)

2720 17TH STREET
SAN FRANCISCO
CALIFORNIA 94110
415 558 - 0600
FAX 415 621-0755

90

up a special fund that will be used exclusively to feed people with AIDS.

It's called the 100% Food Fund -- and every cent that goes into it will be used to purchase, prepare and deliver food.

Here in the Bay Area -- which is known throughout the world for its cuisine -- it's easy to forget just how basic and important food is. But for the people living with AIDS who depend on Project Open Hand, food isn't just basic -- it's survival. For many of these people, meals and groceries from Open Hand mean the difference between eating and going hungry.

For all of them, the nutritious, appealing food they receive from Open Hand helps them keep up their weight -- and their spirits -- and enables them to better fight their illness and stand up to often drastic medical treatments.

Let me share some "food facts" with you, to give you a better picture of the enormous amount of food it takes to feed over 2,700 people with AIDS -- and why your support of Open Hand is so urgently needed:

FACT #1 -- Every month the Open Hand kitchen goes through 7,000 lbs. of chicken, 1,000 lbs. of rice, 1,600 lbs. of pasta, 800 dozen eggs, hundreds of pounds of fresh produce, and much more.

FACT #2 -- The supplies in the Project Open Hand Food Bank's 4,000-square-foot (that's half a football field!) warehouse must be replenished every two weeks.

FACT #3 -- Open Hand's monthly bill for food alone averages $110,000, and it's always growing.

FACT #4 -- Even though Open Hand receives generous donations of food from individuals, restaurants, and food stores, the organization still has to purchase 90% of the food used in its kitchen.

The number of people who depend on Project Open Hand increases every day -- which means that the amount of food needed also increases every day. The fact is, Open Hand can only be there for everyone in need with the help of people like you.

Project Open Hand has been feeding people with AIDS now for eight years. They tell me that every day they re-learn the same humbling lesson: a hand extended to someone in need never comes back empty.

I'm asking you to help Project Open Hand today, by making a special donation. Your donation will help Open Hand provide

(next page, please)

meals and groceries for the growing number of people living with AIDS. It will be like a gift of food for people who urgently need it and greatly appreciate it.

Over 1,900 people with AIDS count on an Open Hand volunteer to knock on their door and deliver a hot meal or a bag of groceries. Hundreds of other people with AIDS depend on the groceries they receive from the Project Open Hand Food Bank.

Altogether, over 2,700 people living with AIDS count on Project Open Hand to be there every day -- which really means they are depending on people like you.

Will you help us feed those who need the proper sustenance to fight their disease, keep up their spirits and better tolerate often drastic medical treatments?

A donation of $35 to the 100% Food Fund will buy enough chicken to feed 80 people with AIDS. $70 will provide 112 portions of beef stew.

On behalf of all the people with AIDS who will receive meals with love as a result of your support, I want to thank you.

Sincerely,

Martin Yan
Yan Can Cook

P.S. Please help Open Hand win the battle against malnutrition for people with AIDS -- send a contribution today!

For Discussion

ABOUT THE CONTENT

1. What is Project Open Hand? What services does it provide?
2. What is funding used for?

ABOUT THE WRITING

1. How does the opening paragraph catch your attention?
2. Why has the writer used underlining?
3. Why has the letter come from Martin Yan, a chef with a popular cooking show on television, rather than the director of the organization?
4. What techniques does the writer use to convince you to donate money?
5. What is the purpose of the "Shopping List" that was included?
6. What techniques are used on the contribution form?

Quickwrite

What organizations do you (or would you like to) give donations to? Why? How do they help the community?

ACTIVITY 3: COLLABORATIVE WRITING FOR PROJECT OPEN HAND

Imagine that you and a group of classmates form a new committee for Project Open Hand. Instead of appealing for money, however, you are appealing for volunteers. People are needed to cook and deliver meals. Your committee has to produce the following materials to send in a mass mailing to your community.

- A letter of appeal
- A volunteer sign-up form
- Any other literature you think will be helpful

Use the information in the "Project Open Hand" reading and the information on effective persuasive techniques to help you write your mailing. Display the materials your committee develops to your class. Whose materials would convince you to donate your time? Why? Discuss the projects with your class.

ACTIVITY 4: PREWRITING—A PERSUASIVE LETTER

Before reading the next section, write a letter to a family member asking for $250. You need the money for textbooks, which are much more expensive than you thought they would be.

The Persuasive Essay

Persuasion is also important in academic writing. It can be used to defend an opinion or justify the analysis of data or other facts. In academic writing, persuasion typically contains three main elements, usually presented in this order:

1. **Background information.** In order to build a convincing argument, you must tell your reader the facts of the case. These facts should be clear, documented, and truthful, but in support of your main argument. For example, in a paper about homelessness, statistics regarding the number of homeless would probably be needed to support your argument. Other types of support are historical facts, personal experience, and quotations or paraphrasing from reading.

2. **Concession.** Every argument has two sides. Although as a writer you may be defending one side of an argument, you need to show your readers that you have considered the opposing side's point of view. This is often called a *concession.* A concession demonstrates that you have taken into consideration the counterargument, but you still believe your argument is stronger. For example, in a paper that argues for the elimination of grading at your school, you might *concede* that some students may do more poorly because they are motivated only by grades, but that overall, you believe students will focus more on their work and not on the grade. A *false concession,* however, merely states that there is another side: "While some students believe that grades should be eliminated, I believe they shouldn't." This "concession" doesn't *concede* anything; it merely states that there are two sides.

3. **The appeal.** The appeal is the main part of the argument, in which you state what you believe and why the readers should believe it, too. Appeals can be subtle or bold, depending on the author's feelings about the subject matter. An effective way of presenting your appeal is to organize your arguments in order of increasing importance. In the appeal, you should make it clear to the reader what you want him or her to do. For example, in an essay that addresses the problem of teenage runaways, you may simply appeal to your readers to be more sympathetic, or you may urge them to take action in their communities by setting up homes for runaways.

ACTIVITY 5: REREAD THE LETTER

Identify the passages in the letter you wrote in Activity 4 that presents the background, concession and appeal. In what order did you present them? Were you surprised to find that you included these three elements without being taught them?

Read the following essay, keeping in mind the elements of persuasive writing.

ROOTLESSNESS
by David Morris

Americans are a rootless people. Each year one in six of us changes residences; one in four changes jobs. We see nothing troubling in these statistics. For most of us, they merely reflect the restless energy that made

Threads

David Morris is the co-director of the Institute for Local Self-Reliance in Washington, D.C. He is the author of *The New City States* (1983) and *Neighborhood Power: The New Localism* (1975), which he wrote with Karl Hess.

America great. A nation of immigrants, unsurprisingly, celebrates those willing to pick up stakes and move on: the frontiersman, the cowboy, the entrepreneur, the corporate raider.

Rootedness has never been a goal of public policy in the United States. In the 1950s and 1960s local governments bulldozed hundreds of inner-city neighborhoods, all in the name of urban renewal. In the 1960s and 1970s court-ordered busing forced tens of thousands of children to abandon their neighborhood schools, all in the interest of racial harmony. In the 1980s a wave of hostile takeovers shuffled hundreds of billions of dollars of corporate assets, all in the pursuit of economic efficiency.

Hundreds of thousands of informal gathering spots that once nurtured community across the country have disappeared. The soda fountain and the lunch counter are gone. The branch library is an endangered species. Even the number of neighborhood taverns is declining. In the 1940s, 90 percent of beer and spirits was consumed in public places. Today only 30 percent is.

This privatization of American public life is most apparent to overseas visitors. "After four years here, I still feel more of a foreigner than in any other place in the world I have been," one well-traveled woman told Ray Oldenburg, the author of the marvelous new book about public gathering spots, *The Great Good Place* (1990, Paragon House). "There is no contact between the various households; we rarely see the neighbors and certainly do not know any of them."

The woman contrasts this with her life in Europe. "In Luxembourg, however, we would frequently stroll down to one of the local cafés in the evening and there pass a very congenial few hours in the company of the local fireman, dentist, bank employee, or whoever happened to be there at the time."

In most American cities, zoning laws prohibit mixing commerce and residence. The result is an overreliance on the car. Oldenburg cites the experience of a couple who had lived in a small house in Vienna and a large one in Los Angeles: "In Los Angeles we are hesitant to leave our sheltered home in order to visit friends or to participate in cultural or entertainment events because every such outing involves a major investment of time and nervous strain in driving long distances. In Vienna everything, opera, theaters, shops, cafés, are within easy walking distance."

Shallow roots weaken our ties in the neighborhood and workplace. The average blue-collar worker receives only seven days' notice before losing his or her job, only two days when not backed by a union. *The Whole Earth Review* unthinkingly echoes this lack of connectedness when it advises its readers to "first visit an electronics store near you and get familiar with the features—then compare price and shop mail order via [an] 800 number."

This lack of connectedness breeds costly instability in American life. In business, when owners have no loyalty to workers, workers have no loyalty to owners. Quality of work suffers. Visiting Japanese management specialists point to our labor turnover rate as a key factor in our relative economic decline. In the pivotal electronics industry, for example, our turnover rate is four times that of Japan's.

American employers respond to declining sales and profit margins by cutting what they regard as their most expendable resource: employees. In Japan, corporate accounting systems consider labor a fixed asset. Japanese companies spend enormous amounts of money training workers. "They view that training as an investment, and they don't want to let the investment slip away," Martin K. Starr of Columbia University recently told *Business Week.* Twenty percent of the work force, the core workers in major industrial companies, have lifetime job security in Japan.

Rootlessness in the neighborhood also costs us dearly. Neighborliness saves money, a fact we often overlook because the transactions of strong, rooted neighborhoods take place outside of the money economy:

- **Neighborliness reduces crime.** People watch the streets where children play and know who the strangers are.
- **Neighborliness saves energy.** In the late 1970s Portland, Oregon, discovered it could save 5 percent of its energy consumption simply by reviving the corner grocery store. No longer would residents in need of a carton of milk or a loaf of bread have to drive to a shopping mall.
- **Neighborliness lowers the cost of health care.** "It is cruel and unusual punishment to send someone to a nursing home when they are not sick," says Dick Ladd, head of Oregon's Senior Services. But when we don't know our neighbors, we can't rely on them. Society picks up the tab. In 1987 home-based care cost $230 a month in Oregon compared to $962 per month for nursing-home care.

Psychoanalyst and author Erich Fromm saw a direct correlation between the decline in the number of neighborhood bartenders and the rise in the number of psychiatrists. "Sometimes you want to go where everybody knows your name," goes the apt refrain of the popular TV show *Cheers*. Once you poured out your troubles over a nickel beer to someone who knew you and your family. And if you got drunk, well, you could walk home. Now you drive across town and pay $100 an hour to a stranger for emotional relief.

The breakdown of community life may explain, in part, why the three best-selling drugs in America treat stress: ulcer medication (Tagamet), hypertension (Inderal), tranquilizer (Valium).

American society has evolved into a cultural environment where it is ever harder for deep roots to take hold. What can we do to change this?

- **Rebuild walking communities.** Teach urban planners that overdependence on transportation is a sign of failure in a social system. Impose the true costs of the car on its owners. Recent studies indicate that to do so would raise the cost of gasoline by as much as $2 a gallon. Recently Stockholm declared war on cars by imposing a $50-a-month fee for car owners, promising to increase the fee until the city was given back to pedestrians and mass transit.
- **Equip every neighborhood with a library, a coffeehouse, a diversified shopping district, and a park.**
- **Make rootedness a goal of public policy.** In the 1970s a Vermont land-use law, for example, required an economic component to environmental impact statements. In at least one case, a suburban shopping mall was denied approval because it would undermine existing city businesses. In Berkeley, citizens voted two to one to permit commercial rent control in neighborhoods whose independently owned businesses were threatened by gentrification.
- **Reward stability and continuity.** Today, if a government seizes property it pays the owner the market price. Identical homes have identical value, even if one is home to a third-generation family, while the other is occupied by a new tenant. Why not pay a premium, say 50 percent above the current market price, for every 10 years the occupant has lived there? Forty years of residence would be rewarded with compensation four times greater than the market price. The increment above the market price should go not to the owner but to the occupant, if the two are not the same. By favoring occupants over owners, this policy not only rewards neighborliness, but promotes social justice. By raising the overall costs of dislocation, it also discourages development that undermines rootedness.
- **Prohibit hostile takeovers.** Japanese, German, and Swedish corporations are among the most competitive and innovative in the world. But in these

countries hostile takeovers are considered unethical business practices or are outlawed entirely.

- **Encourage local and employee ownership.** Protecting existing management is not the answer if that management is not locally rooted. Very few cities have an ongoing economic campaign to promote local ownership despite the obvious advantages to the community. Employee ownership exists in some form in more than 5,000 U.S. companies, but in only a handful is that ownership significant.

- **And above all, correct our history books.** America did not become a wealthy nation because of rootlessness, but in spite of it. A multitude of natural resources across an expansive continent and the arrival of tens of millions of skilled immigrants furnished us enormous advantages. We could overlook the high social costs of rootlessness. This is no longer true.

Instability is not the price we must pay for progress. Loyalty, in the plant and the neighborhood, does not stifle innovation. These are lessons we've ignored too long. More rooted cultures such as Japan and Germany are now outcompeting us in the marketplace and in the neighborhood. We would do well to learn the value of community.

Threads

Definition: A *hostile takeover* is what occurs when a company or group of individuals buys the majority of the stock in a company in order to control it. This can be done without the approval of the company's management (thus the term 'hostile').

For Discussion

ABOUT THE CONTENT

1. List all the advantages that a sense of community gives to a nation, as explained by Morris.
2. Do you disagree with any of these points? Explain your answer.
3. What is Morris's main argument? Phrase it in a single sentence.
4. How would you characterize the neighborliness in your own community? Is it better, the same, or worse than Morris describes?
5. What do you think you could do in your own community to improve neighborliness?

ABOUT THE WRITING

1. In what ways does Morris use authority to support his argument? Find all the instances in this article.
2. How does Morris use persuasive language to convey his point?
3. Does Morris commit any logical fallacies or weaknesses in persuasion?
4. Why does Morris repeat the word "neighborliness" in paragraphs 10–13? What effect does it have on the writing?
5. Morris makes a subtle concession. Can you identify it?
6. Restate Morris's appeal in your own words.

Quickwrite

Have you ever lived in a neighborhood or community that was very close-knit? What was that experience like? If not, would you like to?

You will find additional readings presenting public debate at the end of this chapter.

WRITING THE THIRD ESSAY

For this essay, you will again develop your own writing topic. The subject for the paper is <u>one of your community's most important problems.</u> In your essay, you should provide background about the situation, using information from appropriate authorities (interviews, readings, or whatever is appropriate). In addition, you should explain to your reader that it is an important problem and what might be done to correct it.

Preparation

Use the techniques explained in Chapter 1, such as brainstorming and freewriting, to decide on a topic that interests you. Make a list of all the problems that exist in your community (your community could be your community where your family is, your school community—however you want to define it). Then select a topic. Recall the triangle presented in the last chapter. Fill in the following triangle with your topic and thesis.

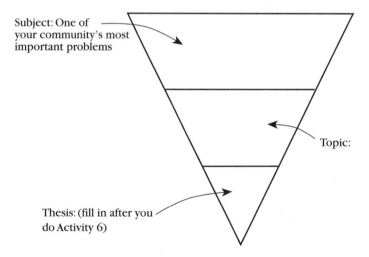

Subject: One of your community's most important problems

Topic:

Thesis: (fill in after you do Activity 6)

ACTIVITY 6: REVIEWING THESIS STATEMENTS

Part I. As you did in Chapter 5, work with a group of classmates to determine which of the following statements are good thesis statements and which are not. Be prepared to explain your decisions to your class.

1. Homelessness is a problem in my community.
2. Family problems cause many teenagers to become dangerously depressed.
3. At the university, cheating on examinations is common.
4. Inadequate public transportation contributes to isolation of the elderly.
5. Competition for high grades causes a breakdown in friendships at our school.

Part II. Now, write a **draft thesis statement** (it doesn't have to be perfect). Put your thesis statement into the triangle. With a partner, discuss the following questions for each of your thesis statements:

- Is it arguable?
- Is it a single sentence?
- Is it interesting?
- Is there enough information to support it?
- Is it grammatical?
- Is it specific (that is, does it make only one point)?

After your discussion, make any changes to your thesis statement that you think are necessary.

Drafting

When you have formulated a good thesis, assemble the materials you will need to begin the drafting process.

- Notes from your reading and class discussion
- Relevant quickwrite topics
- Notes on personal experience that you want to include
- Quotations from your reading that support your thesis
- Facts or information from "experts" or other people whose opinions are important

ACTIVITY 7: PREPARING YOUR ARGUMENT

Use the following table to help you prepare your argument. Briefly describe the main elements of your argument and the support you will provide.

Table 6.2 Outlining your argument

Thesis:	
First argument:	Support: Type of evidence: (historical fact, present experience, etc.)
Second argument	Support: Type of evidence:
Third argument	Support: Type of evidence:
Concession:	
Further arguments:	Support: Type of evidence:

Review the instructions on writing a first draft in the previous chapter. You are now ready to write your first draft.

Peer Response

Exchange drafts with a partner. Read your drafts carefully, and answer the following questions thoroughly and completely:

1. Is the title effective and interesting? Explain.
2. How effective is the introduction? Does it explain the issue? Does it have a thesis that is clear and arguable?
3. What is the writer's argument? Restate his or her main appeal in your own words.
4. Does the writer provide adequate background information? What more would you need to know about the subject in order to be convinced?
5. What concessions does the writer make? Are they effective? Explain.
6. Is the paper well-organized? Are transitions used effectively?
7. Does the conclusion end the paper effectively?
8. What other strengths or problems do you see in this paper?

Discuss your observations with your partner.

Revision

Remember that revision is not merely correcting your spelling and grammar and inserting a few commas. In the revision phase of the writing process, you are reorganizing, cutting, adding detail, and improving your choices. Looking at the review you received from your partner and your response to it, formulate a **revision plan.** Use the following chart to help you identify the areas that need the most improvement.

REVISION PLAN

FEATURE	PROBLEM	POSSIBLE SOLUTION
Title		
Opening paragraph		
Examples		
Organization		
Word choice		
Conclusion		
Other		

Use your revision plan to guide your rewriting.

Final Version

Before turning in your paper, edit and proofread it. Use Chapter 8 of this book to guide you. You may want to look at the results of your last paper and your recent assignments to make changes to your inventory of problem spots. Again, include a writer's memo (page 49) with your paper.

PROBLEM CHECKLIST

PROBLEM	Minor Problem	Major Problem	No Problem	Don't Know	Section
Spelling					
Punctuation					
Subject-verb agreement					
Verb tenses					
Articles and prepositions					
Plurals					
Sentence fragments					
Run-on sentences					
Wordiness					
Transitions					
Relative clauses					

ADDITIONAL READING

The following letter was written in 1963 as a response to a "Public Statement by Eight Alabama Clergymen," which spoke out against the civil rights demonstrations. In particular, they criticized the presence of "outsiders" and urged demonstrators to go through "proper channels" instead of demonstrating on the streets.

LETTER FROM BIRMINGHAM JAIL

by Martin Luther King, Jr.

April 16, 1963

My Dear Fellow Clergymen:

While confined here in the Birmingham city jail, I came across your recent statement calling my present activities "unwise and untimely." Seldom do I pause to answer criticism of my work and ideas. If I sought to answer all the criticisms that cross my desk, my secretaries would have little time for anything other than such correspondence in the course of the day, and I would have no time for constructive work. But since I feel that you are men of genuine good will and that your criticisms are sincerely set forth, I want to try to answer your statement in what I hope will be patient and reasonable terms.

I think I should indicate why I am here in Birmingham, since you have been influenced by the view which argues against "outsiders coming in." I have the honor of serving as president of the Southern Christian Leadership Conference, an organization operating in every southern state, with headquarters in Atlanta, Georgia. We have some eighty-five affiliated organizations across the South, and one of them is the Alabama Christian Movement for Human Rights. Frequently we share staff, educational and financial resources with our affiliates. Several months ago the affiliate here in Birmingham asked us to be on call to engage in a nonviolent direct-action program if such were deemed necessary. We readily consented, and when the hour came we lived up to our promise. So I, along with several members of my staff, am here because I was invited here. I am here because I have organizational ties here.

But more basically, I am in Birmingham because injustice is here. Just as the prophets of the eighth century B.C. left their villages and carried their "thus saith the Lord" far beyond the boundaries of their home towns, and just as the Apostle Paul left his village of Tarsus and carried the gospel of Jesus Christ to the far corners of the Greco-Roman world, so am I compelled to carry the gospel of freedom beyond my own home town. Like Paul, I must constantly respond to the Macedonian call for aid.

Moreover, I am cognizant of the interrelatedness of all communities and states. I cannot sit idly by in Atlanta and not be concerned about what happens in Birmingham. Injustice anywhere is a threat to justice everywhere. We are caught in an inescapable network of mutuality, tied in a single garment of destiny. Whatever affects one directly, affects all indirectly. Never again can we afford to live with the narrow, provincial "outside agitator" idea. Anyone who lives inside the United States can never be considered an outsider anywhere within its bounds.

You deplore the demonstrations taking place in Birmingham. But your statement, I am sorry to say, fails to express a similar concern for the conditions that brought about the demonstrations. I am sure that none of you would want to rest content with the superficial kind of social analysis that deals merely with effects and does not grapple with underlying causes. It is unfortunate that demonstrations are taking place in Birmingham, but it is even more unfortunate that the city's white power structure left the Negro community with no alternative.

In any nonviolent campaign there are four basic steps: collection of the facts to determine whether injustices exist; negotiation; self-purification; and direct action. We have gone through all these steps in Birmingham. There can be no gainsaying the fact that racial injustice engulfs this community. Birmingham is probably the most thoroughly segregated city in the United States. Its ugly record of brutality is widely known. Negroes have experienced grossly unjust treatment in the courts. There have been more unsolved bombings of Negro homes and churches in Birmingham than in any other city in the nation. These are the hard, brutal facts of the case. On the basis of these conditions, Negro leaders sought to negotiate with the city fathers. But the latter consistently refused to engage in good-faith negotiations.

Then, last September, came the opportunity to talk with leaders of Birmingham's economic community. In the course of the negotiations, certain promises were made by the merchants—for example, to remove the stores' humiliating racial signs. On the basis of these promises, the Reverend Fred Shuttlesworth and the leaders of the Alabama Christian Movement for Human Rights agreed to a moratorium on all demonstrations. As the weeks and months went by, we realized that we were the victims of a broken promise. A few signs, briefly removed, returned; the others remained.

As in so many past experiences, our hopes had been blasted, and the shadow of deep disappointment settled upon us. We had no alternative except to prepare for direct action, whereby we would present our very bodies as a means of laying our case before the conscience of the local and the national community. Mindful of the difficulties involved, we decided to undertake a process of self-purification. We began a series of workshops on nonviolence, and we repeatedly asked ourselves: "Are you able to accept blows without retaliating?" "Are you able to endure the ordeal of jail?" We decided to schedule our direct-action program for the Easter season, realizing that except for Christmas, this is the main shopping period of the year. Knowing that a strong economic-withdrawal program would be the by-product of direct action, we felt that this would be the best time to bring pressure to bear on the merchants for the needed change.

Then it occurred to us that Birmingham's mayoral election was coming up in March, and we speedily decided to postpone action until after election day. When we discovered that the Commissioner of Public Safety, Eugene "Bull" Connor, had piled up enough votes to be in the run-off, we decided again to postpone action until the day after the run-off so that the demonstrations could not be used to cloud the issues. Like many others, we waited to see Mr. Connor defeated, and to this end we endured postponement after postponement. Having aided in this community need, we felt that our direct-action program could be delayed no longer.

You may well ask: "Why direct action? Why sit-ins, marches and so forth? Isn't negotiation a better path?" You are quite right in calling for negotiation. Indeed, this is the very purpose of direct action. Nonviolent direct action seeks to create such a crisis and foster such a tension that a community which has constantly refused to negotiate is forced to confront the issue. It seeks so to dramatize the issue that it can no longer be ignored. My citing the creation of tension as part of the work of the nonviolent-resister may sound rather shocking. But I must confess that I am not afraid of the word "tension." I have earnestly opposed violent tension, but there is a type of constructive, nonviolent tension which is necessary for growth. Just as Socrates felt it was necessary to create a tension in the mind so that individuals could rise from the bondage of myths and half-truths to the unfettered realm of creative analysis and objective appraisal, so must we see the need for nonviolent gadflies to create the kind of tension in society that will help men rise from the dark depths of prejudice and racism to the majestic heights of understanding and brotherhood.

The purpose of our direct-action program is to create a situation so crisis-packed that it will inevitably open the door to negotiation. I therefore concur with you in your call for negotiation. Too long has our beloved Southland been bogged down in a tragic effort to live in monologue rather than dialogue.

One of the basic points in your statement is that the action that I and my associates have taken in Birmingham is untimely. Some have asked: "Why didn't you give the new city administration time to act?" The only answer that I can give to this query is that the new Birmingham administration must be prodded about as much as the outgoing one, before it will act. We are sadly mistaken if we feel that the election of Albert Boutwell as mayor will bring the millennium to Birmingham. While Mr. Boutwell is a much more gentle person than Mr. Connor, they are both segregationists, dedicated to maintenance of the status quo. I have hope that Mr. Boutwell will be reasonable enough to see the futility of massive resistance to desegregation. But he will not see this without pressure from devotees of civil rights. My friends, I must say to you that we have not made a single gain in civil rights without determined legal and nonviolent pressure. Lamentably, it is an historical fact that privileged groups seldom give up their privileges voluntarily. Individuals may see the moral light and voluntarily give up their unjust posture; but, as Reinhold Niebuhr has reminded us, groups tend to be more immoral than individuals.

We know through painful experience that freedom is never voluntarily given by the oppressor; it must be demanded by the oppressed. Frankly, I have yet to engage in a direct-action campaign that was "well-timed" in the view of those who have not suffered unduly from the disease of segregation. For years now I have heard the word "Wait!" It rings in the ear of every Negro with piercing familiarity. This "Wait" has almost always meant "Never." We must come to see, with one of our distinguished jurists, that "justice too long delayed is justice denied."

We have waited for more than 340 years for our constitutional and God-given rights. The nations of Asia and Africa are moving with jetlike speed toward gaining political independence, but we still creep at horse-and-buggy pace toward gaining a cup of coffee at a lunch counter. Perhaps it is easy for those who have never felt the stinging darts of segregation to say, "Wait." But when you have seen vicious mobs lynch your mothers and fathers at will and drown your sisters and brothers at whim; when you have seen hate-filled policemen curse, kick, and even kill your black brothers and sisters; when you see the vast majority of your twenty million Negro brothers smothering in an air-tight cage of poverty in the midst of an affluent society; when you suddenly find your tongue twisted and your speech stammering as you seek to explain to your six-year-old daughter why she can't go to the public amusement park that has just been advertised on television, and see tears welling up in her eyes when she is told that Funtown is closed to colored children, and see ominous clouds of inferiority beginning to form in her little mental sky, and see her beginning to distort her personality by developing an unconscious bitterness toward white people; when you have to concoct an answer for a five-year-old son who is asking: "Daddy, why do white people treat colored people so mean?"; when you take a cross-country drive and find it necessary to sleep night after night in the uncomfortable corners of your automobile because no motel will accept you; when you are humiliated day in and day out by nagging signs reading "white" and "colored"; when your first name becomes "nigger," your middle name becomes "boy" (however old you are), and your last name becomes

Threads

Reinhold Niehbar (1892–1971) was an American Prostestant theologian.

"John," and your wife and mother are never given the respected title "Mrs."; when you are harried by day and haunted by night by the fact that you are a Negro, living constantly at tiptoe stance, never quite knowing what to expect next, and are plagued with inner fears and outer resentments; when you are forever fighting a degenerating sense of "nobodiness"—then you will understand why we find it difficult to wait. There comes a time when the cup of endurance runs over, and men are no longer willing to be plunged into the abyss of despair. I hope, sirs, you can understand our legitimate and unavoidable impatience.

You express a great deal of anxiety over our willingness to break laws. This is certainly a legitimate concern. Since we so diligently urge people to obey the Supreme Court's decision of 1954 outlawing segregation in the public schools, at first glance it may seem rather paradoxical for us to consciously break laws. One may well ask: "How can you advocate breaking some laws and obeying others?" The answer lies in the fact that there are two types of laws: just and unjust. I would be the first to advocate obeying just laws. One has not only a legal but a moral responsibility to obey just laws. I would agree with St. Augustine that "an unjust law is no law at all."

Now, what is the difference between the two? How does one determine whether law is just or unjust? A just law is a man-made code that squares with the moral law or the law of God. An unjust law is a code that is out of harmony with the moral law. To put it in the terms of St. Thomas Aquinas: An unjust law is a human law that is not rooted in eternal law and natural law. Any law that uplifts human personality is just. Any law that degrades human personality is unjust. All segregation statutes are unjust because segregation distorts the soul and damages the personality. It gives the segregator a false sense of superiority and the segregated a false sense of inferiority. Segregation, to use the terminology of the Jewish philosopher Martin Buber, substitutes an "I-it" relationship for an "I-thou" relationship and ends up relegating persons to the status of things. Hence segregation is not only politically, economically and socially unsound, it is morally wrong and sinful. Paul Tillich has said that sin is separation. Is not segregation an existential expression of man's tragic separation, his awful estrangement, his terrible sinfulness? Thus it is that I can urge men to obey the 1954 decision of the Supreme Court, for it is morally right; and I can urge them to disobey segregation ordinances, for they are morally wrong.

Let us consider a more concrete example of just and unjust laws. An unjust law is a code that a numerical or power majority group compels a minority group to obey but does not make binding on itself. This is *difference* made legal. By the same token, a just law is a code that a majority compels a minority to follow and that it is willing to follow itself. This is *sameness* made legal.

Let me give another explanation. A law is unjust if it is inflected on a minority that, as a result of being denied the right to vote, had no part in enacting or devising the law. Who can say that the legislature of Alabama which set up that state's segregation laws was democratically elected? Throughout Alabama all sorts of devious methods are used to prevent Negroes from becoming registered voters, and there are some counties in which, even though Negroes constitute a majority of the population, not a single Negro is registered. Can any law enacted under such circumstances be considered democratically structured?

Sometimes a law is just on its face and unjust in its application. For instance, I have been arrested on a charge of parading without a permit. Now, there is nothing wrong in having an ordinance which requires a permit for a parade. But such an ordinance becomes unjust when it is used to maintain segregation and to deny citizens the First-Amendment privilege of peaceful assembly and protest.

I hope you are able to see the distinction I am trying to point out. In no sense do I advocate evading or defying the law, as would the rabid segregationist. That would lead to anarchy. One who breaks an unjust law must

Threads

Paul Tillich (1886–1965) was a German-American Protestant philosopher and theologian.

do so openly, lovingly, and with a willingness to accept the penalty. I submit that an individual who breaks a law that conscience tells him is unjust, and who willingly accepts the penalty of imprisonment in order to arouse the conscience of the community over its injustice, is in reality expressing the highest respect for law.

Of course, there is nothing new about this kind of civil disobedience. It was evidenced sublimely in the refusal of Shadrach, Meshach and Abednego to obey the laws of Nebuchadnezzar, on the ground that a higher moral law was at stake. It was practiced superbly by the early Christians, who were willing to face hungry lions and the excruciating pain of chopping blocks rather than submit to certain unjust laws of the Roman Empire. To a degree, academic freedom is a reality today because Socrates practiced civil disobedience. In our own nation, the Boston Tea Party represented a massive act of civil disobedience.

We should never forget that everything Adolf Hitler did in Germany was "legal" and everything the Hungarian freedom fighters did in Hungary was "illegal." It was "illegal" to aid and comfort a Jew in Hitler's Germany. Even so, I am sure that, had I lived in Germany at the time, I would have aided and comforted my Jewish brothers. If today I lived in a Communist country where certain principles dear to the Christian faith are suppressed, I would openly advocate disobeying that country's antireligious laws.

I must make two honest confessions to you, my Christian and Jewish brothers. First, I must confess that over the past few years I have been gravely disappointed with the white moderate. I have almost reached the regrettable conclusion that the Negro's great stumbling block in his stride toward freedom is not the White Citizen's Counciler or the Ku Klux Klanner, but the white moderate, who is more devoted to "order" than to justice; who prefers a negative peace which is the absence of tension to a positive peace which is the presence of justice; who constantly says: "I agree with you in the goal you seek, but I cannot agree with your methods of direct action"; who paternalistically believes he can set the timetable for another man's freedom; who lives by a mythical concept of time and who constantly advises the Negro to wait for a "more convenient season." Shallow understanding from people of good will is more frustrating than absolute misunderstanding from people of ill will. Lukewarm acceptance is much more bewildering than outright rejection.

I had hoped that the white moderate would understand that law and order exist for the purpose of establishing justice and that when they fail in this purpose they become the dangerously structured dams that block the flow of social progress. I had hoped that the white moderate would understand that the present tension in the South is a necessary phase of the transition from an obnoxious negative peace, in which the Negro passively accepted his unjust plight, to a substantive and positive peace, in which all men will respect the dignity and worth of human personality. Actually, we who engage in nonviolent direct action are not the creators of tension. We merely bring to the surface the hidden tension that is already alive. We bring it out in the open, where it can be seen and dealt with. Like a boil that can never be cured so long as it is covered up but must be opened with all its ugliness to the natural medicines of air and light, injustice must be exposed, with all the tension its exposure creates, to the light of human conscience and the air of national opinion before it can be cured.

In your statement you assert that our actions, even though peaceful, must be condemned because they precipitate violence. But is this a logical assertion? Isn't this like condemning a robbed man because his possession of money precipitated the evil act of robbery? Isn't this like condemning Socrates because his unswerving commitment to truth and his philosophical inquiries precipitated the act by the misguided populace in which they made him drink hemlock? Isn't this like condemning Jesus because his unique God-consciousness and never-ceasing devotion to God's will precipitated the evil act

Threads

The Book of Daniel, in Judaeo-Christian history, tells how Nebuchadnezzar, king of Babylon, cast the three Jewish leaders—Shadrach, Meshach, and Abednego—into a furnace, but released them and praised their God when they emerged unharmed.

Threads

The Hungarian freedom fighters fought against the Soviet troops in 1956, during a revolution against the goverment in Hungary.

of crucifixion? We must come to see that, as the federal courts have consistently affirmed, it is wrong to urge an individual to cease his efforts to gain his basic constitutional rights because the quest may precipitate violence. Society must protect the robbed and punish the robber.

I had also hoped that the white moderate would reject the myth concerning time in relation to the struggle for freedom. I have just received a letter from a white brother in Texas. He writes: "All Christians know that the colored people will receive equal rights eventually, but it is possible that you are in too great a religious hurry. It has taken Christianity almost two thousand years to accomplish what it has. The teachings of Christ take time to come to earth." Such an attitude stems from a tragic misconception of time, from the strangely irrational notion that there is something in the very flow of time that will inevitably cure all ills. Actually, time itself is neutral; it can be used either destructively or constructively. More and more I feel that the people of ill will have used time much more effectively than have the people of good will. We will have to repent in this generation not merely for the hateful words and actions of the bad people but for the appalling silence of the good people. Human progress never rolls in on wheels of inevitability; it comes through the tireless efforts of men willing to be co-workers with God, and without this hard work, time itself becomes an ally of the forces of social stagnation. We must use time creatively, in the knowledge that the time is always ripe to do right. Now is the time to make real the promise of democracy and transform our pending national elegy into a creative psalm of brotherhood. Now is the time to lift our national policy from the quicksand of racial injustice to the solid rock of human dignity.

You speak of our activity in Birmingham as extreme. At first I was rather disappointed that fellow clergymen would see my nonviolent efforts as those of an extremist. I began thinking about the fact that I stand in the middle of two opposing forces in the Negro community. One is the force of complacency, made up in part of Negroes who, as a result of long years of oppression, are so drained of self-respect and a sense of "somebodiness" that they have adjusted to segregation; and in part of a few middle-class Negroes who, because of a degree of academic and economic security and because in some ways they profit by segregation, have become insensitive to the problems of the masses. The other force is one of bitterness and hatred, and it comes perilously close to advocating violence. It is expressed in the various black nationalist groups that are springing up across the nation, the largest and best-known being Elijah Muhammad's Muslim movement. Nourished by the Negro's frustration over the continued existence of racial discrimination, this movement is made up of people who have lost faith in America, who have absolutely repudiated Christianity, and who have concluded that the white man is an incorrigible "devil."

I have tried to stand between these two forces, saying that we need emulate neither the "do-nothingism" of the complacent nor the hatred and despair of the black nationalist. For there is the more excellent way of love and nonviolent protest. I am grateful to God that, through the influence of the Negro church, the way of nonviolence became an integral part of our struggle.

If this philosophy had not emerged, by now many streets of the South would, I am convinced, be flowing with blood. And I am further convinced that if our white brothers dismiss as "rabble-rousers" and "outside agitators" those of us who employ nonviolent direct action, and if they refuse to support our nonviolent efforts, millions of Negroes will, out of frustration and despair, seek solace and security in black-nationalist ideologies—a development that would inevitably lead to a frightening racial nightmare.

Oppressed people cannot remain oppressed forever. The yearning for freedom eventually manifests itself, and that is what has happened to the American Negro. Something within has reminded him of his birthright of freedom, and something without has reminded him that it can be gained. Consciously or unconsciously, he has been caught up by the *Zeitgeist,* and with

Threads

Elijah Muhammad's Muslim movement—The nation of Islam, the members of which were known as "Black Muslims," was an American Islamic sect popular in the 1960s.

his black brothers of Africa and his brown and yellow brothers of Asia, South America, and the Caribbean, the United States Negro is moving with a sense of great urgency toward the promised land of racial justice. If one recognizes this vital urge that has engulfed the Negro community, one should readily understand why public demonstrations are taking place. The Negro has many pent-up resentments and latent frustrations, and he must release them. So let him march; let him make prayer pilgrimages to city hall; let him go on freedom rides—and try to understand why he must do so. If his repressed emotions are not released in nonviolent ways, they will seek expression through violence; this is not a threat but a fact of history. So I have not said to my people: "Get rid of your discontent." Rather, I have tried to say that this normal and healthy discontent can be channeled into the creative outlet of nonviolent direct action. And now this approach is being termed extremist.

But though I was initially disappointed at being categorized as an extremist, as I continued to think about the matter I gradually gained a measure of satisfaction from the label. Was not Jesus an extremist for love: "Love your enemies, bless them that curse you, do good to them that hate you, and pray for them which despitefully use you, and persecute you." Was not Amos an extremist for justice: "Let justice roll down like waters and righteousness like an ever- flowing stream." Was not Paul an extremist for the Christian gospel: "I bear in my body the marks of the Lord Jesus." Was not Martin Luther extremist: "Here I stand; I cannot do otherwise, so help me God." And John Bunyan: "I will stay in jail to the end of my days before I make a butchery of my conscience." And Abraham Lincoln: "This nation cannot survive half slave and half free." And Thomas Jefferson: "We hold these truths to be self-evident, that all men are created equal. . . ." So the question is not whether we will be extremists, but what kind of extremists we will be. Will we be extremists for hate or for love? Will we be extremists for the preservation of injustice or for the extension of justice? In that dramatic scene on Calvary's hill three men were crucified. We must never forget that all three were crucified for the same crime—the crime of extremism. Two were extremists for immorality, and thus fell below their environment. The other, Jesus Christ, was an extremist for love, truth and goodness, and thereby rose above his environment. Perhaps the South, the nation and the world are in dire need of creative extremists.

I had hoped that the white moderate would see this need. Perhaps I was too optimistic; perhaps I expected too much. I suppose I should have realized that few members of the oppressor race can understand the deep groans and passionate yearnings of the oppressed race, and still fewer have the vision to see that injustice must be rooted out by strong, persistent, and determined action. I am thankful, however, that some of our white brothers in the South have grasped the meaning of this social revolution and committed themselves to it. They are still too few in quantity, but they are big in quality. Some—such as Ralph McGill, Lillian Smith, Harry Golden, James McBride Dabbs, Ann Braden, and Sarah Patton Boyle— have written about our struggle in eloquent and prophetic terms. Others have marched with us down nameless streets of the South. They have languished in filthy, roach-infested jails, suffering the abuse and brutality of policemen who view them as "dirty nigger-lovers." Unlike so many of their moderate brothers and sisters, they have recognized the urgency of the moment and sensed the need for powerful "action" antidotes to combat the disease of segregation.

Threads

Amos was a prophet in the Old Testament of the Judaeo-Christian Bible.

Threads

Martin Luther (1483–1546) was a German leader of the Protestant Reformation. He was the founder of Lutheranism, a Christian sect. He spoke the quoted words in response to a demand that he take back his criticisms of Catholic religious practices.

Threads

Governor Ross Barnett was a Governor of Mississippi who believed in segregation of the races.

George Wallace was the governor of Alabama and also a believer in segregation. He later ran unsuccessfully for President and survived an assassination attempt.

Threads

Interposition and nullification is a state's claim that it can cancel any action by the federal government that it believes threatens the state's self-rule.

Let me take note of my other major disappointment. I have been so greatly disappointed with the white church and its leadership. Of course, there are some notable exceptions. I am not unmindful of the fact that each of you has taken some significant stands on this issue. I commend you, Reverend Stallings, for your Christian stand on this past Sunday, in welcoming Negroes to your worship service on a nonsegregated basis. I commend the Catholic leaders of this state for integrating Spring Hill College several years ago.

But despite these notable exceptions, I must honestly reiterate that I have been disappointed with the church. I do not say this as one of those negative critics who can always find something wrong with the church. I say this as a minister of the gospel, who loves the church; who was nurtured in its bosom; who has been sustained by its spiritual blessings and who will remain true to it as long as the cord of life shall lengthen.

When I was suddenly catapulted into the leadership of the bus protest in Montgomery, Alabama, a few years ago, I felt we would be supported by the white church. I felt that the white ministers, priests and rabbis of the South would be among our strongest allies. Instead, some have been outright opponents, refusing to understand the freedom movement and misrepresenting its leaders; all too many others have been more cautious than courageous and have remained silent behind the anesthetizing security of stained-glass windows.

In spite of my shattered dreams, I came to Birmingham with the hope that the white religious leadership of this community would see the justice of our cause and, with deep moral concern, would serve as the channel through which our just grievances could reach the power structure. I had hoped that each of you would understand. But again I have been disappointed.

I have heard numerous southern religious leaders admonish their worshipers to comply with a desegregation decision because it is the law, but I have longed to hear white ministers declare: "Follow this decree because integration is morally right and because the Negro is your brother." In the midst of blatant injustices inflicted upon the Negro, I have watched white churchmen stand on the sideline and mouth pious irrelevancies and sanctimonious trivialities. In the midst of a mighty struggle to rid our nation of racial and economic injustice, I have heard many ministers say: "Those are social issues, with which the gospel has no real concern." And I have watched many churches commit themselves to a completely otherworldly religion which makes a strange, un-Biblical distinction between body and soul, between the sacred and the secular.

I have traveled the length and breadth of Alabama, Mississippi, and all the other southern states. On sweltering summer days and crisp autumn mornings I have looked at the South's beautiful churches with their lofty spires pointing heavenward. I have beheld the impressive outlines of her massive religious-education buildings. Over and over I have found myself asking: "What kind of people worship here? Who is their God? Where were their voices when the lips of Governor Barnett dripped with the words of interposition and nullification? Where were they when Governor Wallace gave a clarion call for defiance and hatred? Where were their voices of support when bruised and weary Negro men and women decided to rise from the dark dungeons of complacency to the bright hills of creative protest?"

Yes, these questions are still in my mind. In deep disappointment I have wept over the laxity of the church. But be assured that my tears have been tears of love. There can be no deep disappointment where there is not deep love. Yes, I love the church. How could I do otherwise? I am in the rather unique position of being the son, the grandson, and the great-grandson of preachers. Yes, I see the church as the body of Christ. But, oh! How we have blemished and scarred that body through social neglect and through fear of being nonconformists.

There was a time when the church was very powerful—in the time when the early Christians rejoiced at being deemed worthy to suffer for what they believed. In those days the church was not merely a thermometer that recorded the ideas and principles of popular opinion; it was a thermostat that transformed the mores of society. Whenever the early Christians entered a town, the people in power became disturbed and immediately sought to convict the Christians for being "disturbers of the peace" and "outside agitators." But the Christians pressed on, in the conviction that they were "a colony of heaven," called to obey God rather than man. Small in number, they were big in commitment. They were too God-intoxicated to be "astronomically intimidated." By their effort and examples they brought an end to such ancient evils as infanticide and gladiatorial contests.

Things are different now. So often the contemporary church is a weak, ineffectual voice with an uncertain sound. So often it is an arch-defender of the status quo. Far from being disturbed by the presence of the church, the power structure of the average community is consoled by the church's silent—and often even vocal—sanction of things as they are.

But the judgment of God is upon the church as never before. If today's church does not recapture the sacrificial spirit of the early church, it will lose its authenticity, forfeit the loyalty of millions, and be dismissed as an irrelevant social club with no meaning for the twentieth century. Every day I meet young people whose disappointment with the church has turned to outright disgust.

Perhaps I have once again been too optimistic. Is organized religion too inextricably bound to the status quo to save our nation and the world? Perhaps I must turn my faith to the inner spiritual church, the church within the church, as the true *ekklesia* and the hope of the world. But again I am thankful to God that some noble souls from the ranks of organized religion have broken loose from the paralyzing chains of conformity and joined us as active partners in the struggle for freedom. They have left their secure congregations and walked the streets of Albany, Georgia, with us. They have gone down the highways of the South on tortuous rides for freedom. Yes, they have gone to jail with us. Some have been dismissed from their churches, have lost the support of their bishops and fellow ministers. But they have acted in the faith that right defeated is stronger than evil triumphant. Their witness has been the spiritual salt that has preserved the true meaning of the gospel in these troubled times. They have carved a tunnel of hope through the dark mountain of disappointment.

I hope the church as a whole will meet the challenge of this decisive hour. But even if the church does not come to the aid of justice, I have no despair about the future. I have no fear about the outcome of our struggle in Birmingham, even if our motives are at present misunderstood. We will reach the goal of freedom in Birmingham and all over the nation, because the goal of America is freedom. Abused and scorned though we may be, our destiny is tied up with America's destiny. Before the pilgrims landed at Plymouth, we were here. Before the pen of Jefferson etched the majestic words of the Declaration of Independence across the pages of history, we were here. For more than two centuries our forebears labored in this country without wages; they made cotton king; they built the homes of their masters while suffering gross injustice and shameful humiliation—and yet out of bottomless vitality they continued to thrive and develop. If the inexpressible cruelties of slavery could not stop us, the opposition we now face will surely fail. We will win our freedom because the sacred heritage of our nation and the eternal will of God are embodied in our echoing demands.

Before closing I feel impelled to mention one other point in your statement that has troubled me profoundly. You warmly commended the Birmingham police force for keeping "order" and "preventing violence." I doubt that you would have so warmly commended the police force if you had seen its dogs sinking their teeth into unarmed, nonviolent Negroes. I doubt that you would so quickly commend the policemen if you were to observe their ugly and inhumane

Threads

Definition: *ekklesia* (Greek) is an assembly or church

Threads

T.S. Eliot (1888–1964) was an American poet who converted to Christianity.

Threads

James Meredith was the first black to be accepted and graduate from the University of Mississippi, despite much harassment.

treatment of Negroes here in the city jail; if you were to watch them push and curse old Negro women and young Negro girls; if you were to see them slap and kick old Negro men and young boys; if you were to observe them, as they did on two occasions, refuse to give us food because we wanted to sing our grace together. I cannot join you in your praise of the Birmingham police department.

It is true that the police have exercised a degree of discipline in handling the demonstrators. In this sense they have conducted themselves rather "nonviolently" in public. But for what purpose? To preserve the evil system of segregation. Over the past few years I have consistently preached that nonviolence demands that the means we use must be as pure as the ends we seek. I have tried to make clear that it is wrong to use immoral means to attain moral ends. But now I must affirm that it is just as wrong, or perhaps even more so, to use moral means to preserve immoral ends. Perhaps Mr. Connor and his policemen have been rather nonviolent in public, as was Chief Pritchett in Albany, Georgia, but they have used the moral means of nonviolence to maintain the immoral end of racial injustice. As T. S. Eliot has said: "The last temptation is the great treason: To do the right deed for the wrong reason."

I wish you had commended the Negro sit-inners and demonstrators of Birmingham for their sublime courage, their willingness to suffer, and their amazing discipline in the midst of great provocation. One day the South will recognize its real heroes. They will be the James Merediths, with the noble sense of purpose that enables them to face jeering and hostile mobs, and with the agonizing loneliness that characterizes the life of the pioneer. They will be old, oppressed, battered Negro women, symbolized in a seventy-two-year-old woman in Montgomery, Alabama, who rose up with a sense of dignity and with her people decided not to ride segregated buses, and who responded with ungrammatical profundity to one who inquired about her weariness: "My feets is tired, but my soul is at rest." They will be the young high school and college students, the young ministers of the gospel and a host of their elders, courageously and nonviolently sitting at lunch counters and willingly going to jail for conscience' sake. One day the South will know that when these disinherited children of God sat down at lunch counters, they were in reality standing up for what is best in the American dream and for the most sacred values in our Judaeo-Christian heritage, thereby bringing our nation back to those great wells of democracy which were dug deep by the founding fathers in the formulation of the Constitution and the Declaration of Independence.

Never before have I written so long a letter. I'm afraid it is much too long to take your precious time. I can assure you that it would have been much shorter if I had been writing from a comfortable desk, but what else can one do when he is alone in a narrow jail cell, other than write long letters, think long thoughts, and pray long prayers?

If I have said anything in this letter that overstates the truth and indicates an unreasonable impatience, I beg you to forgive me. If I have said anything that understates the truth and indicates my having a patience that allows me to settle for anything less than brotherhood, I beg God to forgive me.

I hope this letter finds you strong in the faith. I also hope that circumstances will soon make it possible for me to meet each of you, not as an integrationist or a civil-rights leader but as a fellow clergyman and a Christian brother. Let us all hope that the dark clouds of racial prejudice will soon pass away and the deep fog of misunderstanding will be lifted from our fear-drenched communities, and in some not too distant tomorrow the radiant stars of love and brotherhood will shine over our great nation with all their scintillating beauty.

Yours for the cause of Peace and Brotherhood,
Martin Luther King, Jr.

For Discussion

ABOUT THE CONTENT

1. Why do you think King says that he doesn't usually reply to criticism?
2. Why is King in jail?
3. King emphasizes "self-purification" as an important step leading to "nonviolent direct action." Is this spiritual requirement also a practical suggestion?
4. Find examples where King has anticipated criticism of his argument. Does he present a concession? Find it.
5. What is King's distinction between just and unjust laws? Do you understand his position? Can you apply it to a circumstance in society today?
6. Why does King think "the white moderate" is perhaps a greater threat to racial progress than the obvious racist?
7. What is meant by Niebuhr's quotation that "groups tend to be more immoral than individuals"?

ABOUT THE WRITING

1. Find passages where King appeals to authority. Describe the variety of authorities he appeals to. What does this say about his approach to persuasion?
2. Describe the tone of this letter. How does he maintain this tone?
3. Can you identify examples of writing that indicate that King writes as a preacher? Are you familiar with that style of writing or speech?
4. How does King use concrete examples to make segregation more real to the reader?
5. Why does King introduce black nationalism to his audience? What purpose does this example serve in his argument?
6. If King had written an essay instead of a letter, how might it have been different, in your opinion?

DEATH BY DECREE: AN ANTHROPOLOGICAL APPROACH TO CAPITAL PUNISHMENT

by Colin Turnbull

Anthropologists, particularly when in the field, try to be as detached as possible, eschewing value judgments, looking at social institutions in their context. Sometimes I think they become too detached and lose sight of their own social values and responsibilities. Sometimes I think they become detached from humanity itself. Yet anthropology is as much a humanity as a science, if not more so. If we are dealing exclusively with society as a system of interrelated social institutions, then we can achieve a greater legitimate measure of detachment, and indeed we should. But we are also dealing with human beings with human values, and we have to recognize that human emotions and the need for their expression are powerful forces in shaping the structure of any society. To be truly holistic, which is one of our claims, we must be subjective as well as objective in our quest for truth and meaning. It is not always a comfortable quest, least of all when dealing with an issue such as capital punishment.

Threads

Colin Turnbull is an anthropologist who has studied and written about the tribal peoples of Africa. He worked as an instructor in the Virginia State Penitentiary for three years.

In all societies and all legal systems, and certainly in our own, persons are distinguished from things. To persons we attribute inalienable human rights. The institution of slavery was justified, even by Christian moralists, by the simple denial of that basic tenet. We classified one group of persons as things and from that moment on had no moral obligation to them as humans. Joseph Towles, a black American anthropologist, who has some experience of what it is to be treated as a thing, recently pointed out to me the similarity of the process as applied to slaves and as applied to prisoners, particularly those on death row today. He was thinking not only of the deprivation suffered by, and the injury done to, the slaves but also of the deprivation and injury experienced by the masters. (It is now recognized that the institution of slavery eroded the most basic human values throughout the system, brutalizing and dehumanizing both slave and master.) As an anthropologist, he was seeking a structural comparison that would at least explain, although not necessarily justify, the brutalization and dehumanization that take place on death row, recognizing that the tragedy is as great for those in authority as for those subject to it and that, as with slavery, the effects permeate society throughout, threatening our very understanding of the word humanity.

One frequently heard argument is that those on death row are not human. They are often referred to as savages, beasts, subhuman, beyond redemption, animals. The word *animal* is of particular significance to the anthropologist who knows that in many "primitive" societies this is the word used most often to distinguish people from "nonpeople," or "the others." Exactly the same concept of exclusivity underlies racism, religious factionalism, economic warfare, political chauvinism, and other similar characteristics that exist in our modern society, however much we wish it were otherwise.

Threads

In 1995, New York State instituted the death penalty.

We cannot avoid recognizing that this concept permeates our society just as strongly as the belief that to classify persons as things is wrong. Why then do we legitimize it in our prison system? Look at the process for a moment if you deny it is so. On entry into prison, a prisoner's name is taken away from him. He is bathed; often his hair is cut. He is disinfected, given a prison uniform, and deprived of contact with the outside world, the world of the living. It is a ritual death of his entire being as a human, comparable in remarkable detail to initiation rituals in which children who are candidates for adulthood are similarly separated from their earlier existence, from family and friends. Their names are taken from them, and they are ritually cleansed and given new uniforms appropriate to their limbo state, until they are ready for induction as the reborn, the final rite being a ritual of rebirth into adulthood. On death row, however, the process is reversed. The candidate enters as a man, is systematically separated from all that manhood is, and placed in limbo until the moment of induction into his new status, death. To the structuralist, the process makes sense. As a humanist, however much I may despise a man who commits murder, I am still bothered about taking away his humanity. Taking his life is bothersome enough; taking his humanity not only seems logically unjustified (unless we can show that he has *no* human qualities) but far more important, it legalizes the dangerous concept that under certain circumstances—those convenient to society—we may classify certain groups of persons as things and treat them accordingly. Disposable things.

However, let us set about finding the reason for this concept through an examination of the process.

My research has only begun; like all fieldwork it is intensely involving: at times it depresses; at times it inspires. As a humanist I am as much concerned with the families of murder victims, with the lives of prison officials, with those who pass sentence and those who implement it, as with the lives of the condemned men and women, their families, and the life of society at large. This is not an argument for or against capital punishment. It is an attempt to understand and to provoke the kinds of questions we all ought to be trying to answer. Field research spreads like a weed, and like a weed it occasionally blossoms into flower. Let me give an example so that you can see what I mean.

In the field I enter an African village, and in my notebook I hastily sketch an outline of the village—the disposition of houses and meeting places. Later I supplement these sketches with information about who lives where. I have no idea what the significance will be. I only know that, more likely than not, it will be significant.

So my first visit to death row produced a sketch of a dark, cramped, unventilated basement. There was one corridor, with the ten cells facing each other. Directly behind them was the chamber housing the electric chair. Such light as there was came from an inadequate supply of electricity; ironically, across one end of the corridor ran a huge thick cable carrying an ample supply to the chair.

The next death row I saw was light and airy, up on the second floor. There were some ninety cells (my notes would tell me exactly, but that is close enough for the moment), in two double rows, each back to back, so that each cell looked out only on a heavily barred and empty corridor and through that to the sunny skies of the world beyond. The electric chair was on the ground level, where another, smaller double row of cells, similarly back to back, housed men within one week of execution. At the time, these cells were empty; the second floor was full.

A third was similar in most respects to the second example, except that beyond the empty corridor there were no windows letting in a flood of sunlight; instead yet another heavily barred corridor was patrolled by armed guards, and behind that was a high wall topped by windows that let in some diffused daylight. And there was no large waiting area way down below (this was the top floor), just two tiny cells, barely large enough for a cot, in which the condemned spent their last night prior to taking the short walk to the gas chamber a few feet away. But there was another, more curious difference in the last instance: up on the top floor each empty corridor was spaced with television sets, one to every three cells, and each cell had a control.

These sketches corresponded to my initial sketches of an African village. I began to look for significance and instantly I was drawn in several different directions, which is why it is impossible to do more than begin to tell the story in such a short account. The significance lay not just with the obvious difference in quality of living conditions: the amount of fresh air, the adequacy of natural light, the sanitation, and the degree of isolation (the back-to-back cells each had a buttress that projected about three feet beyond the inner cell door, so that from one cell you could not even see the outstretched arm of the person next door). The architecture and furnishings also had to do with security and, in this connection, inmate morale, as well as with the antiquity of the building, which gave little leeway to prison authorities who might have wished for a different design, different living conditions.

A connection was made in my mind between security and morale. I began to look, for instance, at the varied functions of television. For those prisoners who were not semicatatonic, that is, those who were not lying on the cold floor of their cell staring at me with unblinking eyes but not seeing, not moving a muscle as I tried to engage their attention, television provided entertainment and relaxation. But the TV sets also served a much less obvious function; they bound inmates who could not even see each other into social units, within which there was cooperation, caring, and understanding. Each unit came to its own agreement as to which shows to watch and when. These units were rather like sublineages; the lineage as a whole manifests itself during exercise periods when half of one row at a time is taken to the roof for exercise. The television also served to anesthetize, as indeed it does in our living rooms. It drained the

Threads

John Grisham's 1994 bestselling novel, *The Chamber,* details the conditions and psychological profile of a death row inmate.

energy and sapped the will to think. It thus functioned (which is not to say that it was necessarily installed for this purpose) to take away the will to live. A man about to die surely has something better to do with his time than watch "I Love Lucy." For this very reason, a number of inmates refused television.

The small basement death row, with cells facing each other, with all its disadvantages (it is one of the oldest buildings in the country still used as a penitentiary) at least afforded the possibility of continual visual communication, but for many years the men were forbidden to talk above a whisper in an attempt to minimize any interaction. It had the disadvantage of being in such proximity to the death chamber that the sound and smell of death was ever present, whereas in other prisons the men were removed from that, at least until the final week or day. . . .

The first step in classical anthropological observation and analysis is descriptive ethnography—to observe and describe without academic or personal prejudice. This is where anthropologists demand of themselves an objectivity that is as complete and free of value judgments as possible. This is also where our holistic concept is important, for since we are unencumbered by theoretical considerations at this stage, we have no preconceptions as to what might be significant or insignificant —we observe and note everything around us, however trivial it might seem at the time, for we are interested in the total social system, not just one part of it.

In this case, although I am concerned with capital punishment as an institution and its interrelationships with other institutions. I am also concerned with the value system within which it operates and therefore interested in opinions, which are value statements, regarding it. As an observer then, without initial judgment concerning capital punishment itself, I look at: (1) the common arguments *for* capital punishment; (2) the common arguments *against* capital punishment; (3) the nature of capital punishment.

Only then am I in a position to assess and interpret the role of the institution in our society and determine just how far it affects the lives of every one of us in that society.

THE ARGUMENTS FOR CAPITAL PUNISHMENT

1. It is a deterrent.
2. It prevents recurrence.
3. It is a moral duty.
4. It is more economical than life imprisonment.
5. It is kinder than life imprisonment.
6. Those sentenced to death are only the worst offenders and are beyond rehabilitation.
7. Those sentenced to death are beyond humanity and therefore deserve no consideration as such (a counterargument to "cruel and unusual punishment").
8. "We don't know what else to do, and we have to do something," an argument first stated to me by a prominent judge who, as a lawyer, had successfully won the restoration of the death penalty in one state, yet was willing to concede all arguments except this one.

THE ARGUMENTS AGAINST CAPITAL PUNISHMENT

1. It is not a deterrent. Here again it is necessary to stress the best-informed opinion within the legal system is, at best, divided, since the argument is as impossible of proof as it is of disproof. Every murder committed where subject to the death penalty is positive proof that in that case the penalty was *not* a deterrent. Clifton Duffy, who as warden of San Quentin witnessed ninety executions and dealt with many of the most hardened

criminals in the country, said of the death penalty, "It is not a deterrent to crime. . . . I have yet to meet the man who let the thought of the gas chamber stop him from committing a murder." Hard data support this view. There has been a slightly higher murder rate in some states having the death penalty. The abolition or introduction of the penalty does not make *any* significant difference in the rate of commission of capital crimes; in any case, such fluctuation can only be assessed in relationship to other considerations as well, such as changing social context. The only valid rational verdict on deterrence, then, is "not proved."

2. It does not necessarily prevent recurrence. The only validity of the "prevention" argument for the death penalty is that in killing a murderer we prevent the possibility of that one man murdering again. Of the more than four hundred men and women on death row at this moment or of the thousands executed in this country recently (about four thousand in the last forty years) few had committed more than one murder or showed evidence they were likely to do so. The great majority were crimes of passion of a single moment, and although such people need to be restrained, confinement would do that as well as execution and would seem more appropriate.

3. It is not a moral duty. Those who try to justify capital punishment on moral grounds can only cite ancient Hebraic law ("Eye for an eye . . .") which, in itself, is susceptible to different interpretations and was in any case applicable in a totally different context some two thousand years ago. Further, the major churches have argued strongly *against* capital punishment. The significant discrepancy between church leadership and the extent to which it is followed by nominal adherents has to be explained, and the explanation is probably that the churches, no more than other anti–capital-punishment bodies, have failed to come up with an effective alternative or even with effective arguments other than a direct moral commitment.

4. It is not more economical, necessarily, to execute a criminal than to keep him in confinement for life. The cost to the state of a capital offense trial and of all the subsequent appeals is exorbitant, as is the added cost of maintaining a prisoner on death row for what might be many years of appeal. Summary execution would of course reduce that cost and would add something to the possibility of the penalty acting as a deterrent, but is unacceptable under our present concept of justice and due process. For those unwilling to accept that anyone in authority would consider mere economics in an issue of such gravity, I cite the recent case where the warden of a state penitentiary asked for legalization of lethal injection as a means of execution because it would cost only one dollar per head. Against that kind of thinking there is no refutation.

5. It is not "kinder" than keeping a man in prison for life unless prison conditions are admittedly inhumane. In any case, it is inconsistent to invoke "kindness" in this one respect, yet ignore it when it comes to consideration of the extreme deprivation, physical and psychological, under which prisoners live on death row. There might be an argument for giving a choice, but that would be legalizing suicide in the same sense that execution legalizes murder.

6. It has been clearly demonstrated and confirmed by prison officials that those sentenced to die are not beyond rehabilitation. Faced with this extreme crisis, many prisoners often reflect on life and sociality in a way they might never have done otherwise. In cases where such men have had their sentence commuted they sometimes become model prisoners and form a constructive and stable element of the general prison population. It is almost as though, by accident, we have discovered the

secret of rehabilitation, in rather a drastic way. Such data might be of the greatest significance in the wider area of prison reform and rehabilitation. Murderers and other prisoners I have talked with frequently express a deep frustration at being denied the possibility of making effective atonement. Punishment alone is not atonement.

7. The experience of prison wardens alone demonstrates that convicted murderers may, at least, have human potential. That is a negative way of stating the issue, which is of much greater significance. I refer to the concept of justice found in most primitive societies, where an offender is judged not only for the offense but also for his positive attributes. Even a murderer, after all, might be a good father, an admirable husband, a cooperative and productive craftsman, and a devoutly religious person. In executing that part of him that is "bad" we also execute the good. Even if that had to be so, then should we not continue to grant the condemned person the right to be treated as a human being until the moment of his death, and give him the opportunity to prepare for and meet his death with the decency and dignity our law demands for all human beings?

8. We may not know what else to do, but there is no way that we can demonstrate that nothing else can be done. We have examples of alternatives even within our own country, let alone in foreign countries that have completely abandoned the death penalty. We cannot declare that an equally effective solution to murder is impossible, since one cannot logically deny the existence of that which is not known. If successful alternatives have been found in other societies and if we value the sanctity of all human life, even that of humans who have committed crimes, then we are logically bound to search for such alternatives. Regrettably, it is both easier and cheaper not to do so, and this places in question whether our stated human values are any longer valid. Such a quest for an alternative is within our intellectual ability and our financial capability; it is merely a matter of choice and will.

While the above constitute refutations of arguments in support of capital punishment, opponents of capital punishment have two irrefutable arguments. The first is the possibility of a mistake. We know that innocent victims have been executed; fortunately, others condemned to death have been found innocent prior to execution. And we have to face the very real possibility that other mistakes have never been discovered because following execution, the incentive for costly investigation to prove innocence is largely gone; in nearly all instances the cases of those who maintained their innocence until the moment of death are dropped at that time.

The other irrefutable argument against capital punishment is the existence of two prime factors—caprice and selectivity—that effectively determine who shall die and who shall not. Let me cite three of the most obvious demonstrations of this process at work. The proportion of black Americans on death row is totally inconsistent not only with their numbers in relation to the total population but with the numbers of all convicted murderers, black or white. Furthermore, although more than half the murder victims in the United States are black, Dr. Riedel, of the University of Pennsylvania, has shown that in 87 percent of the cases where the death penalty was given, the victim was white. And there is virtually a total absence of persons of any wealth, even moderate, on death row. The penalty clearly selects poor and black, those least able to afford the expert defense such a charge necessitates and whose guilt is most likely to be accepted without protest by the general public. Finally the death penalty discriminates heavily against males. Few women have faced a capital charge, and fewer still have been executed.

There is more—so much more—but this has to be enough. What sense does capital punishment make? It exists in this particular form and therefore, the anthropologist says it is likely to have reason, to make sense, somehow to be necessary for the survival of our society. Perhaps so, but I refuse to admit there is no alternative, for that would be to admit there is an end to humanity. I think back to the final reasoning of the judge who successfully fought to have the death penalty reinstated: What else can we do?

There *is* a desperate situation. Murder seems to have become a pastime. We all want to feel safe on the streets, safe in our homes. We are not in authority, so we have the right to demand of those who are that "something be done." I have just described what they do. The deliberate taking of human life is sensational, perhaps the most dramatic act that can be performed.

All other considerations aside, our system is supremely inefficient. We are only accomplishing the disposal of a number of human beings, many of whom are perfectly good people who may have, in a moment of passion, committed a single crime; some may even be totally innocent. We do this in a way that is singularly barbaric, enormously expensive to the public at large, and more particularly, detrimental to the mental and physical health of all those involved. And while we do all this in the name of society at large, the focus is kept firmly on the individual crime and the individual criminal, who is disposed of without any opportunity for atonement. If the entire process were more public; indeed if judge and jurors were compelled to participate in the execution, and if their attention as well as the attention and concern of the rest of society were focused on the need for goodness in society instead of the mere sordid destruction of one individual, then perhaps something might be accomplished by capital punishment.

But if we were concerned with the well-being of society, there would be little or no need for capital punishment in the first place. Meanwhile it persists merely to provide the public with the illusion that something is being done.

For Discussion

ABOUT THE CONTENT

1. Why does Turnbull compare slavery to capital punishment?
2. How do architecture and furnishings contribute to the "dehumanization" of prisoners?
3. In your own words, restate Turnbull's two "irrefutable" arguments. Do you agree with him on these points? Is he persuasive? Why or why not?
4. Do you find any logical fallacies or weaknesses in his argument? Explain.
5. What concessions does Turnbull offer? Are they effective?
6. What does he mean by the "illusion that something is being done" in the last paragraph?
7. What is the importance of the idea of "atonement" in Turnbull's argument?

ABOUT THE WRITING

1. What is the purpose of the first paragraph?
2. Why do you think Turnbull repeats the phrase "as a humanist"?
3. Locate passages where Turnbull uses appeals to authority to support his argument.
4. How would you characterize Turnbull's tone and use of language? Does it help the persuasiveness of his argument?
5. Contrast the way that Turnbull presents the "pro" and "con" sides of the argument. Why has he done this, in your opinion?
6. What words or phrases show that Turnbull is "writing as an anthropologist"?

Quickwrite

What is dehumanization? Was there ever a time you witnessed a dehumanizing event? Describe it.

Writing to Inform: Science and Medicine

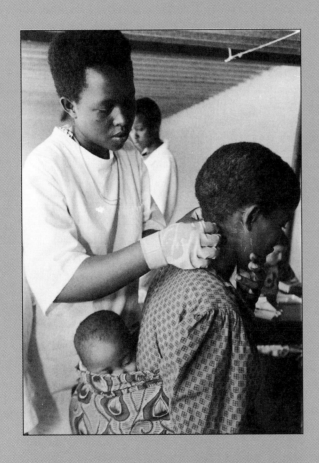

We use informative writing to give our readers information that they will find helpful. Many kinds of informative writing exist: journalism, research papers, and instruction manuals, to name

> ### Think about . . .
> What major diseases concern you?
> How do you think governments should respond to the spread of disease?

just a few. However, all informative writing involves organizing facts and data and presenting it to the reader in a format that will be clearly understood.

In this chapter we will look at writing in the fields of science and medicine to see how information is organized and presented so that the reader can make sense of it. The following reading about malaria and its effects presents both a personal story and a scientific one. As you read it, ask yourself the following questions:

- What do I know about malaria?
- What is the author's main purpose in writing this?
- How does he accomplish that purpose?

Take notes on your reading (refer to Chapter 2).

LEARNING STRATEGY

Forming Concepts: Exploring your knowledge of a reading topic helps you to better understand the reading.

THE MALARIA CAPERS

by Robert S. Desowitz

In Another Village a Mother Dies

On the Buffalo River—the River Kwai—at the town of Kanchanaburi, the big familiar relic, the bridge, still remains; it is an unremarkable structure spanning the river to nowhere (shortly after the war the Thais tore up the tracks to the Burmese border). The festive, touristy scene around the bridge—souvenir stands, food stalls, touts for boats with bongo drums—is an unseemly commercial celebration of the unspeakable atrocities committed here. In what year will T-shirts be sold in tourist shops of Auschwitz? The ultimate relics, the bones of the fallen and felled, lie in the immaculate graveyard of the British and in the quiet, more jungly cemetery of the Dutch and Australians.

One hundred miles to the west, the Kwai begins its flow from the jungle-covered, not-quite-mountainous hills at the Burmese border. A great dam has been built across the upper Kwai and a valley flooded into a lake. At the head of the lake is the new, raw town of Sangklaburi. Three Pagoda Pass is ten miles or so from Sangklaburi. It was through this pass that the Burmese armies with their "tanks"—the war elephants—spumed forth to ravish and pillage the early kingdoms of the Thais, first at Sukhothai and then at Ayuthia. Now, when you walk to the Burmese side of Three Pagoda Pass (there are no Customs or immigration barriers at this remote border), signs and banners proclaim this to be the headquarters of the Karen and Mon Liberation Armies. The streets are patrolled by menacing child-soldiers who carry AK-47s. It is wild country, disturbed by civil strife and ecological change.

The last relics of the Kwai's Japanese rail line to oblivion lie in the schoolyard of a Thai village several roadless miles north of Three Pagoda Pass. The schoolmaster shows the visitor the remnants of the depot and the termite-ridden remains of the ties. The school assembly bell, hanging by a rope from a limb of a mango tree, is the nose cone from an unexploded bomb. Next to the school, raised on pillars, is the wooden residence of a group of monks. On this late morning in June their prayers have ended; only the unceasing anguished cries of a monk dying from throat cancer break the subdued quiet of the village. In a one-room, wood-framed, tin-pan-roofed house at the village edge, Amporn Punyagaputa, twenty-three years old and big with child, sits alone, feverish and confused by the searing pain in her head.

Amporn is not an ethnic Thai. She is a woman of the hill tribes, a Karen, born and raised in a mountain village near that dodgy border between Thailand and Burma. As a child she had a few years of education in a Thai primary school located in a nearby village, but she was forced to leave when only marginally literate. The Thai officials decided that education was a privilege reserved for Thai citizens, not for the tribal peoples who had no real national affiliation. Also, when Amporn was eleven years old the family had to migrate to another part of the forest. The ten-year cycle of land use was at an end. Now it was a time to allow the exhausted plot to regenerate to nurturing forest. It was time to move, to slash and burn a new clearing for their modest crops of maize, beans, mountain rice, and—maybe—a little opium poppy.

That was when she was a child and the traditional life style of the hill tribe swidden farmer remained unchanged. A relatively stable tribal population size permitted this. The cost of that stability was a fearful childhood mortality that exceeded 40 percent. The desire of fathers to have large families balanced this wastage and ensured tribal survival. The fathers wanted large families to expand and work the plots so that more cash crops could be raised. They wanted the money, $800 to $1,000, to buy the ultimate status symbol of a Karen male—an elephant. They craved ownership of an elephant as other men yearn for fast cars, large homes, and many young wives. The ratiocination being that the elephant could be let out to hire by the timber concessionaires; but really this didn't make economic sense considering the cost of the animal's care and feeding. In truth, Karen men simply like elephants.

Increased access to, and usage of, primary health facilities gradually upset the population size so delicately balanced between a father's demands for a large family and the death of many small children. As always, the children frequently became sick, but now fewer died. Now, they could be taken to health stations staffed by nurses and medical assistants dispensing life-saving medicines to those acutely ill with diarrheas and respiratory infections. Family size and tribal populations rapidly increased. Fathers thought that the elephant was finally within their grasp. They failed to reckon on the realities of demography and the capacities of swidden agriculture. The swidden plots and the farming methods that had served so well for countless generations failed to provide the food for a population that had nearly doubled within a generation. The farmers tried to shorten the fallow time, but this only quickened the

Threads

The film "The Bridge over the River Kwai" portrays a fictionalized history of this area.

Threads

Burma was renamed Myanmar in 1989.

Threads

Definition: *ratiocination* means logical reasoning

Myanmar

Thailand

exhaustion of the land. There was less and less forest available that could be cleared for farming. The forest was being drastically reduced by timber concessionaires on behalf, mostly, of the Japanese, who wanted the Thai and Burmese forests in order to maintain the "wooden" aesthetic of their culture. Some of Amporn's family, like so many other of the close-knit Karen families, were forced to the heartbreaking necessity of leaving the tribal group to seek life and employment elsewhere. Amporn and her husband—she had been married the year before—were amongst those who made the exodus from the high hills of their birth.

Not long after their marriage they moved to this village on the Thai side of the border near Sangklaburi. Most of the villagers were also displaced Karens trying to eke a livelihood from one or two acres of land leased from Thai landlords. Amporn and her husband were wise and careful farmers, and they leased a two-acre tract in the expectation that it would provide sufficient food and cash crops to meet their modest needs and, eventually, give them enough savings to buy their "elephant"—a television set. But the Thai owner had extracted so heavy a lease rent that Amporn's husband had to supplement their income by working for the sugar estates bordering the lower Kwai seventy-five miles away. Amporn was now alone most of the time. She bore the full responsibility of the farm. And she had conceived four months after her marriage.

The joy and stoicism that Karen women have in bearing their first child was diminished for Amporn. Here in this valley village she felt so alone and so unrelievedly tired. So far, she had been fortunate not to sicken with malaria as did so many of her neighbors. In the highlands of her home malaria was virtually unknown, but here it seemed to attack everyone. Many would have died if it were not for the medicine dispensed by the health center in the neighboring village. It must be the bad waters of this place. In school they tried to tell her some nonsense about mosquito bites and malaria. Every Karen knew that drinking the corrupted waters of the lowlands was the cause of malaria. When she first came to the village, a year ago, there was so much malaria and the village headman was so angry with the state of affairs that he sent water samples to the health officials in Sangklaburi, demanding that the water be analyzed for whatever it was that caused the sickness. To its credit, the government responded promptly and sent a malaria office team to the village; but these men, instead of treating the water as they should have done, sprayed all the houses in the village with an insecticide. A strange thing happened after that: most of the village cats died.[1] After the cats died, there were many more rats, and people began losing a good part of their food crops to the rodents.

Two weeks ago, when the maize began to ripen, Amporn started sleeping in the shelter she and her husband had built at the edge of their fields. There were so many rats that any additional loss from marauding wild pigs and the occasional bear would bankrupt her fragile economy. During those watchful nights on guard she would clang the gong to drive the wild animals away. She slept fitfully in the shelter; the attack of mosquitoes was unrelenting. Her neighbor, an elderly lady of long residence in the village, had told her that before the loggers came to cut the forest and before the dam was built and the impounded lake formed, there were not so many mosquitoes. In that former time, sleeping out in the shelters of their fields, as is customary for farmers in Thailand, was not a problem. The old lady now slept under a mosquito net and advised Amporn to do the same. A net was expensive, but Amporn thought they could afford one after the baby was born.

Amporn had been reasonably healthy during her pregnancy. She was a modern, informed woman, and last month had gone to the "mothers-to-be"

---

[1] The insecticide was DDT, which has no significant toxicity for humans. Cats are more susceptible, and there are numerous reports of village cats dying within one week after malaria-control teams have sprayed DDT onto household walls.

clinic at the nearby health center. The nurse had given her some vitamin pills, told her the baby within her was doing fine, although Amporn, like most pregnant women in the district, was anemic and the nurse gave her more pills for that. Amporn wasn't sure what "anemic" was, but she knew it was something to do with her not having enough blood. That was probably why she felt so tired and had to drag herself through the day's work. The nurse at the clinic also told her that she should go to the hospital at Sangklaburi to have the baby. There she would have expert care and it would only cost 100 baht ($4).

Amporn may have thought of herself as a modern woman, but she was also a Karen and she had consulted the friendly old village midwife. The midwife too, after prodding Amporn's abdomen, predicted a normal delivery and advised that she be called when labor began. Even at this late stage of pregnancy Amporn was still undecided where she would give birth. However, since her husband would likely not be there to arrange transport to the hospital in Sangklaburi, she probably would have the baby at home, attended by the traditional midwife. She would also then be in familiar surroundings, amongst the people she knew, and the proper rituals would be performed to protect the newborn's soul from harm.

Amporn's world—her personal concerns and joys, the comfort of the day's domestic routine—had begun to vanish yesterday morning, submerged under a sudden wave of sickness. The child within her became an insupportable burden, her back ached, there was a nausea so intense that it made her choke breathlessly. The attack came with surprising ferocity. In a moment the nausea yielded to a chill that made Amporn feel her body was encased in a shroud of ice. Under the blazing tropical sun she shook uncontrollably. During this "freezing" rigor, Amporn's temperature had risen to 104°F. After an hour of tooth-chattering shakes the rigor abated, and for a few moments in the eye of this parasitic storm Amporn thought she might yet live. The brief respite was followed by a feverishness that was as intense as the sensation of cold she had experienced during the rigor. Amporn's temperature was now 106°F. Her senses reeled; consciousness blurred. She crawled into her house and collapsed upon the cool dirt floor, her sarong sodden with the sweat pouring from her burning body.

In the early evening, the fever broke, and Amporn, exhausted, drained of all strength, fell into a fitful sleep. The cries of the dying monk woke her in the first light of the new day. Still lying on the floor, she sensed a foreboding communion of death with the tortured holy man. She was too dispirited to eat but had a great thirst. As she staggered to the large water-storage klong jar, the frightening premonitory signs of another rigor began. Amporn realized that it was malaria. She knew she needed medical help, but her weakness and confusion prevented her from even calling to her neighbor. The malaria again seized her. It was at this point we began our story: Amporn Punyagaputa, twenty-three years old and big with child, sits alone, feverish and confused by the searing pain in her head.

Now there was another terrifying aspect of the malaria attack: she felt her womb contracting. The pains of childbirth were beginning. But the baby was not due for another two months yet. What was happening? The headache became unbearable; she lost sense of time, of place, of her person; her vision blurred; she felt herself being swept into a dark vortex. Then there was nothing. Amporn lay unconscious on the hard dirt floor, her womb, propelled into premature labor by the malarial fever, starting its rhythm of birth.

Amporn's good neighbor, Lek, was also a Karen woman displaced from her hill tribe village. Most mornings Amporn and Lek would grind their grain in the stone mortar mills in front of their houses. They would exchange gossip and commiserate on their lonely lives. Lek's husband too was away a good deal of the time, working as a logger in the deep forest. Amporn's failure to appear worried Lek, and at mid-morning she decided to see if all was well at the house next door. All was not well: Lek found her friend collapsed on the floor unconscious, her clammy skin an ominous gray pallor. Lek quickly realized that

Amporn had to be brought to the hospital at Sangklaburi . . . she was beyond the help of traditional medicine.

At that time of day the men were away working in the fields. Only the women were in the village to give assistance. The monks could offer their advice and prayers, but they were forbidden to touch a woman, even a dying woman. There was no formal village civil defense unit or Red Cross chapter, but over the years of too frequent emergencies—the wounds of the agriculturists, the sudden life-threatening fevers, the births gone bad—the women had developed their own efficient disaster drill. Responding to Lek's summons, the women gently placed Amporn on the canvas stretcher that had been stored in the Headman's house. Then they set off on a walk-trot, spelling each other as bearers, over the two miles of path to the rutted dirt track that served as a road to the surrounding villages.

Once at the road, the women had to wait almost a half hour before a samlor taxi putt-putted by. The samlor is a motorcycle converted to a tricycle with a bench seat for the passengers. It is an uncompromising, hard ride, but reliable and economical—the proletarian transport of Thailand. Packing a comatose, seven-month-pregnant lady and her traveling companion into a samlor with its four-foot bench required some shoving and folding. Amporn's head rested on Lek's lap; only her occasional groans gave sign that she still lived. In this manner they finally came to a jolting stop under the portico of the Sangklaburi hospital.

The portico of the country hospital is an intersection of old and new Thailand. The Sangklaburi hospital was but a few years old; it was the standard twenty-bed rural affair, of standard government-dictated architecture, plain and functional except for the portico which graced it with a pleasant elegance. A large gilt Buddha sat smiling, in bronze solidity, at one side of the portico facing the garden. Traditional and reassuring. The hospital "kitchen" was also housed under the portico—a "noodle lady" and her steaming cart. The noodle lady's pet gibbon, a furry blond baby, sat pensively in the Buddha's lap.

The nurses came running to their patient and carried Amporn across the portico into the examination room. Amporn was now in the care of the new Thailand. This small, immaculately maintained hospital in a far corner of the kingdom was remarkably well suited to serve the health needs of the local population. There was a pharmacy stocked with a broad and adequate supply of drugs and biologicals. There was an X-ray machine, an efficient laboratory, and an ambulance to take patients to the Provincial General Hospital if their problems were beyond the capabilities of the young staff and their resources.

The people of Sangklaburi, like the rural populations everywhere in the Third World, were served by the least experienced and youngest physicians. The government sent the new medical graduates to staff the rural hospitals and health centers. After a few years in the country they were brought back to the cities for specialist training, to enter private practice, or to continue government service at the general hospitals. In the balance, in Thailand at least, service by the youthful was not necessarily a disservice to the sick. It requires the energy and enthusiasm of youth to be a country doctor in the Third World. And by no means are these young doctors incompetent. They receive intensive training in basic clinical medicine—family care—as part of their medical curriculum. Once posted to the rural health facility, the government does not abandon them. They are brought to the Provincial General Hospital for frequent short courses and meetings with senior specialists, who can also be relied upon for assistance with the difficult cases. The young Thai doctors are given decent housing, decent pay. Equally important, the nurses and technicians working with them are also given decent housing and decent pay. This makes for an egalitarian camaraderie, a harmony and vitality in working a full-time patient care. Nor do these kids remain inexperienced for long. They are bright and learn from the exigencies of daily practice. And for what they haven't learned, there are the older nurses to keep the young doctors from doing too much harm.

In the examination room, a team of doctor and midwife nurses quickly came to the provisional diagnosis of premature labor brought on by acute malaria. Amporn was not an unusual case. Each week during the early rains (the height of the malaria transmission season) one or more young women, pregnant and gravely ill with malaria, were brought to the hospital. Malaria of the malignant tertian type caused by the parasite *Plasmodium falciparum* was always of concern because of the rapidity with which it could develop into a life-threatening infection; but pregnancy imposed a degree of vulnerability even beyond the fearful "natural" risk.

To be pregnant is to have within your person a growing foreign body that meets many of the biological definitions of a parasite. The mother makes all sorts of immunologically dampening adjustments so that this particular foreign body, the fetus, will not be rejected. While it is not an AIDS-like depression, the immune compromise is such as to make a pregnant woman of the tropics more likely to contract malaria and to die of the infection.[2] A woman of the Third World may face a four hundred times greater risk of dying each time she becomes pregnant than a pregnant woman of an industrialized country. In regions of malarial hyperendemicity, a high proportion of this mortality can be attributed, directly or indirectly, to falciparum malaria. Survivors tend to have a severe anemia (malaria, hookworm, and nutritional factors, all present in the pregnant peasant, can turn blood into "water") and the spontaneous abortion rate is as high as 50 percent. The babies that *are* born to the malarious usually have a birth weight 200 grams or more below normal. A low-birth-weight baby who doesn't "catch up" has a puny immune system, and these children frequently die during childhood of all sorts of infections. The death certificate (when there is one) may read diarrhea or pneumonia, but the real cause of death was malaria of the mother.

There were other fevers, other causes of coma—the virus of Japanese encephalitis and a group of bacterial pathogens capable of invading the central nervous system—that were old familiars in western Thailand. Thus, before treatment could be given, the presumptive diagnosis that Amporn's fever and coma was caused by malaria had to be confirmed. The laboratory technician pricked Amporn's unfeeling finger and from the droplet of blood she made a film on a glass microscope slide and filled a glass capillary tube. Thirty minutes later the technician returned to the group gathered about their dying patient to give them a report that more than 15 percent of Amporn's red blood cells held the tiny signet ring-like forms characteristic of *Plasmodium falciparum.* This was an intensity of infection considered to be potentially lethal and too often beyond the curative power of antimalarial therapy. The technician also reported that the reading of the centrifuge tube gave a hematocrit of 17 percent—Amporn was so anemic that she hardly had enough red blood cells left to oxygenate a mouse.

So the young doctor was confronted with a conglomeration of three emergencies requiring immediate attention. The overwhelming malaria infection had to be brought rapidly under control by a chemotherapeutic agent. The anemia, so profound as to be nearly insupportable of life, had to be

---

[2]The mechanisms responsible for pregnancy-related enhanced malaria are still not fully understood. One important cause of this pathogenicity is brought about by a characteristic of the malignant tertian malarial parasite, Plasmodium falciparum. Red blood cells infected with this parasite congregate in the placental blood vessels—sometimes one can hardly find the parasitized erythrocytes in the "finger-stick" peripheral blood while at the same time the placental blood is, literally, thick with infected erythrocytes.

reversed. And the premature labor had to be halted if the unborn child, if not already dead in the womb, was to be saved. Nor were there any simple textbook solutions to this triple threat. Twenty years ago Amporn could have been given an intravenous injection of chloroquine and within hours this remarkably efficient antimalarial drug would have begun killing the parasites. However, over the years the widespread use of chloroquine had led to the selection of resistant strains of *Plasmodium falciparum* that no longer responded to the drug.

The doctor didn't even consider using chloroquine. Instead, to treat Amporn, he opened a vial containing a solution of a plant alkaloid that had first been used to treat malaria more than 350 years ago—quinine. Quinine was all he had in his therapeutic armamentarium. It was all there was to treat severe falciparum malaria. But quinine was toxic, relatively slow-acting and, importantly in this case, tended to induce abortion. Quinine also had a side effect of stimulating the pancreas to produce more insulin. The insulin could "burn off" what sugar Amporn had left in her blood and send her into a state of shock and irreversible coma. Still, all chemotherapy, be it taking an aspirin or taking quinine, is a chancy clinical compromise. Necessity dictated that a nurse prepare the syringe to infuse the quinine slowly into Amporn's nearly collapsed vein.

Amporn urgently needed new blood. In Sangklaburi hospital there is no refrigerated blood bank; the blood for medical emergencies is stored in the original containers—on the hoof, so to speak. The laboratory identifies the patient's blood type and matches it with that of a relative from whom blood is drawn. When there are no relatives, as in Amporn's case, the hospital staff selflessly act as donors. Amporn was found to have a common blood type shared by several of the nurses. One of those nurses, Chalong, immediately volunteered to give his blood. Chalong is a young man, the same age as Amporn, who had spent two years in a nurses' training program at a government general hospital. He loved nursing and was the first to volunteer for any job. He was the hospital's dynamo, completely and single-mindedly devoted to taking care of the ill. His smiling, calm, youthful presence seemed always there, at any time of the night or day, when needed.

A unit of blood was withdrawn from Chalong and transferred into Amporn's vein. Within minutes her blood pressure rose—there was yet hope that she could be saved. Later that day another unit of blood was given to Amporn, this one collected from a vivacious, slender nurse known affectionately as Gop, Thai for "the fox."

The third problem, the premature labor, posed a special dilemma. Drugs could be given in an attempt to stop the early birth process. However, the doctor could not detect a fetal heart beat—the unborn baby was probably already dead.[3] It might even be better to encourage the abortion, although this was an ethical and legal decision the young doctor had to make each time he treated a pregnant woman suffering from severe malaria. His, and others', observation had been that if they induced abortion to remove the heavily parasitized, "toxic" placenta, the mother would have a much better chance of surviving, of responding to the antimalarial chemotherapy. But this was only an observation, it was not prescribed medical practice. Abortion, although frequently performed by private practitioners, is in fact illegal in Thailand. However, Amporn was already in labor, the baby was probably already dead, and it was decided to allow nature to take its quinine-accelerated course.

---

[3]What kills the fetus when the mother has severe malaria is not known with any certitude. The malaria parasites rarely cross from the placental into the fetal circulation, so it is not a malarial infection in the unborn baby that is the cause. Probably, it is a combination of the high fever of the mother, which makes the womb a cauldron, and the deficiency in transferring oxygen from the placenta, where blood circulation is impaired by the parasite and inflammation clogs blood vessels, that leads to the death of the fetus.

Amporn was taken to the women's ward, screens placed around her bed. The ward nurse was almost constantly with her. Near midnight, Amporn, still comatose, showed signs that she was about to give birth. She was quickly moved to the delivery room where, with the midwife-nurse in attendance, she gave birth to a dead premature infant. It was a boy.

In the morning, Amporn opened her eyes. The coma receded; the fever abated. The blood film now showed fewer parasites—they were still there but the quinine was working. The hematocrit had risen to 25 percent—still very anemic, but improving after the blood transfusions and the continued intravenous infusion of a glucose-saline solution. The doctor came to her bedside and tried to explain what had happened. Amporn's mind was still blurred; it was difficult for her to form thoughts, but somehow she understood that she was in a hospital and was being cared for.

Throughout the day Amporn's condition remained stable; the parasites in her blood continued to diminish. The staff's mood brightened from the somber tension that pervaded whenever they were dealing with a critically ill patient whose life was in the balance . . . Amporn might yet make it, they now thought. Gop talked about a party she was organizing—a boat would take them on a cruise around the lake. There would be a mountain of food, singing, swimming. Hospital activities returned to a less stressful normal; outpatients were seen by the two doctors, prescriptions filled, a fractured arm set. In the late afternoon, their busy day finished, the staff gathered in one nurse's house for a heated card game. Another nurse cooked a big pot of green curry chicken for a communal dinner.

Sometime in the very early morning hours Amporn died. Her tired heart just stopped beating. The night-duty nurse called the doctor who, still in his sleeping "sarong," came running from his nearby house to the hospital. Everything possible was done to revive Amporn. The staff worked quietly and efficiently for over a half hour to no avail. At four in the morning, feeling a great, futile depression, they left, and Amporn was taken to the morgue to rest beside her dead son.

During that night, a child was born to another Karen woman. What the personal tragedy or circumstances of this woman were will never be known, but at first light she painfully rose from her bed and fled the hospital, abandoning her newborn infant. In the morning sunlight, Chalong sat on the bench on the hospital veranda tenderly holding the baby and sobbing, the tears streaming down his young face.

The M&M's: Monkey, Man, and Malaria

In the 1960s, malariologists were preoccupied, consumed, by the global campaign to eradicate malaria. In those busy, heady days, little attention was given to the possible zoonotic potential of the simian malarias. The general feeling was that the monkeys were in *their* trees being bitten by *their* mosquitoes and the humans were on *their* turf being bitten by *their* mosquitoes—the two primates neatly separated by the vertically stratified ecosystem compartments. However, in 1960 a mini-outbreak of monkey malaria in humans turned attention to evaluating the zoonotic potential of the Asian monkeys. The infected humans were malariologists, and the outbreak was in Bethesda, Maryland.

Scientists at the National Institutes of Health in Bethesda had been studying the biology of *Plasmodium cynomolgi,* a malaria parasite of Asian monkeys. Under the microscope, *Plasmodium cynomolgi* is an almost exact doppelganger of the human benign tertian parasite, *Plasmodium vivax.* The inability of *Plasmodium vivax* to infect Asian monkeys indicated that it was a different species, although it was not then known whether or not *Plasmodium cynomolgi* could infect humans. One facet of the research concerned the way the parasite developed in the anopheline mosquito and how it was transmitted

Threads

Definition: Zoonotic, related to diseases of animals.

Threads

Definition: doppelganger (German), a living double.

by the mosquito from monkey to monkey. To do this, the entomologists had a "domesticated" anopheline that mated and bred readily in caged captivity, and from the Institute's insectary these mosquitoes were supplied for experimental infection. It was all rather a relaxed undertaking, and if you visited the National Institutes of Health malaria research laboratory in those days you were likely as not to be bitten by the escapees buzzing about. No one worried about the stray anophelines—even if they were infected, it was only with the monkey *Plasmodium cynomolgi,* which was thought to be of no health risk to the laboratory workers.

On May 5, 1960, one of those laboratory workers, Dr. Don Eyles, called from Memphis, Tennessee, to his friend and colleague at the Institute in Bethesda, Dr. Bob Coatney, to tell him that he had had a fever and headache and that he had examined his blood film and that he had malaria—the malaria, in his opinion, was definitely *Plasmodium cynomolgi.* A few days later several technicians in Coatney's laboratory became febrile and experienced the teeth-chattering rigor of a malaria attack. They too were infected with *Plasmodium cynomolgi.* They had been infected by a mosquito vector in the same manner as if they had been natives of a jungle in Malaya.

For almost twenty years Coatney had been testing the efficacy of new antimalarials and how they might be used in the prevention and treatment of malaria. The bottom line was always, would it work in the infected human? To get that bottom line, a remarkable program had been established at the Atlanta Federal Prison, in which prisoner volunteers were infected and then treated with experimental antimalarial drugs. It was a program of high American altruism. Malaria was no longer an American health problem, but Americans were offering their bodies and suffering from an uncomfortable, sometimes dangerous, illness in the service of tropical peoples. No deals were cut; the prisoner volunteers were not offered better conditions of their imprisonment or promised any remission of their sentence. Equally astonishing, this program was not only condoned by the government but actually legitimized by an act of Congress (section 4162 of title 18 U.S. Code; Public Law 772 of the 80th Congress). The United States has been the *only* country in the entire world ever to pass a law facilitating human research on malaria.

Coatney, with access to the prisoner volunteers in Atlanta and intrigued by the possible implications of the accidental infections, began infecting humans with *Plasmodium cynomolgi.* These experimental infections quickly revealed that clinically it produced symptoms very much like those of *Plasmodium vivax* malaria—a high fever every forty-eight hours, headache, frequent abdominal pain, and, after a time, enlargement of the spleen. If a Malayan "local" had been infected with *Plasmodium cynomolgi,* there would be no practical way to distinguish it from *Plasmodium vivax.* The zoonotic cloud began to loom on the epidemiological horizon.

In 1965 another event occurred which made the cloud a little darker. It is also a cautionary tale for tourists and business people returned from the tropics and seeking medical care for "weekend" malaria or some other acute travel-related illness. This is the tale of a young American surveyor, a civilian employee of the U.S. Army, who spent five days surveying (at night!) in the Malayan jungle. What a U.S. Army surveyor was doing in a Malayan jungle and what he was surveying at night was never satisfactorily explained. Anyway, after making what must have been a night map of the jungle, he emerges and goes to Kuala Lumpur, where he spends a week being debriefed. Now he's ready to fly home but decides to do this via Bangkok and a few days of intensive R & R. Three days later and well hung-over—there's no town to be on quite like Bangkok—he takes the "flying tunnel" (a Military Air Transport 707 with no windows, seats facing backward, and cheese sandwich/cookie catering) to Travis Air Force Base in California. The plane lands and our surveyor feels bloody awful—chills, sweating, headache, and sore throat. He attributes this to natural phenomena—the indiscretions of Bangkok and the long, steerage-class ride in the flying tunnel—but nevertheless feels sufficiently bad to visit the Base aid station. The busy young physician there summarily diagnoses an upper respiratory infection, gives him some antibiotic pills, and advises him to get the next plane to his home in Silver Spring, Maryland, where he can recuperate from the wear and tear of the Malayan jungle, Patpong Road, and the virus of the URI.

He wakes the next morning, a Saturday, back in Silver Spring, and, if anything, he feels worse than the day before. Worried, he calls his personal physician, a general practitioner. The doctor vaguely remembers from one of the three lectures he had on parasitic diseases in medical school that fever, malaria, and tropical visits go together. He makes a blood film from his patient, and being one of the few doctors still doing some of his own microscopic examinations he sees what he believes to be numerous malaria parasites within the red blood cells. The physician has insufficient knowledge to make an accurate diagnosis, but his reference book tells him that if it is *Plasmodium falciparum* it can be rapidly fatal. The patient needs expert diagnosis, care, and treatment, and because this is a "Government" case, he sends him to the nearby Walter Reed Army Hospital. Reeling from fever, our patient gets to Walter Reed Hospital only to be told that patients are not admitted on the weekend. The Army physician advises him to go cross-town to the National Institutes of Health Clinical Center in Bethesda—they like malaria there and maybe they can treat him. Nauseous, with 103°F temperature and a blinding headache, our pilgrim makes his way to Bethesda and, finally, to a hospital bed and treatment.

Before beginning antimalarial therapy, the species of parasite—and indeed, whether it was a malarial parasite that was responsible—had to be identified. The laboratory technologist makes a stained blood film and sees malaria parasites that he thinks are *Plasmodium malariae,* a non-fatal quartan infection (fever peaking every seventy-two hours). The attending physician remembers that Bob Coatney at the National Institutes of Health Malaria Unit in Atlanta wants a strain of *Plasmodium malariae* to test its response to antimalarial drugs in prison volunteers. So, before chloroquine is given, some blood is drawn from the patient's vein, stored in a fridge, and sent by air to Atlanta on Monday.

On Monday, Coatney inoculates the blood into a prisoner volunteer. A few days later, the volunteer develops the expected fever and Coatney makes a blood smear, expecting to see the red cells infected with *Plasmodium malariae.* To his amazement, Coatney sees the unmistakable morphology of *Plasmodium knowlesi*—a monkey malaria. Clinical confirmation came with the typical daily spiking of fever in the prisoner volunteer. No wonder the surveyor had felt so continuously ill since he left Bangkok. When the story of the infection unfolded, Coatney realized that this was the first confirmed example of zoonotic malaria. A series of improbable events and medical miscalculations had led the parasite into Coatney's expert hands and precipitated the discovery that in nature a monkey malaria *could* infect humans.[4]

Potential to infect was not enough to constitute a health hazard; someone had to return to Malaya to determine whether monkey malaria was actually being transmitted to people living in the *kampongs* (villages) within the jungle. What better man to head the research team assembled by the National Institutes of Health than that wise malariologist with so personal an experience of monkey malaria—Don Eyles? During the 1960s Eyles's team, established at the Institute of Medical Research in Kuala Lumpur, were busy looking at blood films from all sorts of monkeys and gibbons, and they were discovering all sorts of new species of primate malaria. Members of Eyles's team inoculated themselves

---

[4]There is a bizarre and cautionary postscript to the story that gives insight to the mixed messages between physicians and patients. The surveyor not only suspected that he had malaria but he had chloroquine with him the entire time from the day he entered the Malayan jungle. He didn't take the chloroquine because he remembered that a doctor had told him never to take a drug of any sort without a physician's explicit advice.

132

Threads

The OSS, the Office of
Strategic Services, is
now the CIA, the Cen-
tral Intelligence Agency,
of the United States.

with infected monkey/gibbon blood, and the subsequent chills and shakes amply proved that at least some of the new species, such as the gibbon malaria parasite (later named *Plasmodium eylesi*), were indeed capable of infecting the human animal. These self-inflicted infections made the necessity for field studies even more convincing.

Field work in the Malayan jungle had never been easy. There are trackless expanses, thickly forested mountains, and large rivers whose rapids flow into jungle swamps. This is the ecosystem in which the holidaying Thai silk entrepreneur/wartime OSS agent Jim Thompson went for a morning stroll down a jungle path and disappeared forever without a trace. And the natives were unfriendly (to malaria workers). Malaya was then in the throes of its national malaria eradication campaign and the *kampong* dwellers were tired of having their fingers stuck repeatedly in the service of the promise of a malaria-free life that never seemed to arrive. What was even worse than a sore finger was the strange phenomenon of their roofs collapsing within a month of their houses being sprayed with DDT.

Malaria they knew, but falling roofs were something else again, and the sophisticated biological explanations offered by the malaria workers didn't put back the cover on the house. What was happening was that the roofs were made of *attap* (palm fronds) and there was an *attap*-devouring caterpillar that dwelt in the roof. Under normal conditions a parasitic wasp preyed on the caterpillars and kept the pests at low, non-destructive numbers. Unfortunately, the wasp was highly sensitive to DDT while the caterpillar was resistant. The malaria workers sprayed the houses, the wasps died, the caterpillars proliferated . . . and the roofs came tumbling down. Malaria workers were told that they weren't welcome in the *kampongs* and forcibly ejected if the polite dismissal wasn't heeded.

The problems of epidemiological diplomacy were more than equaled by the experimental problems that would be needed to determine whether monkey-to-man transmission of malaria was taking place in its natural setting. It was one thing to conduct tidy transmission studies under laboratory and hospital conditions, but quite another matter to enter a village, bleed the populace, and prove that some of the infections were of monkey origin. There was, at that time, no genetic-marker, biotechnical methods to distinguish look-alike species from one another. The only, and still the most convincing, method was to take blood from the villagers and inoculate "clean" monkeys (which would have to be rhesus imported from an area of India where primate malaria doesn't exist). Any consequent infections in the recipient animals would be proof of zoonotic monkey malaria (since, you may recall, truly human malaria parasites are not infective to Asian monkeys).

This Herculean experiment was actually carried out by a group of the National Institutes of Health team, led by MacWilson Warren, an affable young man. Mac gained the trust of the villagers by his genuine concern and affection for all things Malay, and by passing the trial by fire—the ability to consume, with relish, the mega-chili curries of the Malayan village cuisine. The monkeys were obtained from India and housed at the Kuala Lumpur Institute. Then the team drew venous blood from twelve hundred jungle *kampong* dwellers (an extraordinary feat in itself, considering the great reluctance of the rural Malay to have blood drawn from the vein). The blood supplies were iced, rushed back to Kuala Lumpur, and inoculated into the rhesus. No monkey ever became infected. Humans were not infected with any monkey malaria. The research team came to the conclusion that in Malaya, at least, monkeys were not giving malaria to man and that antimalaria campaigns did not have to incorporate strategies to control transmission from lower primates.

Malaria: From the Miasma to the Mosquito

The infection in humans begins when an infected female anopheline mosquito (only the lady mosquito partakes of blood; the male, gentle fellow that he is, flies about in a lifelong pursuit of sex and nectar) injects into the bloodstream, during the act of feeding, threadlike malaria parasites (the *sporozoites*) that have been stored in her salivary glands. Thousands of sporozoites are usually injected (Figure 1) and they are carried in the bloodstream to the liver, where they leave the circulatory system and each sporozoite penetrates a "building block" cell of the liver tissue. Within the liver cell the sporozoite rounds up and transforms into a "spore." For about two weeks this spore replicates repeatedly (a process known as *schizogony*), until there are many thousand "spores" (*merozoites*) within a cystlike structure, the host liver cell having been destroyed by the proliferating parasites (Figure 2).

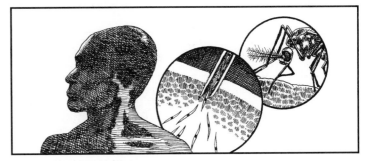

Figure 1

Those two weeks are a clinically quiescent period for the person within whom the seeds of malaria are undergoing repeated division. There is no fever, no sign of the illness that is to descend so swiftly. The first clinical attack—the intense rigor and sweating with high fever—develops when the cyst bursts to release the myriad of "spores" (merozoites) into the bloodstream (Figure 3). Each merozoite now attaches to the surface of a red blood cell and then enters it. Inside the red blood cell the young parasite appears as a minute circlet with a nucleus-dot (the ring stage). The parasite feeds avidly by engulfing, in amoeba-like fashion, the red cell's hemoglobin. The parasite grows the "body" cytoplasm increasing until it fills more than half the red cell (the *trophozoite* stage).

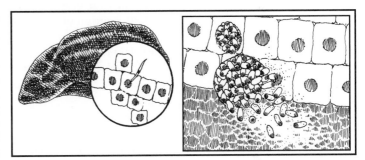

Figure 2

The next developmental event is the asexual "shattering" of the nucleus (*schizogony*) into eight to twenty-four discrete bits (the number depending on

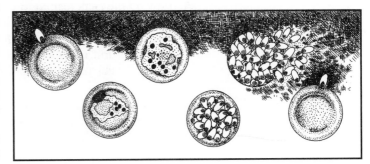

Figure 3

the species of malaria parasite) within the cytoplasmic matrix. There then occurs a complex reorganization in which the cytoplasm coalesces around each nuclear bit to form a "spore," that is, a merozoite. The demolished red cell bursts; the merozoites are released into the bloodstream to attack and invade new red blood cells.

This process is repeated over and over again with more and more red cells becoming parasitized until natural or acquired immunity, or antimalarial chemotherapy, or death (in the case of untreated *Plasmodium falciparum* infections in non-immunes) brings the repetitive process to an end. Moreover, there is a marvelous synchrony in development. The growing malaria parasites are a *corps de ballet* moving together in their growth cycle; all are at the ring stage simultaneously, all are at the trophozoite stage simultaneously, all burst, as merozoites, form their millions of invaded red blood cells simultaneously. This synchronicity of development is responsible for the characteristic periodicity of malarial fever cycles in the infected human; the forty-eight hours between fever peaks for *Plasmodium falciparum, Plasmodium vivax,* and *Plasmodium ovale,* and seventy-two hours between peaks for *Plasmodium malariae* malaria.

For Discussion

ANALYZING INFORMATIVE WRITING

Although we have defined informative writing as writing that tries to relate information, in fact it frequently does more than that. In "The Malaria Capers," the author's decision to start the reading with a narrative shows that he has a particular interest and sentiment about malaria and its effects.

Look over your notes, and reread this selection; then answer the following questions with a group of classmates.

1. This selection comes from two separate chapters of the book *The Malaria Capers.* Why do you think the author chose the story of Amporn to begin his discussion of the malaria parasite? What do you think his feelings are about malaria?
2. What are the symptoms of malaria? Why has the author presented them in this way?
3. What facts did you learn about malaria and its treatment from the first part of the reading?
4. How are the second and third parts of the reading different from the first?
5. How do the facts that are presented in the second and third sections of the reading relate to the first? Why are the sections found in the order that they are?
6. What is your opinion about this reading? Did it interest you? Did you learn new facts and ideas about malaria? Did the author seem knowledgeable about his subject matter? How did he convince you of this knowledge?

Quickwrite

What disease concerns you? Why?

WRITING THE FOURTH ESSAY

For this essay, you will investigate some aspect of a fight against a major disease that interests you. You may further investigate malaria, or you may choose another subject, such as the subject of your previous quickwrite.

Checklists throughout this section will help you fulfill the assignment. Fill in the due dates assigned by your instructor.

Choosing a Topic

The obvious place to start is at the beginning—that is, choosing a topic. The most important thing is to choose a subject that interests you. In addition, it must be a subject that is possible to research. While the discovery of a new virus reported in this morning's newspaper may be fascinating, you might have difficulty finding much information on such a recent finding. To assure yourself that there is adequate information, go to the library and do preliminary research. Remember, although you may select a well-researched area, you should keep in mind how much information *your* library has.

Checklist 1: Proposed Topic: _____

_____ The topic fulfills the assignment.

_____ There is adequate information on this topic.

_____ My instructor has approved my choice.

Defining Your Approach

An **approach** in writing means your unique way of looking at a topic. For example, if you choose to research AIDS, there will be many different points of view to examine: the scientific explanation, its social impact, prevention, and so on. As you narrow the focus of your subject, there are three principles to consider in choosing an approach:

- *Completeness* concerns your choice of subject matter. In choosing your topic, make sure you can cover your topic adequately. That is, you need to make your topic specific and manageable. For a six-page essay, you probably don't want to take on the entire history of malaria research throughout the world.
- *Surprise value* means you should find something new or interesting to say about your topic. In other words, your topic should reflect your own interests and point of view.
- *Factuality* means that as the writer of information, you are responsible for relating an accurate story that sufficiently documents sources and facts.

These three stages are not completely separate. At each stage, you will probably be doing (or at least thinking about) the other parts of the task.

Checklist 2: Approach

_____ I have narrowed my subject area.

_____ The aspect of my subject I'm most interested in is

_____

_____ I've discussed this approach with classmates or my instructor

Conducting the Research

Before you go the library to begin more serious research, take a few minutes to freewrite or map out what you already know about your subject matter. Use this time to ask yourself questions, jot down ideas, and explore what interests you.

LEARNING STRATEGY

Managing Your Learning: Using resources to support your position makes your writing more convincing.

From your prewriting and reading notes, identify as many **keywords** as you can to help you with your library search. For example, if malaria eradication efforts interest you, looking up the keyword "DDT" might be useful.

If you have never searched for information in your library, you should ask the reference librarian for assistance. Reference librarians are experts at finding information and can help you start an efficient search. Use the card catalogue or computerized catalogue searching program and look under a subject heading with the name of the disease you are researching. Then, check to see what is actually available in your library.

In order to familiarize yourself with your library, for each of the following possibilities, find out and write where you can find each of the items:

1. If you are familiar with your library's computer or card catalog, you can begin there. Do a "subject" search, using your keywords. Some library systems list books only, others have computer databases that list articles as well.

   List the card catalogues or computer programs that are available in your library.
2. Use *Readers' Guide* and newspaper indexes to find articles that appear in magazines and newspapers. For back issues, your library probably has newspapers on microfilm or microfiche.

   In your library, where can you find . . .
   a. *Readers' Guide*?
   b. Newspaper Indexes?
   c. Newspapers on microfilm or fiche?
3. Use computer databases and CD-ROM to find current articles in specific areas. Many libraries have access to specialized databases that are available through the computer. In addition, your library may have information on CD-ROM, which will give you access to articles in a variety of fields.
   a. What computer databases can you access in your library?
   b. Does your library have CD-ROM? What discs are available?

4. Find out if your library has a collection of government documents. Many large public libraries have these, but smaller or private libraries do not.

Does your library have a government documents room? Where is it located?

To begin your search, find at least three sources on your topic. If you photocopy your sources, be sure to write the full reference of your article somewhere on the copy: author, title, publisher, city, date, and page numbers, if they don't show on the copy. It is also helpful to write the call number (the library identification number that tells where the book can be found) of the book or journal you took the copy from, so that you can return to it easily if necessary.

You can use your sources as sources, too. At the end of most articles and books, you will find a bibliography of the sources the author used. Look them over to see if there is something that would be useful to your own research. If so, see if they are available in your school's library.

NOTETAKING

If you use sources in the library and take notes from them, be sure you keep <u>perfect</u> records of your sources. Index cards are a good way to keep both bibliographic records and reading notes. Two examples follow; the first is a bibliographic entry, the second a quotation card.

Bibliography Card

Desowitz, Robert S.	← Author
————————————	
<u>The Malaria Capers</u>	← Title
W.W. Norton & Co., New York	← Publishing information
1992	← Date

Be sure to put only one entry on each card. Be absolutely accurate in everything you note. It will make a difference later.

Cards can also be used to note useful quotations or paraphrases. Use a quotation when the words the author wrote are unique and interesting. Otherwise, use a paraphrase card, on which you put the author's words into your own—copying quotations is time-consuming.

Quotation Card

Title →	<u>The Malaria Capers</u>
Author and page numbers →	Desowitz, p. 143
Quotation (use exact wording) →	"Dead men tell no tales, and when malaria has caused their death the microscopic killers vanish without a trace."
Indicate quotations →	Quotation

Paraphrase Card

Include a subject heading →	Malaria's Effects
Author and page number →	Desowitz, p. 143
Paraphrase of information →	Once a person has died, it's often unclear that the cause was malaria.
Add questions or comments → you have in brackets. Follow up on them.	[What are the ways to detect whether malaria caused a person's death?]
Indicate whether it's a → paraphrase or a quotation.	Paraphrase

Write a summary card when you want to recall the *meaning* of a passage or reading.

Summary Card

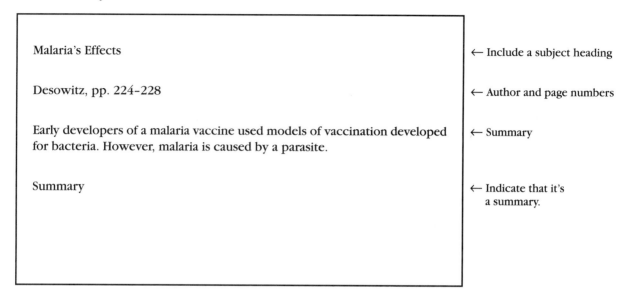

Malaria's Effects   ← Include a subject heading

Desowitz, pp. 224–228   ← Author and page numbers

Early developers of a malaria vaccine used models of vaccination developed for bacteria. However, malaria is caused by a parasite.   ← Summary

Summary   ← Indicate that it's a summary.

When you finish your notecards, you can sort them, arrange them, and use them to help you think in a more organized fashion about your topic.

Checklist 3: Conducting Research

_____ I explored my topic through freewriting.

_____ I identified keywords in my notes and freewriting.

_____ I asked the librarian how to begin my search.

_____ I checked for sources on the computer or card catalog.

_____ I looked at *Reader's Guide* or other indexes for sources.

_____ I recorded my sources on index cards.

_____ I looked at the bibliographies of my sources for books or articles I might use.

Evaluation

At this phase in your research, you need to read your sources carefully, take notes, and decide if further sources may be needed. Once again, use index cards to record the following information:

- a short summary of each source
- useful quotations and their locations
- paraphrases of important information and your questions, opinions, or ideas about it

Be sure to keep very careful records of your sources on each card, in order to avoid **plagiarism.**

Managing Your Learning: Learning how to cite your sources correctly will help you avoid plagiarism.

AVOIDING PLAGIARISM

Plagiarism, in brief, is the misrepresentation of someone's ideas or words as your own. There is a range of plagiarism, starting with the most severe cases, such as copying someone else's writing word for word to unintentional failure to credit your sources. In either case, in colleges and universities, the penalties for plagiarism are very serious. A writer's words are his or her property and are protected by law. Thus, in your writing, you need to show that you are aware of the **conventions of scholarship** and cite your sources.* Use the following techniques to avoid plagiarism:

- When you quote directly from a text, place those words within quotation marks and include the source (see the following instructions on format).
- When you paraphrase passages from your reading, make sure you rewrite the passage completely in your own words. Rearranging words or substituting synonyms isn't adequate. To be certain, close the book or turn the page and paraphrase without consulting the original text. Then check that your facts are correct.
- Provide documentation for each borrowed idea or phrase.
- Include a bibliography with your writing.

For something that is considered "common knowledge" you do not need to provide documentation. For example, if you say that polio threatened the lives of many people, it would not be necessary to give a source, as it is a fact that you can assume most people would know. However, it can be difficult to determine what is common knowledge and what isn't. A good guideline to follow is that if you knew a fact before you did your research, or any reasonably educated person should know it, it is probably common knowledge. But, if you learned it from your reading, you need to cite it. If you have any question about it, check with your instructor.

ACTIVITY 1: IDENTIFYING PLAGIARISM

Here is an original passage from a reading, followed by three different student paraphrases—Versions A, B, and C. Only one of the paraphrases is acceptable. Determine which one it is, and explain what makes it a good paraphrase. Also highlight the specific features that make the other two passages unacceptable.

---

*Chapter 9 gives the various conventions for quoting and referencing sources.

Original passage:

It is clear that American health-care costs must be contained. But HMOs—which do nothing to contain the 23 percent of health-care dollars that cover the costs of administering 1,500 different insurance plans—are not the answer. Even the minuscule savings they claim in their first few years are not genuine: the General Accounting Office recently reported that some of the cost savings realized by HMOs are the result of skimming—subscribing healthier patients—rather than cost containment. And, insurance companies' concentration on the quarterly profit statement ignores the fact that patients denied care and treatment get sicker—and thus cost more—in the long run. ("Cutting Care," by Suzanne Gordon and Judy Shindul-Rothschild. *Mother Jones,* January/February 1994, p. 72.)

Version A:

American health-care costs must be lowered. However, HMOs—which do nothing to contain the 23 percent of health-care dollars that cover the costs of administering 1,500 different insurance plans—are not the answer. They misrepresent their profits and patient data. Also, their concentration on the quarterly profit statement ignores the fact that patients denied care and treatment get sicker—and thus cost more—in the long run.

Version B:

Health care costs are out of control. Many people have suggested HMOs as a way to reduce costs. However, according to a recent article in *Mother Jones,* HMOs "are not the answer" (Gordon and Shindul-Rothschild, 1994, p. 72). The authors claim that the savings that HMOs do show are the result of "skimming"—the practice of subscribing healthy patients in order to lower the average cost of treatment. The authors also argue that insurance companies are more concerned with their profit margins, and this results in higher costs over time (p. 72).

Version C:

American health-care costs must be contained, but HMOs are not the answer. They have minor savings in their first few years, and even those are not genuine. The U.S. General Accounting Office recently reported that some of the HMOs' cost savings are the result of "skimming"—subscribing healthier patients—rather than cost cutting. And, insurance companies' care more about profits than patient care, which results in higher costs anyway. (Gordon & Shindul-Rothschild, p. 72.)

Checklist 4: Evaluation

_____ I wrote summaries of my readings on index cards.

_____ I included some direct quotations on index cards.

_____ Each source has a separate card and is fully recorded.

_____ I have noted some of my questions and opinions on cards as well.

_____ I have avoided plagiarism by keeping good records and paraphrasing completely.

_____ I have evaluated my notes and determined I have enough information to begin organizing my paper.

Organization

It is now time to start planning your paper. The first step is to write your thesis statement. Review the procedures on thesis writing in Chapters 4, 5 and 6, then write a compelling and arguable thesis. Draft a thesis statement to share with your class.

Peer Evaluation: Share your thesis with your classmates and discuss its arguability, specificity, and interest level. Rework your thesis until it is satisfactory.

What kind of organization will you use? You have many choices, or even a combination of choices. Table 7.1 shows you a few of the possibilities and the reasons for their choice.

TABLE 7.1 ORGANIZATIONAL METHODS

ORGANIZATIONAL METHOD	DESCRIPTION
Cause to Effect (or vice versa)	Shows the links between an event and its outcome, or examines an effect and determines what might have caused it. Beware of making *post hoc* claims— that is, believing that because event A happened before event B, event A caused event B. (Review Table 6.1 of Chapter 6)
Chronological Order	Shows the development of an event or process over time.
Compare and Contrast	Shows the relationship between two or more events or ideas. Typically, comparison concentrates on similarities, and contrast focuses on differences. However, most papers using this organizational strategy use both.
Known to Unknown	Starts with concepts that are familiar to the reader in order to explain new ideas. In reverse, begins with the unfamiliar concept and works towards the familiar one.
Problem to Solution	Begins by defining a problem and then demonstrating a possible solution, or in reverse, showing how a particular problem was solved.

ACTIVITY 2: ORGANIZATIONAL STRATEGIES

With a partner or group of classmates, discuss what kind of organizational strategy or strategies you might use for each of the following possible paper topics. Use Table 7.1 to help you.

1. The history of polio in North America
2. Preventing AIDS in teenagers
3. The difference between the common cold and influenza
4. The influence of stress on arthritis
5. The development of the Salk vaccine
6. Genetic therapy as a cure for cancer

After you have decided upon an organizational strategy (or strategies) for your paper, an outline will be helpful. What are the main points you want to make to support your thesis? How will you use your note cards and other evidence to develop your main points? Create an outline and check to make sure each item on it relates to your thesis. You may use a traditional outline form, such as the following, or any other form that is useful to you.

I.   Major Heading
   A. First main idea
      1. First topic
      2. Second topic
         a. first sub-topic
         b. second sub-topic
            etc.
   B.
   C.
II.
   A.
   B.
      1.
         a.
         b.
      2.

Checklist 5: Organization

_____ I wrote a compelling thesis statement.

_____ I decided on an organizational strategy or strategies.

_____ I created an outline to help keep my work organized.

_____ I have discussed my work with classmates and my instructor.

Writing the Initial Draft

Even though you are reporting research, it is still important to write an interesting opening paragraph. Avoid the following "traps" in writing an opening to a research paper.

TABLE 7.2 TRAPS IN OPENING RESEARCH PAPERS

Avoid . . .	because . . .	Instead . . .
repeating the title	the reader has already read your title. Now he/she would like to know more about it.	Open with an interesting sentence that will spark your reader's interest.
announcing your topic	it's more effective to write about your topic directly. In other words, don't say "In this paper, I will discuss malaria . . ."	State your thesis or opening paragraph directly: "Malaria is one of the most deadly diseases in the world today . . ."
giving too much information	the reader may be more interested if you don't tell everything you know in the first paragraph.	Give your reader a reason to continue reading—that is, to find out the results.
asking a question	the reader will be more interested in learning from you than in answering your questions. If you begin with a rhetorical question (a question you assume your reader would answer in the same way you would), you may be making an unfair assumption.	Offer interesting facts and ideas.
using a dictionary definition	dictionary definitions aren't very interesting. Unless it's an unusual word, the reader probably knows the definition.	Define difficult terms in the body of the paper, if necessary.
being too broad	the reader will want to know specifically what your paper is about. If you start with an overly general statement, the reader won't see what you are going to write about.	Make your topic and position clear in the opening of your paper.
being too informal	readers expect a certain degree of formality in researched writing. This doesn't mean that you shouldn't be creative, or that you should use "inflated" vocabulary but neither should you start off by writing jokes or overly personal experiences.	Use "middle voice"—a level of formality that avoids slang and overly emotional language.

Use your note cards and outline to guide the rest of your writing. Bring your draft to class on the date assigned by your instructor.

Peer Response

Exchange your paper with a partner, and read each other's drafts. Then provide the following information.

Writer's name: _____

Reader's name: _____

Title: _____

Author: _____

Part A.

1. Recopy the thesis statement here:

   Is it arguable, interesting, specific, and grammatical? If not, suggest changes.

2. Is the introduction compelling? Do you know clearly what the paper will be about?

3. Describe the organizational technique(s) the author uses. Is it effective? Are there transitions?

4. Is the logic of the paragraph order clear? Write a short sentence that summarizes each paragraph. Does each paragraph relate to the thesis in some way?

5. Do you see any flaws in the reasoning? Explain.

6. Does the author incorporate quotations and citations from his/her sources? Do they make sense?

7. What did you learn from reading this paper? What would you still like to know about this topic?

8. Other comments:

Part B. When your partner returns your paper and the comments, respond to each of the following questions.

1. Did your partner correctly identify your thesis? If not, do you think you need to make it clearer?

2. Do you agree with the comments concerning your introduction? If changes were suggested, which will you make?

3. Was your organization clear? What improvements can you make?

4. Were any of your paragraphs off topic, or poorly ordered? What adjustments will you make?

5. How can you improve your reasoning, if necessary?

6. What additional citations and quotations are necessary? Will you do any more research? Explain.

7. Other comments:

Revision

In the revision phase of your research paper, you are reorganizing, cutting, adding development of examples, and improving your citations. As with previous essays, looking at the review you received from your partner and your response to it, formulate a **revision plan.** You may use the following chart to help you identify the areas that need the most improvement.

REVISION PLAN

FEATURE	PROBLEM	POSSIBLE SOLUTION
Title		
Opening paragraph		
Use of sources		
Organization		
Development of ideas		
Word choice		
Conclusion		
Other		

Use your revision plan to guide your rewriting.

Final Version

After you have solved the problems identified in your revision plan, you can focus on editing and proofreading your paper. The editing phase includes double-checking your grammar, spelling, punctuation, citation format, and so forth. Use Chapter 8 of this book to guide you. Again, take an inventory of problems you have experienced with previous essays.

Check the appropriate column; then use the section listed at the right to guide your editing. Include a writer's memo (see page 49).

PROBLEM CHECKLIST					
PROBLEM	**Minor Problem**	**Major Problem**	**No Problem**	**Don't Know**	**Section**
Spelling					
Punctuation					
Subject-verb agreement					
Verb tenses					
Articles and prepositions					
Plurals					
Sentence fragments					
Run-on sentences					
Wordiness					
Transitions					
Relative clauses					

If you have checked more than three as a "major problem," decide which three you would like to work on first. It's easier to concentrate on a few problem areas at a time.

The last step should be proofreading—that is, looking for careless mistakes: misspellings, leaving out words, typing words twice in a row, and so forth. Before you turn your paper in, proofread it carefully.

THE MAN WHO MISTOOK HIS WIFE FOR A HAT

by Oliver Sacks

Threads

Oliver Sacks is a neurologist who has written widely about the effects of neurological disorders. The movie *Awakenings,* starring Robin Williams, was based on his book by the same name.

Dr. P. was a musician of distinction, well-known for many years as a singer, and then, at the local School of Music, as a teacher. It was here, in relation to his students, that certain strange problems were first observed. Sometimes a student would present himself, and Dr. P. would not recognize him; or, specifically, would not recognize his face. The moment the student spoke, he would be recognized by his voice. Such incidents multiplied, causing embarrassment, perplexity, fear—and, sometimes, comedy. For not only did Dr. P. increasingly fail to see faces, but he saw faces when there were no faces to see: genially, Magoo-like, when in the street he might pat the heads of water hydrants and parking meters, taking these to be the heads of children; he would amiably address carved knobs on the furniture and be astounded when they did not reply. At first these mistakes were laughed off as jokes, not least by Dr. P. himself. Had he not always had a quirky sense of humor and been given to Zen-like paradoxes and jests? His musical powers were as dazzling as ever; he did not feel ill—he had never felt better; and the mistakes were so ludicrous—and so ingenious—that they could hardly be serious or betoken anything serious. The notion of there being "something the matter" did not emerge until some three years later, when diabetes developed. Well aware that diabetes could affect his eyes, Dr. P. consulted an ophthalmologist, who took a careful history and examined his eyes closely. "There's nothing the matter with your eyes," the doctor concluded. "But there is trouble with the visual parts of your brain. You don't need my help, you must see a neurologist." And so, as a result of this referral, Dr. P. came to me.

It was obvious within a few seconds of meeting him that there was no trace of dementia in the ordinary sense. He was a man of great cultivation and charm who talked well and fluently, with imagination and humor. I couldn't think why he had been referred to our clinic.

And yet there *was* something a bit odd. He faced me as he spoke, was oriented towards me, and yet there was something the matter—it was difficult to formulate. He faced me with his *ears,* I came to think, but not with his eyes. These, instead of looking, gazing, at me, "taking me in," in the normal way, made sudden strange fixations—on my nose, on my right ear, down to my chin, up to my right eye—as if noting (even studying) these individual features, but not seeing my whole face, its changing expressions, "me," as a whole. I am not sure that I fully realized this at the time—there was just a teasing strangeness, some failure in the normal interplay of gaze and expression. He saw me, he *scanned* me and yet . . .

"What seems to be the matter?" I asked him at length.

"Nothing that I know of," he replied with a smile, "but people seem to think there's something wrong with my eyes."

"But *you* don't recognize any visual problems?"

"No, not directly, but I occasionally make mistakes."

I left the room briefly to talk to his wife. When I came back, Dr. P. was sitting placidly by the window, attentive, listening rather than looking out. "Traffic," he said, "street sounds, distant trains—they make a sort of symphony, do they not? You know Honegger's *Pacific 234?*"

What a lovely man, I thought to myself. How can there be anything seriously the matter? Would he permit me to examine him?

"Yes, of course, Dr. Sacks."

I stilled my disquiet, his perhaps, too, in the soothing routine of a neurological exam—muscle strength, coordination, reflexes, tone. . . . It was while examining his reflexes—a trifle abnormal on the left side—that the first bizarre experience occurred. I had taken off his left shoe and scratched the sole of his foot with a key—a frivolous-seeming but essential test of a reflex—and then, excusing myself to screw my ophthalmoscope together, left him to put on the shoe himself. To my surprise, a minute later, he had not done this.

"Can I help?" I asked.

"Help what? Help whom?"

"Help you put on your shoe."

"Ach," he said, "I had forgotten the shoe," adding, *sotto voce,* "The shoe? The shoe?" He seemed baffled.

"Your shoe," I repeated. "Perhaps you'd put it on."

He continued to look downwards, though not at the shoe, with an intense but misplaced concentration. Finally his gaze settled on his foot: "That is my shoe, yes?"

Did I mis-hear? Did he mis-see?

"My eyes," he explained, and put a hand to his foot. "*This* is my shoe, no?"

"No, it is not. That is your foot. *There* is your shoe."

"Ah! I thought that was my foot."

Was he joking? Was he mad? Was he blind? If this was one of his "strange mistakes," it was the strangest mistake I had ever come across.

I helped him on with his shoe (his foot), to avoid further complication. Dr. P. himself seemed untroubled, indifferent, maybe amused. I resumed my examination. His visual acuity was good: he had no difficulty seeing a pin on the floor, though sometimes he missed it if it was placed to his left.

He saw all right, but what did he see? I opened out a copy of the *National Geographic* magazine and asked him to describe some pictures in it.

His responses here were very curious. His eyes would dart from one thing to another, picking up tiny features, individual features, as they had done with my face. A striking brightness, a color, a shape would arrest his attention and elicit comment—but in no case did he get the scene-as-a-whole. He failed to see the whole, seeing only details, which he spotted like blips on a radar screen. He never entered into relation with the picture as a whole—never faced, so to speak, *its* physiognomy. He had no sense whatever of a landscape or scene.

I showed him the cover, an unbroken expanse of Sahara dunes.

"What do you see here?" I asked.

"I see a river," he said. "And a little guest-house with its terrace on the water. People are dining out on the terrace. I see colored parasols here and there." He was looking, if it was "looking," right off the cover into mid-air and confabulating nonexistent features, as if the absence of features in the actual picture had driven him to imagine the river and the terrace and the colored parasols.

I must have looked aghast, but he seemed to think he had done rather well. There was a hint of a smile on his face. He also appeared to have decided that the examination was over and started to look around for his hat. He reached out his hand and took hold of his wife's head, tried to lift it off, and put it on. He had apparently mistaken his wife for a hat! His wife looked as if she was used to such things.

I could make no sense of what had occurred in terms of conventional neurology (or neuropsychology). In some ways he seemed perfectly preserved, and in others absolutely, incomprehensively devastated. How could he, on the one hand, mistake his wife for a hat and, on the other, function as apparently he still did, as a teacher at the Music School?

I had to think, to see him again—and to see him in his own familiar habitat, at home.

A few days later I called on Dr. P. and his wife at home, with the score of the *Dichterliebe* in my briefcase (I knew he liked Schumann), and a variety of odd

Threads

Definition: fin-de-siècle, style characteristic of the late 19th century

objects for the testing of perception. Mrs. P. showed me into a loft apartment, which recalled fin-de-siècle Berlin. A magnificent old Bösendorfer stood in state in the center of the room, and all around it were music stands, instruments, scores. . . . There were books, there were paintings, but the music was central. Dr. P. came in, a little bowed, and, distracted, advanced with outstretched hands to the grandfather clock, but, hearing my voice, corrected himself, and shook hands with me. We exchanged greetings and chatted a little of current concerts and performances. Diffidently, I asked him if he would sing.

"The *Dichterliebe*!" he exclaimed. "But I can no longer read music. You will play them, yes?"

I said I would try. On that wonderful old piano even my playing sounded right, and Dr. P. was an aged but infinitely mellow Fischer-Dieskau, combining a perfect ear and voice with the most incisive musical intelligence. It was clear that the Music School was not keeping him out of charity.

Dr. P.'s temporal lobes were obviously intact: he had a wonderful musical cortex. What, I wondered, was going on in his parietal and occipital lobes, especially in those areas where visual processing occurred? I carry the Platonic solids in my neurological kit and decided to start with these.

"What is this?" I asked, drawing out the first one.

"A cube, of course."

"Now this?" I asked, brandishing another.

He asked if he might examine it, which he did swiftly and systematically. "A dodecahedron, of course. And don't bother with the others—I'll get the icosahedron, too."

Abstract shapes clearly presented no problems. What about faces? I took out a pack of cards. All of these he identified instantly, including the jacks, queens, kings, and the joker. But these, after all, are stylized designs, and it was impossible to tell whether he saw faces or merely patterns. I decided I would show him a volume of cartoons which I had in my briefcase. Here, again, for the most part, he did well. Churchill's cigar, Schnozzle's nose: as soon as he had picked out a key feature he could identify the face. But cartoons, again, are formal and schematic. It remained to be seen how he would do with real faces, realistically represented.

I turned on the television, keeping the sound off, and found an early Bette Davis film. A love scene was in progress. Dr. P. failed to identify the actress—but this could have been because she had never entered his world. What was more striking was that he failed to identify the expressions on her face or her partner's, though in the course of a single torrid scene these passed from sultry yearning through passion, surprise, disgust, and fury to a melting reconciliation. Dr. P. could make nothing of any of this. He was very unclear as to what was going on, or who was who or even what sex they were. His comments on the scene were positively Martian.

It was just possible that some of his difficulties were associated with the unreality of a celluloid, Hollywood world; and it occurred to me that he might be more successful in identifying faces from his own life. On the walls of the apartment there were photographs of his family, his colleagues, his pupils, himself. I gathered a pile of these together and, with some misgivings, presented them to him. What had been funny, or farcical, in relation to the movie, was tragic in relation to real life. By and large, he recognized nobody: neither his family, nor his colleagues, nor his pupils, nor himself. He recognized a portrait of Einstein because he picked up the characteristic hair and mustache; and the same thing happened with one or two other people. "Ach, Paul!" he said, when shown a portrait of his brother. "That square jaw, those big teeth—I would know Paul anywhere!" But was it Paul he recognized, or one or two of his features, on the basis of which he could make a reasonable guess as to the subject's identity? In the absence of obvious "markers," he was utterly lost. But it was not merely the cognition, the *gnosis*, at fault; there was something radically wrong with the whole way he proceeded. For he approached these faces—even of those near and dear—as if they were abstract puzzles or tests. He did not relate to them, he did not behold. No face was familiar to him, seen as a "thou," being just identified as a set of features, an "it." Thus, there was formal, but no trace of personal, gnosis. And with this went his indifference, or blindness, to expression. A face, to us, is a person looking out—we see, as it were, the person through his *persona,* his face. But for Dr. P. there was no *persona* in this sense—no outward *persona,* and no person within.

I had stopped at a florist on my way to his apartment and bought myself an extravagant red rose for my buttonhole. Now I removed this and handed it to him. He took it like a botanist or morphologist given a specimen, not like a person given a flower.

"About six inches in length," he commented. "A convoluted red form with a linear green attachment."

"Yes," I said encouragingly, "and what do you think it *is,* Dr. P.?"

"Not easy to say." He seemed perplexed. "It lacks the simple symmetry of the Platonic solids, although it may have a higher symmetry of its own. . . . I think this could be an inflorescence or flower."

"Could be?" I queried.

"Could be," he confirmed.

"Smell it," I suggested, and he again looked somewhat puzzled, as if I had asked him to smell a higher symmetry. But he complied courteously, and took it to his nose. Now, suddenly, he came to life.

"Beautiful!" he exclaimed. "An early rose. What a heavenly smell!" He started to hum "*Die Rose, die Lillie . . .*" Reality, it seemed, might be conveyed by smell, not by sight.

I tried one final test. It was still a cold day, in early spring, and I had thrown my coat and gloves on the sofa.

"What is this?" I asked, holding up a glove.

"May I examine it?" he asked, and, taking it from me, he proceeded to examine it as he had examined the geometrical shapes.

"A continuous surface," he announced at last, "infolded on itself. It appears to have"—he hesitated—"five outpouchings, if this is the word."

"Yes," I said cautiously. "You have given me a description. Now tell me what it is."

"A container of some sort?"

"Yes," I said, "and what would it contain?"

"It would contain its contents!" said Dr. P., with a laugh. "There are many possibilities. It could be a change purse, for example, for coins of five sizes. It could . . ."

I interrupted the barmy flow. "Does it now look familiar? Do you think it might contain, might fit, a part of your body?"

No light of recognition dawned on his face.[1]

No child would have the power to see and speak of "a continuous surface . . . infolded on itself," but any child, any infant, would immediately know a glove as a glove, see it as familiar, as going with a hand. Dr. P. didn't. He saw nothing as familiar. Visually, he was lost in a world of lifeless abstractions. Indeed, he did not have a real visual world, as he did not have a real visual self. He could speak about things, but did not see them face-to-face. Hughlings Jackson, discussing patients with aphasia and left-hemisphere lesions, says they have lost "abstract" and "propositional" thought—and compares them with dogs (or, rather, he compares dogs to patients with aphasia). Dr. P., on the other hand, functioned precisely as a machine functions. It wasn't merely that he displayed the same indifference to the visual world as a computer but—even more strikingly—he construed the world as a computer construes it, by means of key features and schematic relationships. The scheme might be identified—in an "identi-kit" way—without the reality being grasped at all.

---

[1]Later, by accident, he got it on, and exclaimed, "My God, it's a glove!" This was reminiscent of Kurt Goldstein's patient "Lanuti," who could only recognize objects by trying to use them in action.

The testing I had done so far told me nothing about Dr. P.'s inner world. Was it possible that his visual memory and imagination were still intact? I asked him to imagine entering one of our local squares from the north side, to walk through it, in imagination or in memory, and tell me the buildings he might pass as he walked. He listed the buildings on his right side, but none of those on his left. I then asked him to imagine entering the square from the south. Again he mentioned only those buildings that were on the right side, although these were the very buildings he had omitted before. Those he had "seen" internally before were not mentioned now; presumably, they were no longer "seen." It was evident that his difficulties with leftness, his visual field deficits were as much internal as external, bisecting his visual memory and imagination.

What, at a higher level, of his internal visualization? Thinking of the almost hallucinatory intensity with which Tolstoy visualizes and animates his characters, I questioned Dr. P. about *Anna Karenina*. He could remember incidents without difficulty, had an undiminished grasp of the plot, but completely omitted visual characteristics, visual narrative, and scenes. He remembered the words of the characters, but not their faces; and though, when asked, he could quote, with his remarkable and almost verbatim memory, the original visual descriptions, these were, it became apparent, quite empty for him and lacked sensorial, imaginal, or emotional reality. Thus, there was an internal agnosia as well.[2]

But this was only the case, it became clear, with certain sorts of visualization. The visualization of faces and scenes, of visual narrative and drama—this was profoundly impaired, almost absent. But the visualization of *schemata* was preserved, perhaps enhanced. Thus, when I engaged him in a game of mental chess, he had no difficulty visualizing the chessboard or the moves—indeed, no difficulty in beating me soundly.

Luria said of Zazetsky that he had entirely lost his capacity to play games but that his "vivid imagination" was unimpaired. Zazetsky and Dr. P. lived in worlds which were mirror images of each other. But the saddest difference between them was that Zazetsky, as Luria said, "fought to regain his lost faculties with the indomitable tenacity of the damned," whereas Dr. P. was not fighting, did not know what was lost, did not indeed know that anything was lost. But who was more tragic, or who was more damned—the man who knew it, or the man who did not?

When the examination was over, Mrs. P. called us to the table, where there was coffee and a delicious spread of little cakes. Hungrily, hummingly, Dr. P. started on the cakes. Swiftly, fluently, unthinkingly, melodiously, he pulled the plates towards him and took this and that in a great gurgling stream, an edible song of food, until, suddenly, there came an interruption: a loud, peremptory rat-tat-tat at the door. Startled, taken aback, arrested by the interruption, Dr. P. stopped eating and sat frozen, motionless, at the table, with an indifferent, blind bewilderment on his face. He saw, but no longer saw, the table; no longer perceived it as a table laden with cakes. His wife poured him some coffee: the smell titillated his nose and brought him back to reality. The melody of eating resumed.

How does he do anything? I wondered to myself. What happens when he's dressing, goes to the lavatory, has a bath. I followed his wife into the kitchen and asked her how, for instance, he managed to dress himself. "It's just like the eating," she explained. "I put his usual clothes out, in all the usual places, and he dresses without difficulty, singing to himself. He does everything singing to

---

[2]I have often wondered about Helen Keller's visual descriptions, whether these, for all their eloquence, are somehow empty as well? Or whether, by the transference of images from the tactile to the visual, or, yet more extraordinarily, from the verbal and the metaphorical to the sensorial and the visual, she did achieve a power of visual imagery, even though her visual cortex had never been stimulated, directly, by the eyes? But in Dr. P.'s case it is precisely the cortex that was damaged, the organic prerequisite of all pictorial imagery. Interestingly and typically he no longer dreamed pictorially—the "message" of the dream being conveyed in nonvisual terms.

himself. But if he is interrupted and loses the thread, he comes to a complete stop, doesn't know his clothes—or his own body. He sings all the time—eating songs, dressing songs, bathing songs, everything. He can't do anything unless he makes it a song.

While we were talking my attention was caught by the pictures on the walls.

"Yes," Mrs. P. said, "he was a gifted painter as well as a singer. The School exhibited his pictures every year."

I strolled past them curiously—they were in chronological order. All his earlier work was naturalistic and realistic, with vivid mood and atmosphere, but finely detailed and concrete. Then, years later, they became less vivid, less concrete, less realistic and naturalistic, but far more abstract, even geometrical and cubist. Finally, in the last paintings the canvasses became nonsense, or nonsense to me—mere chaotic lines and blotches of paint. I commented on this to Mrs. P.

"Ach, you doctors, you're such Philistines!" she exclaimed. "Can you not see *artistic development*—how he renounced the realism of his earlier years, and advanced into abstract, nonrepresentational art?"

"No, that's not it," I said to myself (but forbore to say it to poor Mrs. P.). He had indeed moved from realism to nonrepresentation to the abstract, yet this was not the artist, but the pathology, advancing—advancing towards a profound visual agnosia, in which all powers of representation and imagery, all sense of the concrete, all sense of reality, were being destroyed. This wall of paintings was a tragic pathological exhibit, which belonged to neurology, not art.

And yet, I wondered, was she not partly right? For there is often a struggle, and sometimes, even more interestingly, a collusion between the powers of pathology and creation. Perhaps, in his cubist period, there might have been both artistic and pathological development, colluding to engender an original form; for as he lost the concrete, so he might have gained in the abstract, developing a greater sensitivity to all the structural elements of line, boundary, contour—an almost Picasso-like power to see, and equally depict, those abstract organizations embedded in, and normally lost in, the concrete. . . . Though in the final pictures, I feared, there was only chaos and agnosia.

We returned to the great music room, with the Bösendorfer in the center, and Dr. P. humming the last torte.

"Well, Dr. Sacks," he said to me. "You find me an interesting case, I perceive. Can you tell me what you find wrong, make recommendations?"

"I can't tell you what I find wrong," I replied, "but I'll say what I find right. You are a wonderful musician, and music is your life. What I would prescribe, in a case such as yours, is a life which consists entirely of music. Music has been the center, now make it the whole, of your life."

This was four years ago—I never saw him again, but I often wondered about how he apprehended the world, given his strange loss of image, visuality, and the perfect preservation of a great musicality. I think that music, for him, had taken the place of image. He had no body-image, he had body-music: this is why he could move and act as fluently as he did, but came to a total confused stop if the "inner music" stopped. And equally with the outside, the world. . . .[3]

In *The World as Representation and Will*, Schopenhauer speaks of music as "pure will." How fascinated he would have been by Dr. P., a man who had wholly lost the world as representation, but wholly preserved it as music or will.

And this, mercifully, held to the end—for despite the gradual advance of his disease (a massive tumor or degenerative process in the visual parts of his brain) Dr. P. lived and taught music to the last days of his life.

Threads

Arthur Schopenhauer (1788–1860) was a German philosopher who believed that the will to live is the fundamental reality.

---

[3]Thus, as I learned later from his wife, though he could not recognize his students if they sat still, if they were merely "images," he might suddenly recognize them if they moved. "That's Karl," he would cry. "I know his movements, his body-music."

For Discussion

ABOUT THE CONTENT

1. Summarize Dr. P.'s problem. What are the symptoms? What might be the cause?
2. What are "gnosis," "agnosia," and "persona"? How are they important to Sacks's thoughts about his patient?
3. What role did music play in Dr. P.'s life?
4. What did Sacks think Dr. P.'s paintings showed? How did it differ from Dr. P.'s wife's opinion? Who do you think was right?
5. What do you think of Sacks's advice to his patient?

ABOUT THE WRITING

1. For whom is Sacks writing? What features of the writing tell you this?
2. Sacks is an accomplished writer as well as doctor. Can you find specific passages in the writing that are examples of his writing skill?

Quickwrite

Dr. P. compensated for his neurological problem through his music. How does music comfort us? What role does it play in your life?

NAMING A KILLER

by Randy Shilts

Freeze Frames, December 23, 1980
Beth Israel Medical Center, New York City

With a sense of weariness, Dr. Donna Mildvan studied the autopsy report of a thirty-three-year-old German chef to whom she had devoted so much of the past five months. His death had been particularly grisly. Plagued by the cytomegalovirus that had spread its virulent herpes throughout his body, the young man had simply curled into a ball and finally died one day, as the late December cold descended on Manhattan. Mildvan grimaced as she surveyed the last CAT scan of the man's brain. It was shrunken and atrophied, like the brain of a senile old man. She wondered whether she would ever understand what she had missed, what had so cruelly torn away this man's life.

Two weeks later, a Beth Israel nurse appeared in the emergency room, suffering from *Pneumocystis*. Within ten days, he was dead. It turned out that he was also homosexual. When the pathologist told Mildvan that an autopsy had revealed widespread infection with cytomegalovirus, the physician's thinking crystallized quickly: There were too many coincidences. Two men had died of infections that should be

mere nuisances, not brutal killers. Their immune systems had collapsed. This also explained why she had ten other patients, all gay men, who were suffering from a strange enlargement of their lymph nodes. Something was wrong with their immune systems too.

Mildvan quickly arranged a meeting with the city's best-known gay physician, Dan William.

"I'm very concerned too," said William. "I have lots of patients with lymphadenopathy."

Mildvan went quickly to the point. This was all connected, she was convinced, and in the early weeks of 1981 she became one of the first doctors to begin conceiving a larger picture.

"Whatever that lymphadenopathy is, I think it's the same thing that just killed those two other guys," Mildvan said. "There is a new disease going around homosexual men."

The Prettiest One, June 16, 1981
Centers for Disease Control, Hepatitis Laboratories, Phoenix

Although he was only thirty-eight, Dr. Don Francis was one of the most eminent experts on epidemics at the CDC, having been among the handful of epidemiologists who literally wiped smallpox off the face of the earth in the 1970s. In recent years he had worked with the gay community on the hepatitis vaccine project, which he was now wrapping up.

Don called his old Harvard mentor, Myron Essex, as soon as he heard about how PCP [Pneumocystis pneumonia] and Kaposi's sarcoma victims suffered from a strange depletion in T-lymphocytes. It was with Essex that Francis had studied the mechanisms of feline leukemia virus for his virology doctorate.

"This is feline leukemia in people," Francis began.

Essex knew Francis had a penchant for quick conclusions stated in the most dramatic terms; he also knew that his former student had gained an international reputation for singular brilliance. After spending eight years studying feline leukemia, the major cause of cat deaths, Essex was more than casually interested in links between this disease and human disease. He and Francis were among the small minority of scientists who believed that viruses would one day be linked to cancer and other serious human ailments. Together, they had published eight articles on feline leukemia as well as a controversial piece suggesting that some human lymphomas, leukemias, and cancers of the immune system might be linked to viral infections. Essex settled back to listen to Francis's logic.

Cancer and immune suppression, Francis said. Both feline leukemia and this new gay disease were marked by a trail of opportunistic infections that seemed to take advantage of an immune system weakened by a primary infection. In cats, the infection was a leukemia virus that knocked out the cats' immune systems and left them open to a number of cancers. Clearly, some similar virus was doing the same thing to these homosexual men, and they were getting cancer too. Secondly, feline leukemia has a long incubation period; this new disease must have long latency too, which is the only way it was killing people in three cities on both coasts before anybody even knew it existed.

His years of battling epidemics in Africa, Asia, and America had imbued Francis with the idea that viruses were crafty little creatures constantly trying to outsmart humans in their bid for survival. Long latency periods were one of the most clever ways to thwart detection and extermination. Francis didn't think the gay health problems were being caused by cytomegalovirus or the other familiar viruses under discussion. They had been around for years and hadn't killed anybody. It was something new; it could even be a retrovirus, Francis said.

Essex was intrigued, although he knew most scientists would consider Francis's suggestion farfetched. As a subgroup of viruses, retroviruses were, at

Threads

Definition: retrovirus is any of a group of viruses, many of which cause tumors, that contain the genetic material RNA.

Threads

Mark Conant is a dermatologist affiliated with the University of California at San Francisco.

Threads

Cleve Jones is a gay activist and organizer of the Kaposi's Sarcoma Research and Education Foundation.

best, a quaint and exotic group of viruses. Last year, a National Cancer Institute researcher, Dr. Robert Gallo, had shown that a retrovirus caused a leukemia common in Japan, the first time any virus had been linked to a human cancer. That was something of a backward scientific affair, however. Gallo had first discovered the virus and then searched worldwide for a disease that it might cause. By chance, Japanese researchers were studying the T-cell leukemia, assuming it was a contagious cancer, but they hadn't identified a viral culprit. Identifying Human T-cell Leukemia virus, or HTLV, as the cause, had forged a major scientific breakthrough in virology; it also had frightened scientists because of its long incubation period. Such a virus could be spread all over before it caused disease and anybody would even know it existed.

Many scientists remained dubious about the future of retroviral research, however, and many still believed retroviruses to be animal bugs because virtually all of them were linked to diseases in chickens, pigs, or cats. Essex figured that this was wishful thinking. Francis's idea, Essex thought, was a hypothesis that bore watching.

Francis was already convinced. He quickly became the leading CDC proponent of the notion that a new virus that could be spread sexually was causing immune deficiencies in gay men.

Enemy Time, January 14, 1982
University of California, San Francisco

Mark Conant told Cleve Jones that he needed advice from somebody political. They'd talk about it over dinner, but first there was someone Conant wanted Cleve to meet.

Simon Guzman smiled shyly at Cleve Jones when the young activist entered the room on the top floor of the UC Medical Center. As they talked, Simon pulled out a snapshot of himself from Before. Smooth brown skin was pulled taut over well-developed muscles. Clad only in a tight pair of yellow Speedos, Simon was everything that Cleve had considered hot; he knew he could have fallen for the hunky Mexican in the photo.

Simon Guzman's body now, however, was barely more than a skeleton with sallow, lesion-covered skin sagging loosely, and tubes coursing in every conceivable orifice and vein. Simon explained that he hadn't made many friends in his two years working as a printer in the suburb of Hayward. Yes, he had been popular but that kind of, uh, popularity didn't put one in line for best buddies, not in this time and place. Now he had this horrible diarrhea that wouldn't stop; the doctors couldn't even tell him what was causing it. He was embarrassed that his mother would learn he was gay because he had gay cancer, and sometimes he felt so alone he wished he would just die. It would be over then.

Cleve left the room feeling sick to his stomach. He wanted a drink.

This was real; this was the future.

* * *

Over dinner, Conant began carefully laying out what he saw ahead. He had been thinking about this since he left the National Cancer Institute meeting in September. The forty-four-year-old dermatologist leaned back in his chair. His face showed a certain weariness, but his voice never quavered. He was going through his lecture with a slow, smooth southern cadence that subtly revealed his roots in Jacksonville, Florida. Years of giving lectures as a clinical professor at UCSF had also taught him how to meter his sentences and pause to let a significant piece of information sink in.

This is an infectious disease, Conant began. The CDC case-control study may offer some definitive word on how it was spread, but that research was stalled, probably for lack of resources. We are losing time, and time is the enemy in any epidemic. *The disease is moving even if the government isn't.*

It was at this dinner that Cleve Jones first heard the technical jargon that would become the stuff of his nightmares in the years ahead—terms like geometric progression and exponential increases. Some scientist had come up with a new name for the syndrome: Gay-Related Immune Deficiency, or GRID. Conant, however, wasn't sure how gay-related this immune deficiency would stay. Viruses tend not to respect such artificial divisions among humans. Lymphocytes were lymphocytes, and clearly they were major taste treats for the new virus, whether they happened to live in gay bodies or straight.

"This is going to be a world-class disaster," Conant said. "And nobody's paying attention."

Cleve's thoughts had drifted off while he merged Conant's frightening tale of a new virus with what he knew about gay community sexual mores; hell, with what he knew about his own sexual exploits. His face turned white, and he ordered a drink.

"We're all dead," Cleve said.

Patient Zero, April 2, 1982
Atlanta

By now, a dizzying array of acronyms was being bandied about as possible monikers for an epidemic that, though ten months old, remained unnamed. Besides GRID, some doctors liked ACIDS, for Acquired Community Immune Deficiency Syndrome, and then others favored CAIDS, for Community Acquired Immune Deficiency Syndrome. The CDC hated GRID and preferred calling it "the epidemic of immune deficiency." The "community" in other versions, of course, was a polite way of saying gay; the doctors couldn't let go of the notion that one identified this disease by whom it hit rather than what it did.

Whether CAIDS, ACIDS, or GRID, the epidemic had by April 2, 1982, struck 300 Americans and killed 119. In the past two weeks, cases had been detected in two more states and two more European nations, indicating that the epidemic had now spread across nineteen states and seven countries. Of the 300 cases in the United States, 242 were gay or bisexual men, 30 were heterosexual men, 10 were heterosexual women, and 18 were men of unknown sexual orientation. Since transmission through unclean needles had yet to be proven scientifically, the cautious CDC statisticians had not yet roped off addicts as a separate risk group. By now, somebody was dying almost every day in America from an epidemic that still did not have a name.

Entropy, July 27, 1982
Washington, D.C.

If you don't abide by scientific principles, chaos will ensue.

It was a fundamental tenet of Dale Lawrence's world. It was an idea that also recurred to him after he had flown up from Atlanta to join his boss, Dr. Bruce Evatt, and Don Francis and a gathering of leaders of the blood industry, hemophiliac groups, gay community organizations, and assorted luminaries from the National Institutes of Health and the Food and Drug Administration. The Centers for Disease Control had hoped the new evidence of blood transmission would incite the blood industry's two major components, the voluntary blood banks and the for-profit manufacturers of blood products, to move quickly to stem the tide of blood contamination.

The CDC privately preferred launching the only available preventive measure: donor deferral guidelines, asking people who fit into the high-risk groups, such as gay men, Haitians, and drug users, not to donate blood. The logical science of GRID demanded that logical steps be taken, the CDC thought, or people would die needlessly. However, as would be the case with just about every policy aspect of the epidemic, logic would not be the prevailing modus operandi.

Threads

Dale Lawrence conducted early studies of AIDS in hemophiliacs and blood transfusion recipients for the CDC.

The hemophiliac groups immediately attacked the data that linked the immune suppression to the contamination of Factor VIII. They had read that some scientists believed gay men contracted the immune suppression simply because they were overloaded with infections. With all their exposure to blood-borne viruses, hemophiliacs also might be suffering from such immune overload, they argued. Isn't it too early to say with scientific certainty that this thing is hitting hemophiliacs? The National Hemophilia Foundation was also nervous about the accusations directed at Factor VIII, the product that had done so much to improve the hemophiliacs' quality of life in recent years. Did the CDC want these 20,000 stricken Americans to go back to the less sophisticated techniques of stopping bleeding with attendant hemorrhagic fatalities?

For their part, the CDC hands wondered whether the hemophiliacs were reluctant to have their blood disorder linked in any way to a disease the homosexuals got; it created a terrible public relations problem.

Gay community leaders were even more public relations-oriented than hemophiliacs. A New York City gay physician, Dr. Roger Enlow, argued persuasively that it was too soon to push for guidelines. Any such moves would have implications for the civil rights of millions of Americans, gay leaders noted. Only Dr. Dan William argued that such deferral of gay blood donors might be an entirely appropriate step toward saving lives, and that observation marked the beginning of his loss of popularity in the gay community.

The agency with the authority to actually enforce any donor guidelines on the blood industry was the Food and Drug Administration. Already, the FDA was keenly aware of maneuvers for control of turf in this meeting. Some FDA regulators resented the CDC's brash invasion of what was plainly their territory, the blood industry. Moreover, many at the FDA did not believe that this so-called epidemic of immune suppression even existed. Privately, in conversations with CDC officials, FDA officials confided that they thought the CDC had taken a bunch of unrelated illnesses and lumped them into some made-up phenomenon as a brazen ruse to get publicity and funding for their threatened agency. Bureaucrats have been known to undertake more questionable methods to protect their budgets. Given the Reagan administration's wholesale budget slashing, this would not be all that drastic a reaction.

In the end, everybody agreed that they should do one thing: Wait and see what happens. The situation would clarify itself and then they would move. How could the government be expected to forge national policy for more than 220 million Americans just because three hemophiliacs got sick?

The meeting, however, did accomplish one memorable achievement. It was more than one year since Michael Gottlieb and Alvin Friedman-Kien had reported their cases of pneumonia and skin cancer, and the epidemic still did not have one commonly agreed-upon name. Different scientists were using different acronyms in an alphabet soup that further confused the already befuddled story of a strange new disease of unknown origin. The staffers at the CDC despised the GRID acronym and refused to use it. With the advent of hemophiliac cases, Jim Curran argued that any references to "gay" or "community" should be dropped and something more neutral be adopted. Besides, Curran thought ACIDS was a little grotesque.

Somebody finally suggested the name that stuck: Acquired Immune Deficiency Syndrome. That gave the epidemic a snappy acronym, AIDS, and was sexually neutral. The word "acquired" separated the immune deficiency syndrome from congenital defects or chemically induced immune problems, indicating the syndrome was acquired from somewhere even though nobody knew from where.

This bit of resolution, however, did not keep Dale Lawrence from fretting about the vacuum in policy on AIDS blood transmission. Immune overload didn't fit with the facts, Lawrence thought. Hemophiliacs had been getting transfusions for decades, and only now did three of them pop up with

Threads

Dr. James Curran is an epidemiologist and director of AIDS research efforts at the CDC in Atlanta.

Pneumocystis pneumonia in a matter of months, showing identical immunological profiles to those of the gay AIDS patients.

Gays were worried about public relations, and hemophiliacs were skittish about being involved with anything having to do with homosexuals. The FDA was worried about turf and was largely unconvinced there was a disease at all, much less something that merited the kind of serious scrambling those CDC hotshots wanted.

There was something else from the meeting that also troubled Dale Lawrence. Jim Curran and others discussed that AIDS cases were turning up in prisons, and a commercial plasma manufacturer had admitted that a lot of blood had been drawn in state prisons. They were a good source of plasma, he said. Lawrence could think only, "Oh God."

* * *

By mid-1982, there was much to be ignored; the epidemic was spreading faster than the official pronouncements indicated. Science was not working at its best, accepting new information with an unbiased eye and beginning appropriate investigations. The handful of scientists who ignored their elders' advice and worked on the newly christened AIDS epidemic found themselves not only struggling against a baffling disease but against the indifference of science, government, mass media, most gay leaders, and public health officials.

In the Bronx, Dr. Arye Rubinstein was now treating eleven babies stricken with AIDS, but few scientists would believe his diagnosis. After holding his article on the infants for six months, the *New England Journal of Medicine* had returned it to Rubinstein with the firm conclusion that these kids most certainly did not have AIDS, the homosexuals' disease. By now, at least, the CDC doctors were interested in his findings, but they were moving cautiously. Jealously watched by other federal health agencies that were worried that the CDC might use the epidemic to cut into the already restricted flow of federal money, every CDC-announced development had to be entirely sound, or enemies in the government would use it to discredit them.

In his lab at the Albert Einstein College of Medicine, Rubinstein was frantic with worry. He had to make people believe him; the science establishment obsession with the sex lives of most of the AIDS victims was blinding it to the horror that could unfold in other pockets of America. Given the projections of new AIDS cases, it was clear that many more such babies would be born to infected mothers. Many of these mothers would die. Who would take care of their babies? How would society cope with supporting a population that seemed born to die of such a horrible disease? Yet, pondering such solutions would happen only after he had convinced somebody important that there was a problem, that these babies even existed.

August 2
New York City

Dan Rather put on his somber face as he stared into the cameras of the "CBS Evening News."

"Federal health officials consider it an epidemic. Yet you rarely hear a thing about it. At first, it seemed to strike only one segment of the population. Now, Barry Peterson tells us, this is no longer the case."

The story, one of the first network news pieces to appear on AIDS had all the right elements: Bobbi Campbell talked about how he wanted to survive; Larry Kramer said the lack of government research was because it was perceived as a gay disease; Jim Curran provided the hopeful note that solving AIDS could lead to the elimination of all cancer.

"But there is almost no money being spent so far," concluded reporter Peterson. "For Bobbi Campbell, it is a race against time. How long before he and others who have this disease, finally have answers, finally have the hope of a cure?"

Of all the sentences in this story, probably none was so pointedly directed at the fundamental problem than Rather's own lead-in, "you rarely hear a thing about it." A managing editor of the "CBS Nightly News," Rather passed the news judgment that made AIDS a disease that one rarely heard anything about. Three years later, television commentators would still be talking about AIDS as that disease you rarely heard anything about, as if they were helpless bystanders and not the very people who themselves had decreed the silence in the public media.

Because nobody heard much about the disease, nobody in 1982 really did very much about it, save for a few heroic souls. And they were too few to make much a difference, ensuring that Bobbi Campbell, like thousands of other Americans, would lose his race against time.

For Discussion

ABOUT THE CONTENT

1. What is the significance of retroviruses in the research on AIDS?
2. Why do you think the CDC disliked the name GRID for the disease?
3. Why do you think there was such difficulty in finding a name for the disease? What factors might have influenced this?
4. How did hemophiliacs affect the emerging epidemic?
5. Why did Dr. Rubinstein have difficulty convincing people that there were babies with AIDS?
6. How has reporting and knowledge about AIDS changed since 1982? Do you know what the current state of the research is?

ABOUT THE WRITING

1. Why do you think Shilts chose the "date/place" format for his writing?
2. How would you characterize Shilts's tone? Give specific examples.
3. What effect does the interweaving of more personal stories have on the reporting of the facts? Do you think this is an effective technique for this type of writing? Why or why not?
4. Compare Shilts's style with Desowitz's. In what ways are they similar? How are they different?

Quickwrite

What effect has the AIDS epidemic had on society, in your opinion?

A Guide to Editing with Practice Exercises

*T*he following sections are intended to help you identify and correct areas where you make errors in your writing. It is not necessary to read this chapter by starting at the beginning and ending at the end. Locate the topics that concern you and focus on one or two sections at a time.

LEARNING STRATEGY

Managing Your Learning: Identifying major grammar problems will help you to write more effective sentences and paragraphs.

AGREEMENT

Subject-Verb Agreement

A basic rule of English is that a singular subject takes a singular verb, and a plural or compound subject takes a plural verb. Unfortunately, it isn't always easy to determine the subject and whether or not it is plural. In addition, usage varies in spoken English, making the "rule" less clear.

The first thing to do is identify the true subject of a sentence. Sometimes the subject can be a whole phrase, but there is one word in that phrase that can be identified as the true subject. In the following example, the italicized phrase is the full subject phrase, but the underlined noun is the true subject:

The <u>reason</u> that my dogs, ten German shepherds, bark so much
<u>is</u> they are trained to listen for intruders.

The full subject is "the reason that my dogs bark so much," but the true subject is the word "reason," which is singular, and takes the singular verb "is." Don't be confused by long phrases that come between the subject and the verb.

However, even when you identify the true subject correctly, whether it is singular or plural can be confusing. The following table lists ten common sources of confusion.

TABLE 8.1 AGREEMENT PITFALLS

SUBJECT WORD	NUMBER	EXAMPLE
each, every, everybody, everyone	singular	*Each of the students <u>is</u> expected to attend.*
who, which, that, what	singular if the word it refers to is singular, plural if it is plural.	*a. Who <u>is</u> going with me tonight?* *b. What <u>are</u> your ten favorite books?*
enough, none	singular if the word it refers to is singular, plural if it is plural	*a Enough information <u>is</u> available.* *b. Enough <u>are</u> present at the rally to make an impact.*
there	when used as a subject, the verb agrees with the noun that comes after it.	*a. There <u>is</u> no reason to panic.* *b. There <u>are</u> no eggs in the refrigerator.*
either . . . or neither . . . nor	the verb agrees with the noun closest to it	*a. Either that man or those women <u>have</u> the class notes.* *b. Neither the dogs nor the cat <u>is</u> making all that noise.*
expression of a unitary quantity before a plural	singular	*a. Twenty-six miles <u>is</u> a long way to run.* *b. Forty-five dollars <u>is</u> too expensive.*
A quantifier (lot, much, many) with "of"	singular if the noun that follows "of" is singular, plural if it is plural	*a. Much of the book <u>is</u> hard to understand.* *b. A lot of the men here <u>are</u> tall.*
the number of **a** number of	singular plural	*a. The number of students here today <u>is</u> ten.* *b. A number of students <u>are</u> going to the museum.*
names of countries, companies, institutions, and areas of study ending in -s, and the word *news*	singular	*a. Physics <u>is</u> my favorite class this term.* *b. The Philippines <u>was</u> an important location during the war.* *c. The United Nations <u>is</u> an influential organization.*
titles	singular	*"Heroes" <u>is</u> my favorite song.*

Cartoon by Bill Watterson, © 1994 Andrews and McMeel, a Universal Press Syndicate Company.

"Denominalized" Verbs: English allows frequent "denominalization"—the turning of nouns (or even adjectives) into verbs. What does the "Calvin & Hobbes" cartoon imply about this practice?

In your writing, check verb forms carefully.

ACTIVITY 1: SUBJECT-VERB AGREEMENT

Underline the full subject of each sentence. Circle the word that serves as the true subject. Then, in the blank, write the correct present tense verb form of the verb in brackets [ ].

1. "All the preceding, except the last few sentences [be] _____

   exposition that should've been done earlier or interspersed with the present

   action instead of lumped together."

   —John Barth, "Lost in the Funhouse"

2. "Friday night. Girls in dark skirts and white blouses [sit] _____ in

   ranks and scream in concert."

   —William H. Gass, "In the Heart of the Heart of the Country"

3. "No one, including my father, [seem] _____ to have known exactly

   how old he was, but his mother had been born during slavery."

   —James Baldwin, "Notes of a Native Son"

4. "What [be] _____ we going to do, what [be] _____ going to

   become of us, what [be] _____ the future?"

   —Tennessee Williams, *The Glass Menagerie*

5. "Omaha. Great cumulus clouds, from coppery churning to creamy to silvery

   white, [trail] _____ brown skirts of rain over the hot plains."

   —John Dos Passos, "The Big Money"

Self-Correction: In a recent piece of writing, identify areas where you had difficulty with subject-verb agreement. Copy any sentences with agreement errors in them, then rewrite each sentence correctly.

Pronoun Agreement

A pronoun must agree with its <u>antecedent</u>, that is, the word or phrase to which it refers. For example:

The boys ate *their* lunches quickly.

antecedent   pronoun

The book was missing *its* cover.

antecedent   pronoun

Some difficulties arise in English pronoun use, however, resulting from the lack of a neuter pronoun to refer to any individual, whether male or female. Thus, there are variations in pronoun usage (see page 30 to review this).

In the past, it was generally considered appropriate to use a sentence like the following: *Everyone should bring his books to class.* However, this is less acceptable in current writing practice. Here are some ways to avoid this problem:

1. Use plurals: *Students should bring their books to class.*
2. Use "he or she," "him or her," or "his or her": *Everyone should bring <u>his or her</u> books to class.*
3. Avoid pronouns: *Everyone should bring the necessary books to class.*
4. Use a plural pronoun (nonstandard): *<u>Everyone</u> should bring <u>their</u> books to class.*

Note that substitution #4 is more commonly used in speaking than in writing; therefore, some instructors may disapprove of its use.

It is important to be consistent with your choice of pronouns. Don't switch between "one," "you," and "he/she" without a reason for doing so.

ACTIVITY 2: PRONOUN AGREEMENT

Underline the antecedent of the pronoun, then write the correct pronoun in the blank.

1. "The postman left a letter. Richards glanced listlessly at the superscription and the postmark—unfamiliar, both—and tossed the letter on the table and resumed _____ might-have-beens and _____ hopeless dull miseries where _____ had left _____ off."

    —Mark Twain, "The Man That Corrupted Hadleyburg"

2. "The sun, keeping _____ strength here even in winter, stayed at the top of the sky, and every time Bowman stuck his head out of the dusty car to stare up the road, _____ seemed to reach a long arm down and push against the top of _____ head, right through _____ hat—like the practical joke of an old drummer, long on the road."

    —Eudora Welty, "Death of a Traveling Salesman"

3. "Macomber's wife had not looked at him nor _____ at _____ and he had sat by _____ in the back seat with Wilson sitting in the front seat. Once he had reached over and taken _____ wife's hand without looking at _____ and she had removed _____ hand from _____."

—Ernest Hemingway, "The Short Happy Life of Francis Macomber"

4. "Elisa Allen, working in _____ flower garden, looked down across the yard and saw Henry, _____ husband, talking to two men in business suits. The three of _____ stood by the tractor shed, each man with one foot on the side of the little Fordson."

—John Steinbeck, "The Chrysanthemums"

5. "But Charlie did not relax; _____ heart sat up rigidly in _____ body and he drew confidence from _____ daughter, who from time to time came close to _____, holding in _____ arms the doll he had bought."

—F. Scott Fitzgerald, "Babylon Revisited"

Self-Correction: In a recent piece of writing, identify areas where you had difficulty with pronoun agreement. Copy any sentences with agreement errors in them; then rewrite each sentence correctly.

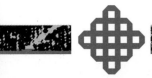

ARTICLES

Before nouns or noun phrases you can find the articles *a/an* or *the,* or no article at all. Determining which articles are appropriate is "natural" for native speakers of English, but, if English is not your first language, you may find articles difficult.

The following generalizations may help if you have problems with article use. However, keep in mind there are exceptions to many, perhaps all, of these generalizations. Pay close attention to any unusual uses of articles you find in your reading and ask your instructor about them.

TABLE 8.2 ARTICLE USE

GENERALIZATION	COMMON EXCEPTIONS
Single, countable nouns usually require an article. *There's a car in the driveway.*	Another type of determiner is used, such as a possessive, a demonstrative, or a quantifier. *That is her car.*
Plural, specific, countable nouns usually require the article "the." *I put away the dishes.*	If they refer to generic categories of items, do not use an article. *Dogs bark too much.* *(Note: this refers to all dogs, not a specific group of dogs.)*
Abstract or generic nouns usually do not require an article. *Life is sweet.*	When used as examples of specific instances, use an article. *The life of a student is difficult.*

Other uses of articles:

A/an can be used

to classify a noun:	*"Carmen" is an opera.*
instead of "per" or "each":	*Take one vitamin a day.*
in the idiom "many a" (meaning "many"):	*There was many a time I had no money to spend.*

The should be used with names of

deserts	*The weather in the Gobi Desert is often cold.*
regions	*The South has a complex history.*
mountain ranges	*It is snowing in the Sierra Nevada.*
groups of islands	*I would like to go to the Bahamas.*
buildings or structures	*U.S. Military strategy is planned at the Pentagon.*
oceans	*The Atlantic Ocean is very cold.*
rivers	*Mark Twain wrote about the Mississippi River.*
seas	*Can you locate the Black Sea on a map?*
groups of lakes	*The Finger Lakes are in New York.*
gulfs and canals	*The Gulf of California is also called the Sea of Cortez.* *The Panama Canal is an important shipping channel.*
plural country names	*Amsterdam is in the Netherlands.*
multi-word country names that end in a common noun	*England is just one part of the United Kingdom.*
multi-word proper nouns with "of" in them	*My friend attends the University of Hong Kong.*
adjectives used as nouns	*There are programs to help the poor.*

points in time	*The end of the century is near.*
physical location	*The top of the mountain is covered in snow.*
historical periods or events	*My parents speak often about the Depression.* *The Revolutionary War is still much written about.*
plural family names	*Tonight our family will visit the Kims.*
newspapers	*My favorite newspaper is the Los Angeles Times.*

Do not use an article in

university names (those not containing "of")	*Another friend attends Georgetown University.*
street names	*I live on Spear Street.*
parks	*Last summer we visited Hyde Park in London.*
individual lakes	*The summer before, we went to Lake Victoria.*
bays	*Windsurfers like San Francisco Bay because it's always windy.*
harbors	*Have you seen Boston Harbor on Independence Day?*

ACTIVITY 3: ARTICLES

Insert the correct article (including "none") in the blanks. Different articles may fit correctly. When you finish, compare your answers with your classmates' answers.

1. "One of ___the___ smaller girls did ___a___ kind of puppet dance while her fellow clowns laughed at her. But ___the___ tall one, who was almost ___a___ woman, said something very quietly, which I couldn't hear."

   —Maya Angelou, *I Know Why the Caged Bird Sings*

2. "I was born in ___a___ little village on ___the___ southeast coast. I was fifteen when we moved to ___a___ parcel of _____ land far away still on ___the___ same south coast. My mother was ___a___ widow."

   —Luz Alicia Herrera, "Testimonies of Guatemalan Women"

3. "By ___the___ time we had ridden ___a___ mile upstream, ___the___ water was less than ___a___ foot deep and so crystal clear that we could see our herd of _____ several hundred carp still fleeing from ___the___ splashing, wading, horses."

   —Euell Gibbons, "How to Cook a Carp"

4. "_____The_____ processes to which _____a_____ dead body may be subjected are after all to some extent circumscribed by __(the)__ law. In _____ most states, for instance, _____the_____ signature of _____the_____ next of _____ kin must be obtained before _____an_____ autopsy may be performed, before _____a_____ deceased may be cremated, before _____a_____ body may be turned over to _____a_____ medical school for _____ research purposes; or such _____a_____ provision must be made in _____the_____ decedent's will."

—Jessica Mitford, *The American Way of Death*

5. "For __(the)__ Greeks, beauty was _____a_____ virtue, _____a_____ kind of excellence."

—Susan Sontag, "Beauty"

Self-Correction: In a recent piece of writing, identify areas where you had difficulty with articles. Copy any sentences with article errors in them; then rewrite each sentence correctly.

PLURALS

Some words in English are always plural, some have no plural forms, and some form plurals irregularly. Review the following information if you are having problems with plural formation.

Words that are typically plural

clothes   pants   scissors   shorts

Words not found in plural form (also called noncount nouns)

advice	air	clothing	courage
enjoyment	equipment	evidence	fun
furniture	happiness	homework	honesty
housework	ignorance	information	intelligence
jewelry	knowledge	luck	luggage
machinery	money	music	news
patience	peace	people†	poverty
progress	rain*		

---

*Rain can be made plural in the idiom "the rains," referring to a rainy season: *Then the rains came.*

†people can be made plural when talking about different types of people: *There are many diverse peoples in Canada.*

Food and animal terms

Many food or animal terms can be used as count nouns when they indicate "a type of." For food terms, the plural indicates types of food. Compare these two sentences:

I had bread with my lunch.
There are many breads on the table: wheat, rye, white, and cinnamon.

For meat and animal terms, typically the term for the animal can be made plural when referring to different kinds of animals, but the word for the related meat is singular—for example:

My fish are in an aquarium.
I have many fishes: tetras, angelfish, and guppies.
I don't like to eat fish.

Irregularly formed plurals

Regular English nouns are made plural by adding *-s* or *-es.* However, because English has borrowed vocabulary items from many different languages, some plurals are formed differently.

TABLE 8.3 IRREGULAR NOUNS

SINGULAR	PLURAL	SINGULAR	PLURAL
analysis	analyses	mouse	mice
appendix	appendices *appendixes*	nucleus	nuclei *nucleuses*
basis	bases	ox	oxen
child	children	parenthesis	parentheses
crisis	crises	phenomenon	phenomena
criterion	criteria	radius	radii *radiuses*
foot	feet	stimulus	stimuli *stimuluses*
formula	formulae *formulas*	syllabus	syllabi *syllabuses*
goose	geese	thesis	theses
hypothesis	hypotheses	thief	thieves
index	indices *indexes*	tooth	teeth
man	men	wife	wives
medium *media*	media	woman	women

NOTE   Italicized forms are nonstandard but may be used by some speakers and writers.

ACTIVITY 4: PLURALS

In the blank, write the correct form of the plural of the word in brackets [ ]. Check your spelling! Remember, some words cannot be made plural.

1. "The new earth, freshly torn from its parent sun, was a ball of whirling [gas] _____, intensely hot, rushing through the black [space] _____ of the universe on a path and at a speed controlled by immense [force] _____."

—Rachel Carson, *The Sea Around Us*

2. "One hundred [year] _____ later, the [life] _____ of the Negro is still sadly crippled by the [manacle] _____ of [segregation] _____ and the [chain] _____ of [discrimination] _____."

—Martin Luther King, Jr. "I Have a Dream"

3. "Any home in the arctic, in winter, requires some [fuel] _____—if only for cooking. The coast [people] _____ make use of fat [lamp] _____, for they have an abundance of [fat] _____ from the sea [mammal] _____ they kill, and so they are able to cook in the igloo, and to heat it as well. But the [Ihalmiut] _____ can ill afford to squander the precious [fat] _____ of the [deer] _____, and they dare burn only one tiny lamp for [light] _____."

—Farley Mowat, *People of the Deer*

4. "And her head jerked in [spasm] _____, making a spattering noise; her [antenna] _____ crisped and burned away and her heaving mouth [part] _____ crackled like pistol [fire] _____."

—Annie Dillard, *Holy the Firm*

5. "A further reason for the underdeveloped [quality] _____ of football [personality] _____, and one which gets us to the heart of the game's modernity, is that football is very much a game of modern [technology] _____."

—Murray Ross, "Football Red and Baseball Green"

Self-Correction: In a recent piece of writing, identify areas where you had difficulty with plurals. Copy any sentences with plural errors in them; then rewrite each sentence correctly.

There are so many prepositions and combinations of words with prepositions that it is impossible to cover them here. There are no rules to refer to, and many uses are highly idiomatic, or even vary regionally (for example, New Yorkers "stand *on* line," but Californians "stand *in* line").

Although there are no real "rules" for prepositions, there is a system. This system reflects the way speakers look at objects in the world. Think about the following pair of examples:

Angel got *on* the bus.
Ali got *in* my car.

In both cases, people entered types of transportation—why was one "in" and one "on"? Look at another pair of examples:

Juan is *in* the corner.
Marla is *at* the corner.

Which person is more likely to be outdoors?

These examples show that prepositions relate to the way we see places and surfaces. In the first pair of examples, Angel was *on* a bus because she can walk *on* the floor of it, or move around *on* it. The same applies to airplanes and trains. However, a car is more like a "container"—it's difficult to walk *on* the car unless you are *on* the outside of it. Therefore, we are *in* our cars.

In the second instance, Marla is more likely to be outdoors. Juan is *in*side the two walls that form a corner, so he is probably *in* a room. Marla is *at* the outer point where two walls meet, so she is probably outside. This can be seen in the following simple drawing:

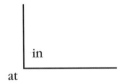

Figure 8.1 The difference between "in" the corner and "at" the corner

Many prepositions are used in **phrasal verbs,** that is, a verb and preposition-like word (called a "particle") combination that has a unique meaning, different from that of the verb and often not predictable from the meaning of the two words themselves.

With true phrasal verbs, you can use two different word orders:

I <u>looked up</u> the word in the dictionary.
I <u>looked</u> the word up in the dictionary.

You cannot do this if the preposition is a true preposition and not a particle.

I looked up at the airplane.
*I looked at the airplane up.

In your journal or notebook, keep track of phrasal verbs or unusual uses of prepositions along with their meanings or examples. If your instructor has marked an incorrect preposition in your writing, ask for an explanation if you don't understand it. Rewrite the correct phrase.

Threads

In many texts about language, ungrammatical sentences are indicated by placing an asterisk at their beginnings.

ACTIVITY 5: PREPOSITIONS

Insert a correct preposition in each blank. Different answers may be possible.

1. "Americans are probably the most pain-conscious people _____ the
   face _____ the earth. _____ years we have had it drummed
   _____ us—_____ print, _____ radio, _____
   television, _____ everyday conversation—that any hint
   _____ pain is to be banished as though it were the ultimate evil."
   —Norman Cousins, *The Anatomy of an Illness*

2. "We got our TV set _____ 1959, when I was 5. So I can barely
   remember life without television. I have spent 20,000 hours _____
   my life _____ front the set. Not all _____ my contemporaries
   watched so much, but many did, and what's more, we watched the same
   programs, heard the same commercials, were exposed _____ the
   same end-_____-show lessons."
   —Joyce Maynard, "I Remember . . ."

3. "As I write this, _____ an airplane, I have run _____
   _____ paper and need to reach _____ my briefcase
   _____ my legs _____ more. I cannot do this until my empty
   lunch tray is removed _____ my lap."
   —William F. Buckley, Jr. "Why Don't We Complain?"

4. "_____ me the most interesting thing _____ a solitary life,
   and mine has been that _____ the last twenty years, is that it
   becomes increasingly rewarding. When I can wake _____ and watch
   the sun rise _____ the ocean, as I do most days, and know that I
   have an entire day ahead, uninterrupted, _____ which to write a few
   pages, take a walk _____ my dog, lie down _____ the
   afternoon _____ a long think (why does one think better
   _____ a horizontal position?), read and listen _____ music, I
   am flooded _____ happiness."
   —May Sarton, "The Rewards of Living a Solitary Life"

5. "A broad expanse _____ the river was turned _____ blood; _____ the middle distance the red hue brightened _____ gold, _____ which a solitary log came floating black and conspicuous; _____ one place a long slanting mark lay sparkling _____ the water; _____ another the surface was broken _____ boiling, tumbling rings, that were as many tinted as an opal. . . ."

—Mark Twain, *Life on the Mississippi*

Self-Correction: In a recent piece of writing, identify areas where you had difficulty with prepositions. Copy any sentences with preposition errors in them; then rewrite each sentence correctly.

COMPLEX AND COMPOUND SENTENCES

Both complex and compound sentences contain more than one clause. A clause is a group of words that has a subject and a verb. (The glossary at the end of this book has definitions of different kinds of clauses, if you aren't familiar with their names.)

Complex and compound sentences offer a way to connect different ideas. However, it is necessary to use the proper connecting words and phrases to show the relationship between the clauses in a sentence.

Coordination

Coordination links two ideas, clauses, or phrases with conjunctions. Coordinated clauses have more or less equal importance, although you can emphasize a clause by putting it first or last in a series. Sentences made up of different independent clauses (and no dependent clauses) are called compound sentences. When conjunctions are used to connect full sentences, semicolons are needed.

Coordinate structures should be parallel; that is, items in a series should be of the same structure, whether they are verb phrases, noun phrases, and so on.

TABLE 8.4 COMMON CONJUNCTIONS AND THEIR FUNCTIONS

CONJUNCTION	FUNCTION
and	joins two equivalent clauses *Verna likes fish and Michiyo likes chicken.*
but	shows a contrast between two clauses *Michiyo likes chicken, but he dislikes lemons.*
for	shows cause and effect *Mariana likes lemons, for they are full of vitamins.*
or	shows choice between two items or issues *Teresa should eat more fruit, or she will have health problems.*
nor	demonstrates contrast *Mariana doesn't like prunes, nor does she like raisins.*
so	shows result *Teresa doesn't like fruit, so she won't eat prunes.*
yet	shows contrast *Michiyo hates tuna, yet he eats it with noodles.*
moreover (see "and")	*Paul likes cheese; moreover, he tells everyone to eat cheese.*
furthermore (see "and")	*Igor eats soup often; furthermore, he makes very good stew.*
however (see "but")	*Michelle prefers potatoes; however, she will eat rice.*
otherwise (see "or," meaning "if not")	*Jun should drink milk; otherwise, he may need calcium supplements.*
therefore (see "so")	*Wei-Li eats a balanced diet; therefore, she doesn't need vitamin supplements.*

Subordination

If a sentence contains a dependent clause, the sentence is called a complex sentence. The dependent clause is not a sentence and must be connected in some way to an independent clause to make a complete sentence. There are three basic types of dependent clauses:

adjective clauses:	which is eaten on Thanksgiving
	whose dinner we ate
adverb clauses:	before we eat breakfast
	because we like chocolate
noun clauses:	whether it was lunchtime
	that we would eat soon

Adverb clause connectors are *because, since, as, when, whenever, while, after, before, wherever, although, though,* and *even though.*

If you have a lot of short sentences in your writing, or if your sentences are of mostly the same type, review these sentence types and think about the connections you need to make between your thoughts. Check the connecting words you use to be sure they are logical. (But beware of too much subordination.) Here are a few examples:

Needs subordination:	*I was taking a shower. I really needed it.*
	I forgot about the cake in the oven.
	The cake was burned.
Subordinated:	*While I was taking a much-needed shower,*
	I forgot about the cake in the oven,
	so it burned.
Over-subordination:	*While I was taking a shower, which I really*
	needed, I forgot about the cake in the oven,
	which was set at 375°, so the cake burned
	because of my carelessness.

ACTIVITY 6: COMPLEX AND COMPOUND SENTENCES

A. In the following sentences, underline each independent clause once and each dependent clause twice.

1. "The idea so possessed my mind that a thrill of fear ran through me, and I wished to exchange the ghastly image of my fancy for the realities around."

   —Mary Shelley, Introduction to *Frankenstein*

2. "Though we wished Lord Tweedsmuir, the Governor-General, a long life each Saturday morning in the synagogue, there were those among us who knew him as Buchanan."

   —Mordecai Richler, *The Street*

3. "That was my worst ride, which left me with a painfully yanked muscle in my shoulder, but I am glad to say it wasn't my last."

   —Peter Schjeldahl, "Cyclone! Rising to the Fall"

4. "I took a highway down the mesa into a valley of the Painted Desert, where wind had textured big drifts of orange sand into rills."

—William Least Heat Moon, *Blue Highways*

5. "The doors were open to the barricaded main steps, and down the steps there was a spill of red paint, lest anyone forget the bloodshed there."

—Joan Didion, *Salvador*

B. Write five sentences, each with two independent clauses joined by a comma plus the coordinating conjunction given in the brackets. A topic is also given for each sentence. Be creative!

> **EXAMPLE** Movies [and]: *I enjoy the movies, and I enjoy plays, too.*

1. Television [and]
2. Music [but]
3. Sports [for]
4. Travel [so]
5. Politics [yet]

Now write five sentences, using two independent clauses joined by a semicolon plus the sentence coordinator given.

6. Television [for example]
7. Music [furthermore]
8. Sports [however]
9. Travel [on the other hand]
10. Politics [thus]

C. Combine the following sets of sentences into one complex sentence. Different possibilities exist for each set of sentences. After you are done, compare your answers with a classmate's.

1. He was unable to read. He entered the world of fantasy through short stories. These stories were read to him from books. His mother read to him.
2. A young man lives in a nearby city. His name is David. I have never met David. I sometimes send him e-mail.
3. Groups of specialized cells arose from one-celled creatures. Next arose creatures with organs for breathing and feeding.
4. I have lived in Africa and Asia. I like Africa and Asia very much. My favorite place to live is South America. I spent three years in Venezuela and Chile as a child.
5. My best friend is Sylvia. Sylvia lives in an apartment above the pharmacy. The pharmacy is on Angelina Street. Sylvia's apartment is small. Sylvia's apartment is also elegant.

Self-Correction: In a recent piece of writing, identify areas where you had difficulty with coordination and subordination. Copy any sentences with coordination and subordination errors in them; then rewrite each sentence correctly.

A run-on sentence is a sentence that has two or more independent clauses that are not coordinated appropriately. You can either separate a run-on into separate sentences or choose the appropriate coordinators or subordinators (see the previous section):

Run-on: I was reading a dull book it was a boring Saturday.

There are two sentences here which need to be made separate. There are two options:

I was reading a dull book; it was a boring Saturday.
I was reading a dull book. It was a boring Saturday.

Joining two independent clauses with a comma is also typically incorrect. These types of sentences are called "comma splices":

Comma Splice: I was reading a dull book, it was a boring Saturday.

These sentences are incorrectly joined with a comma. This can be corrected in the same way the run-ons were. In addition, they can be connected with subordination—showing a relationship between the two clauses:

I was reading a dull book, which made it a boring Saturday.

ACTIVITY 7: INCORRECTLY JOINED SENTENCES

Repair the following sentences by inserting correct punctuation, reducing phrases, or making multiple sentences. If you find some effective as they are, leave them. Be prepared to discuss your choices.

1. "I came, I saw, I conquered."—Julius Caesar
2. Unlike cats, dogs are very social animals, they prefer to run in packs.
3. I had never seen so much lightning in my life I was really frightened.
4. Small computer firms have suffered in the latest economic downturn and IBM and Digital have also experienced losses.
5. Teenagers will become actively involved in the fight against violence on television, they will work to alter attitudes and help work for stricter handgun controls.

Self-Correction: In a recent piece of writing, identify areas where you had difficulty with run-ons. Copy any run-on sentences and then rewrite each sentence correctly.

Sentence fragments lack some word or phrase that is needed to make them a full sentence. Sentence fragments can sometimes be used as a stylistic device, but they should be used intentionally for effect in appropriate kinds of writing. Fragments are typically more acceptable in personal narratives or fiction than they are in researched or expository writing, for example.

If you have identified sentence fragment problems in your writing, ask the following questions about any sentence you write:

1. Does it have a subject?
2. Does it have a main verb?
3. Does it have at least one clause that is not a dependent clause?

FRAGMENT Julio likes potato chips. Which are very fattening.
REVISION Julio likes potato chips, which are very fattening.

FRAGMENT Going down the beautiful winding path on our bicycles.
REVISION Going down the beautiful winding path on our bicycles was fun.
REVISION We were going down the beautiful winding path on our bicycles.

ACTIVITY 8: SENTENCE FRAGMENTS

Repair the following sentence fragments. If you find some effective as they are, leave them. Be prepared to discuss your choices.

1. From a professional point of view, a good résumé is an invaluable tool, according to Dr. Thomas DiPietro. Who teaches business communication at the University of Manitoba.
2. Walking along the river, throwing stones into the clear green water, which looked so inviting that I wanted to jump in.
3. "There was an elder brother described by my father as: 'Too damned clever by half. One of those quick, clever brains . . .'"

   —Doris Lessing, "A Small Personal Voice"

4. "Can such principles be taught? Maybe not. But most of them can be learned."

   —William Zinsser, *On Writing Well*

5. Most banks offer different types of mortgages. The fixed rate mortgage, which guarantees the same rate for the life of the loan, and the adjustable rate mortgage (ARM), which will fluctuate with changing interest rates.

Self-Correction: In a recent piece of writing, identify areas where you had difficulty with fragments. Copy any sentences with fragment errors in them, and then rewrite each sentence correctly.

The complex history of the English language has contributed to many spelling irregularities. There are a few rules that can help you (see the following list of ten), but in general, there are so many exceptions to spelling rules that many people don't find them useful.

Fortunately, there are now better tools for fixing poor spelling: computer spell-checkers and electronic dictionaries can take some of the work out of looking words up. However, it isn't always possible to use these tools, so learning the spelling of common words will make your writing go more smoothly.

In addition to the rules listed here, a list of commonly misspelled words follows. A good strategy is to keep records of words you frequently misspell. Create a section in your journal or notebook. It's also smart to note new words from your reading that you think might be useful.

When you misspell a word, look up the correct spelling, and write it down. It helps to write it several times and to look at it carefully. Research shows that good spellers recognize the *shape* of words, the way they look on the page, not just spelling rules. If you confuse two words that sound alike, write their definitions as well.

Ten spelling rules

1. **Doubling consonants:** With one-syllable words, when adding *-ed, -ing,* or *-y,* double the final consonants of words whose preceding vowel is "short" (*bet→betting*); don't double consonants when the vowel sound is "long" (*beat→beating*).

2. **Plurals:** With regular plurals, add *-es* when a word ends in *-s, -ch, -sh, -x,* or *-z* (*boxes, torches, bushes*). Most words that end in *-y* change to *-ie* before adding *-s* (*tally→tallies*), but words that end in *-ey, -ay,* or *-oy* do not (*holiday→holidays*).

3. **"i before e":** A rule that many people learn is:

   I before e,
   except after c,
   or when sounded like <u>a</u>,
   as in neighbor or weigh.

   Although this works for a small set of words, there are many exceptions, including *neither, science, glacier, either,* and dozens of others.

4. **-able or -ible?** There are more words that end in *-able* than *-ible,* so if you aren't sure, choose *-able.* After a complete word, it's usually *-able;* after a word that ends in *-miss* (*permissible*) or an incomplete word that ends in a "soft" *g* sound (*eligible*), it's usually *-ible.*

5. **Drop final -e:** When you add an ending to a word that ends in *-e,* and the ending begins with a consonant, keep the final *-e* (*sore→sorely*). In other cases, drop the final *-e* (*hope→hoping*).

6. **y or i?** A word that ends in *-y* changes the *-y* to *i* before *-ness* or *-ly* (*happy→happiness; lazy→lazily*). A word that ends in *-ie* changes to *-y* before adding *-ing* (*lie→lying*).

7. **-c or -ck?** A word that ends in a "hard" *-c* adds a *-k* before an ending that begins with a vowel (*picnic→picnicking*).

8. **ful or -full?** The suffix is always *-ful*, never *-full* (*handful, beautiful*). When you add the ending *-ly,* then you have two l's (*thankful→thankfully*).

9. **-sede, -ceed, or -cede?** Supersede is the only common English word that ends in *-sede*. *Exceed, succeed,* and *proceed* are the only common words that end in *-ceed*. The ending for other words is *-cede* (*precede, intercede*).

10. **-ery or -ary?** Only five commonly used English words end in *-ery: stationery* (writing paper), *cemetery, monastery, distillery,* and *confectionery.* The rest end in *-ary.*

Commonly Misspelled and Misused Words

accommodate	exceed	misspell	rhythm
acquaint	existence	misstate	ridiculous
acquire	fascinate	mortgage	sacrilegious
address	February	mosquitoes	sandwich
all right	foreign	necessary	scissors
already	forty	neighbor	secretary
argument	fragile	niece	seize
athletic	freight	noticeable	separate
auxiliary	gauge	nuisance	siege
beginning	government	o'clock	sieve
believe	grammar	obedience	similar
bureau	guarantee	occasion	sincerely
burglar	handkerchief	occur	special
calendar	harass	occurred	squirrel
ceiling	height	offense	straight
cemetery	heir	omitted	strengthen
changeable	hygiene	paid	succeed
chief	hypocrisy	parallel	success
circuit	independence	phenomenon	supersede
concede	indict	physician	susceptible
conceive	indispensable	pneumonia	tariff
counterfeit	irresistible	possess	threshold
debt	judgment*	potato	tobacco
definite	khaki	preferred	tomatoes
dependent	laboratory	privilege	truly
desperate	laugh	probably	Tuesday
develop	league	pseudonym	usually
devise	library	psychology	vaccinate
disappear	license	raspberry	vacuum
disappoint	literature	receipt	villain
dissatisfied	lying	receive	vinegar
eighth	maintenance	recognize	warrant
embarrass	maneuver	recommend	Wednesday
environment	mattress	remittance	weird
equipped	minuscule	resemblance	withhold
especially	mischief	reservoir	yolk
exaggerate	missionary	reverence	

*The preferred American English spelling is *judgment.* British English spells this word *judgement,* a spelling that is gaining some acceptance in American English as well.

Commonly Confused Words:

If you use any of these words in your writing, be sure you are using the right one.

accept/except	formerly/formally	quiet/quite
affect/effect	forth/fourth	stationary/stationery
capital/capitol	idol/idle	than/then
cereal/serial	incite/insight	their/there/they're
colonel/kernel	ingenious/ingenuous	to/too/two
compliment/complement	its/it's	whose/who's
conscience/conscious	lose/loose	you're/your
dessert/desert	precede/proceed	
foreword/forward	principal/principle	

ACTIVITY 9: SPELLING AND MISUSED WORDS

A. Find the mistakes in the following sentences. Explain your answers. Not all sentences have errors.

1. I have a feeling that a storm is about to develope.
2. It was such an embarassing arguement—wether soccer is better than football—who cares?
3. His adress is fourty-four Independance Avenue, near the cemetary.
4. He garantees his morgage will be payed on time.
5. The Library League meets the first Wednesday in February.
6. It is neccessary to protect our fragile enviroment.
7. In order to suceed in your freight business, you must aquaint yourself with all the tarriff and license regulations.
8. The cheif justice of the Eighth Circiut Court handed down her judgment.
9. The physician reccomends that the elderly be vacinnated against pneumonia.
10. I allready have a reciept for the new matress.

B. Explain and correct any misused words in the following sentences.

1. That jacket compliments your skirt perfectly.
2. When I was young, I stole a toy; but my conscious bothered me so much, I returned it the next day.
3. The principal reason its so quite in here is that my stereo is broken.
4. What are the affects of loosing you're job?
5. I'd like chocolate cake for desert—it's better then the pie.

Self-Correction: In a recent piece of writing, identify areas where you had difficulty with spelling or word choice. Copy any sentences with spelling or word choice errors in them; then rewrite each sentence correctly.

The following article by well-known writer Russell Baker addresses the major issues in punctuation.

How to punctuate

By Russell Baker

International Paper asked Russell Baker, winner of the Pulitzer Prize for his book, Growing Up, *and for his essays in* The New York Times *(the latest collection in book form is called* The Rescue of Miss Yaskell and Other Pipe Dreams*), to help you make better use of punctuation, one of the printed word's most valuable tools.*

When you write, you make a sound in the reader's head. It can be a dull mumble—that's why so much government prose makes you sleepy—or it can be a joyful noise, a sly whisper, a throb of passion.

Listen to a voice trembling in a haunted room:

"And the silken, sad, uncertain rustling of each purple curtain thrilled me—filled me with fantastic terrors never felt before . . ."

That's Edgar Allan Poe, a master. Few of us can make paper speak as vividly as Poe could, but even beginners will write better once they start listening to the sound their writing makes.

One of the most important tools for making paper speak in your own voice is punctuation.

When speaking aloud, you punctuate constantly—with body language. Your listener hears commas, dashes, question marks, exclamation points, quotation marks as you shout, whisper, pause, wave your arms, roll your eyes, wrinkle your brow.

In writing, punctuation plays the role of body language. It helps readers hear you the way you want to be heard.

"Gee, Dad, have I got to learn all them rules?"

Don't let the rules scare you. For they aren't hard and fast. Think of them as guidelines.

Am I saying, "Go ahead and punctuate as you please"? Absolutely not. Use your own common sense, remembering that you can't expect readers to work to decipher what you're trying to say.

There are two basic systems of punctuation:

1. The loose or open system, which tries to capture the way body language punctuates talk.

2. The tight, closed structural system, which hews closely to the sentence's grammatical structure.

Most writers use a little of both. In any case, we use much less punctuation than they used 200 or even 50 years ago. (Glance into Edward Gibbon's "Decline and Fall of the Roman Empire," first published in 1776, for an example of the tight structural system at its most elegant.)

No matter which system you prefer, be warned: punctuation marks cannot save a sentence that is badly put together. If you have to struggle over commas, semicolons and dashes, you've probably built a sentence that's never going to fly, no matter how you tinker with it. Throw it away and build a new one to a simpler design. The better your sentence, the easier it is to punctuate.

Choosing the right tool

There are 30 main punctuation marks, but you'll need fewer than a dozen for most writing.

I can't show you in this small space how they all work, so I'll stick to the ten most important—and even then can only hit highlights. For more details, check your dictionary or a good grammar.

Comma [,]

This is the most widely used mark of all. It's also the toughest and most controversial. I've seen aging editors almost come to blows over the comma. If you can handle it without sweating, the others will be easy. Here's my policy.

1. Use a comma after a long introductory phrase or clause; *After stealing the crown jewels from the Tower of London, I went home for tea.*

2. If the introductory material is short, forget the comma: *After the theft I went home for tea.*

3. But use it if the sentence would be confusing without it, like this: *The day before I'd robbed the Bank of England.*

4. Use a comma to separate elements in a series: *I robbed the Denver Mint, the Bank of England, the Tower of London and my piggy bank.*

Notice there is no comma before *and* in the series. This is common style nowadays, but some publishers use a comma there, too.

5. Use a comma to separate independent clauses that are joined by a conjunction like <u>*and, but, for, or, nor, because*</u> or <u>*so*</u>: *I shall return the crown jewels, for they are too heavy to wear.*

6. Use a comma to set off a mildly parenthetical word grouping that isn't essential to the sentence: *Girls, who have always interested me, usually differ from boys.*

184

Do not use commas if the word grouping *is* essential to the sentence's meaning: *Girls who interest me know how to tango.*

7. Use a comma in direct address: *Your majesty, please hand over the crown.*

8. And between proper names and titles: *Montague Sneed, Director of Scotland Yard, was assigned the case.*

9. And to separate elements of geographical address: *Director Sneed comes from Chicago, Illinois, and now lives in London, England.*

Generally speaking, use a comma where you'd pause briefly in speech. For a long pause or completion of thought, use a period.

If you confuse the comma with the period, you'll get a run-on sentence: *The Bank of England is located in London, I rushed right over to rob it.*

Semicolon [;]

A more sophisticated mark than the comma, the semicolon separates two main clauses, but it keeps those two thoughts more tightly linked than a period can: *I steal crown jewels; she steals hearts.*

Dash [–] and Parentheses [( )]

Warning! Use sparingly. The dash SHOUTS. Parentheses whisper. Shout too often, people stop listening;

whisper too much, people become suspicious of you. The dash creates a dramatic pause to prepare for an expression needing strong emphasis: *I'll marry you—if you'll rob Topkapi with me.*

Parentheses help you pause quietly to drop in some chatty information not vital to your story: *Despite Betty's daring spirit ("I love robbing your piggy bank," she often said), she was a terrible dancer.*

Quotation marks [" "]

These tell the reader you're reciting the exact words someone said or wrote: *Betty said, "I can't tango." Or: "I can't tango," Betty said.*

Notice the comma comes before the quote marks in the first example, but comes inside them in the second. Not logical? Never mind. Do it that way anyhow.

Colon [:]

A colon is a tip-off to get ready for what's next: a list, a long quotation or an explanation. This article is riddled with colons. Too many, maybe, but the message is: "Stay on your toes; it's coming at you."

Apostrophe [']

The big headache is with possessive nouns. If the noun is singular, add *'s: I hated Betty's tango.*

If the noun is plural, simply add an apostrophe after the *s: Those are the girls' coats.*

The same applies for singular nouns ending in *s,* like Dickens: *This is Dickens's best book.*

And in plural: *This is the Dickenses' cottage.*

The possessive pronouns *hers* and *its* have no apostrophe.

If you write *it's,* you are saying *it is.*

Keep cool

You know about ending a sentence with a period (.) or a question mark (?). Do it. Sure, you can also end with an exclamation point (!), but must you? Usually it just makes you sound breathless and silly. Make your writing generate its own excitement. Filling the paper with !!!! won't make up for what your writing has failed to do.

Too many exclamation points make me think the writer is talking about the panic in his own head.

Don't sound panicky. End with a period. I am serious. A period. Understand?

Well . . . sometimes a question mark is okay.

ACTIVITY 10: PUNCTUATION

How would you punctuate the following passages? Different answers are possible.

1. I am not one to stand aloof from the rest of humanity in this matter for when I was a university student a gypsy woman with a child in her arms used to appear every year at examination time and ask a shilling of anyone who touched the Lucky Baby that swarthy infant cost me four shillings altogether and I never failed an examination Of course I did it merely for the joke or so I thought then Now I am humbler

—Robertson Davies, "A Few Kind Words for Superstition"

2. A few years ago when I was back in Winnipeg I gave a talk at my old college It was open to the public and afterward a very old man came up to me and asked me if my maiden name had been Wemyss I said yes thinking he might have known my father or my grandfather But no When I was a young lad he said I once worked for your great-grandfather Robert Wemyss when he had a sheep ranch at Raeburn

—Margaret Laurence, *Heart of a Stranger*

Self-Correction: In a recent piece of writing, identify areas where you had difficulty with punctuation. Copy any sentences with punctuation errors in them; then rewrite each sentence correctly.

Transitions let your reader understand your organization and thought processes. The following table shows you some transition signals and how to use them. Good writing has transitions both within and between sentences and paragraphs.

TABLE 8.5 TRANSITIONS			
USAGE	BETWEEN SENTENCES	WITHIN SENTENCES	
		Coordinator	Subordinator
List ideas in order of importance of occurrence	First, Second, Then, Next, Finally, etc.		
Add another idea	Furthermore, Additionally, In addition, Moreover,	and	
Give an example	For instance, For example,		
Give a result or effect	Therefore, Consequently,	so	
Offer an opposing idea	On the other hand, However,	but	although even though
Add a similar idea	Similarly, Likewise, Also,	and	
Give a reason or cause		for	because since as
Supply a conclusion	In conclusion, In summary, In brief,		

ACTIVITY 11: TRANSITIONS

Underline all the transitions in the following passages. Discuss what kind of transitions they are and why they are effective.

1. Then in the nineteenth century, the cell was discovered, and the single machine in its turn was found to be the product of millions of infinitesimal machines—the cells. Now, finally, the cell itself dissolves away into an abstract chemical machine—and that into some intangible inexpressible flow of energy.

—Loren Eiseley, "The Bird and the Machine"

2. In 1980, the media were certainly wrong about television evangelists. Printed estimates of Jerry Falwell's television audience ranged from 18 million to 30 million people. In fact, according to Arbitron's actual counts, fewer than 1.5 million people were watching Falwell. And, according to an Emory University study, those who did watch television evangelists didn't necessarily vote with them.

—Annie Dillard, "Singing with the Fundamentalists"

3. After a time, tired by his dancing apparently, he settled on the window ledge in the sun, and, the queer spectacle being at an end, I forgot about him. He was trying to resume his dancing, but seemed either so stiff or so awkward that he could only flutter to the bottom of the window-pane; and when he tried to fly across it he failed.

—Virginia Woolf, "The Death of the Moth"

Self-Correction: In a recent piece of writing, identify areas where you had difficulty with transitions. Copy any sentences with transition errors in them; then rewrite each sentence correctly.

VERBS AND VERB TENSES

The following lists show a few special verbs that are used with special word forms.

A. Verbs followed by infinitives

I cannot <u>afford</u> to buy a new car.

<u>Verbs followed by an infinitive</u>: afford, agree, appear, arrange, ask, beg, care, claim, consent, decide, demand, deserve, expect, fail, hesitate, hope, intend, learn, manage, mean, need, offer, plan, prepare, pretend, promise, refuse, seem, struggle, swear, threaten, volunteer, wait, want, wish

B. Verbs followed by gerunds (-ing words)

I will <u>practice</u> playing the piano for two hours.

<u>Verbs followed by a gerund</u>: admit, anticipate, appreciate, avoid, consider, delay, deny, detest, discuss, dislike, enjoy, finish, imagine, justify, keep, mention, mind, miss, necessitate, postpone, practice, quit, recall, recollect, recommend, resent, resist, risk, suggest, tolerate, understand

C. Verbs followed by an infinitive phrase

Joanna <u>persuaded</u> Mujibur to wait.

<u>Verbs followed by an infinitive phrase (noun or pronoun + infinitive)</u>: ask,* beg,* cause, challenge, command, convince, dare, enable, expect,* forbid, force, hire, instruct, invite, need, obligate, order, persuade, remind, require, teach, tell, tempt, urge, want,* warn, wish

(* these verbs can be used without the noun/pronoun object as well)

D. Verb phrases followed by a gerund phrase

Phil <u>accustomed himself to</u> drinking tea, though he disliked it at first.

<u>Verb phrases followed by a gerund phrase</u> ("to" + gerund): accustom oneself to, allude to, confess to, confine oneself to, dedicate oneself to, limit oneself to, look forward to, object to, plead guilty to, reconcile oneself to, resign oneself to, resort to, revert to

E. Verbs that can be followed by a gerund or infinitive

I <u>advise</u> you to hurry if you want to catch the bus.
John <u>advises</u> hurrying to the bus station.

<u>Verbs that can be followed by either a gerund or infinitive</u>: advise,* attempt, allow,* begin, continue, encourage,* forget, hate, like, love, permit,* prefer, propose, regret, remember, start, try

(* These verbs need a noun/pronoun with the infinitive form.)

F. Irregular Verbs: Past Tenses and Participles

The following verbs are irregular in their formation in some way. They are grouped together by similarities.

1. Verbs with three different forms, past participle in *-n*

Verb	Past Form	Past Participle
arise	arose	arisen
be	was/were	been
bite	bit	bitten
blow	blew	blown
break	broke	broken
choose	chose	chosen
do	did	done
draw	drew	drawn
drive	drove	driven
eat	ate	eaten
fall	fell	fallen
fly	flew	flown
forbid	forbade	forbidden
freeze	froze	frozen
get	got	got(ten)
give	gave	given
go	went	gone
grow	grew	grown
hide	hid	hidden
know	knew	known
lie (recline)	lay	lain
ride	rode	ridden
see	saw	seen
shake	shook	shaken
show	showed	shown (showed)
speak	spoke	spoken
steal	stole	stolen

Verb	Past Form	Past Participle *(continued)*
swear	swore	sworn
take	took	taken
tear	tore	torn
throw	threw	thrown
wake	woke	woken (waked)
wear	wore	worn
weave	wove	woven
write	wrote	written

2. Verbs with three different forms, vowel changes

Verb	Past Form	Past Participle
begin	began	begun
drink	drank	drunk
ring	rang	rung
run	ran	run
shrink	shrank/shrunk	shrunk
sing	sang	sung
stink	stank	stunk
swim	swam	swum

3. Verbs with two different forms, present and past identical

Verb	Past Form	Past Participle
beat	beat	beaten

4. Verbs with two different forms, present and participle identical

Verb	Past Form	Past Participle
become	became	become
come	came	come

5. Verbs with two different forms, past and participle identical

Verb	Past Form	Past Participle
bend	bent	bent
bleed	bled	bled
breed	bred	bred
bring	brought	brought
buy	bought	bought
catch	caught	caught
creep	crept	crept
deal	dealt	dealt
dig	dug	dug
feed	fed	fed
feel	felt	felt
fight	fought	fought
find	found	found
flee	fled	fled
grind	ground	ground

hang	hung	hung
have	had	had
hear	heard	heard
hold	held	held
keep	kept	kept
lay (put)	laid	laid
light	lit/lighted	lit/lighted
lose	lost	lost
make	made	made
mean	meant	meant
meet	met	met
pay	paid	paid
read	read	read
say	said	said
seek	sought	sought
sell	sold	sold
send	sent	sent
shine	shone	shone (intransitive)
shoot	shot	shot
sleep	slept	slept
slide	slid	slid
spend	spent	spent
stand	stood	stood
stick	stuck	stuck
sting	stung	stung
strike	struck	struck
sweep	swept	swept
swing	swung	swung
teach	taught	taught
tell	told	told
think	thought	thought
weep	wept	wept
win	won	won
wind	wound	wound

6. Verbs with three identical forms

Verb	Past Form	Past Participle
bet	bet	bet
broadcast	broadcast	broadcast
burst	burst	burst
cost	cost	cost
cut	cut	cut
hit	hit	hit
hurt	hurt	hurt
put	put	put
quit	quit	quit
set	set	set
shut	shut	shut
slit	slit	slit
split	split	split
spread	spread	spread

7. Verb Tenses

TENSE/PURPOSE	EXAMPLE

Use the simple present to
a. express feelings, situations, etc.
b. express beliefs
c. describe routines
d. common knowledge
e. indicate the future
f. discuss ideas

He *is* wrong.
I *believe* in justice.
I *swim* regularly.
The sun *rises* in the east.
Class *begins* in March.
Einstein *argues* for
   that theory.

Use the present progressive to
a. describe actions in progress
b. describe an activity taking place
   over a period of time
c. describe a habit
   (with *always*)

It *is raining*.

He *is studying* math.

Lou *is* always *whining*.

Use the present perfect to
a. describe an ongoing activity
   that began in the past
b. describe an event that happened
   at an unspecified or unknown
   time (or did not happen)
c. describe an event that happened
   just before the present
d. describe an activity that has
   happened several times in the past

I *have been* here a year.
I *have visited* that museum
   before.
John *has* never *eaten* eel.

I *have* just *finished* lunch.

I *have eaten* squid three
   times before.

Use the present perfect progressive to
describe an event that started
before the present but continues
into the present and future

Hernando *has been sitting*
   there for hours.

Use the simple past to
a. specify a definite past time

b. describe an event that
   took place over a period of
   time in the past
c. describe events that took
   place at intervals in the past

She *visited* her parents
   yesterday.

I *stayed* in Paris for
   one year.
Kenzo *saw* the doctor each
   Tuesday last month.

Use the past progressive to
a. describe an ongoing activity
   that was happening at the time
   another activity occurred
b. describe an activity that
   was in progress in the past

I *was sleeping* when the
   telephone rang.

We *were walking* around
   the park last night.

Use the past perfect to

a. describe an activity that
   ended before another event
   in the past

Marta *had* already *left*
when Amy arrived.

b. describe a situation that
   happened before a specific
   point in time

Laura *had* never *visited*
a cemetery before today.

Use the past perfect progressive to

describe an ongoing past
activity that was interrupted
by another past activity

Samuel *had been reading*
for six hours before the
movie started.

Use the simple future to

a. express an activity that
   will take place at a definite
   future time

He *will return* at three.

b. express a habitual action
   that will take place in
   the future

May *will practice* on
Saturdays next month.

c. describe a future state
   of being

I *will be* hungry at
one o'clock.

Use the future progressive to

a. describe an event that will
   be taking place at a definite
   time in the future

Hiromi *will be driving* to
school with Marissa
tomorrow.

b. indicate the duration of
   a future event or activity

I *will be reading* this
chemistry chapter for
two hours.

Use the future perfect to

indicate a future action
that will be finished at a
definite time

Yuri *will have finished*
three tests before I
take my first.

Use the future perfect progressive to

describe a future event
that will be interrupted by
another future event

Muhammed *will have been
fishing* for six hours
by the time we get to
the lake.

ACTIVITY 12: VERBS

Cross out any incorrect verb forms and write the correct one(s) in the blank.

1. I use to walk to work every day, but last winter I took the bus.

_____

2. Yesterday, Ginger cut her hair after she finish her homework.

_____

3. Alain admit that he is just a little prejudice, but only against prejudice people!

_____

4. Having just complete washing the car, Alexi is tempted seeing a film.

_____

5. The good news was broadcasted at six o'clock; Devina suggested us to go to dinner to celebrate.

_____

6. I am accustom to practice three hours a day.

_____

7. Pearl swang her purse so hard its contents flown everywhere.

_____

8. I was eating when Michi had arrived.

_____

9. Yesterday, John has been feeling rather ill.

_____

10. In his recent proposal, the president argued for increase taxes.

_____

Self-Correction: In a recent piece of writing, identify areas where you had difficulty with verbs and verb tenses. Copy any sentences with verb errors in them; then rewrite each sentence correctly.

WORDINESS

Effective sentences use exactly the right number of words necessary to get their message across. There is no magic number, however. Charles Dickens' *Tale of Two Cities* starts with a sentence that is 128 words long, yet it is considered a memorable sentence:

It was the best of times, it was the worst of times, it was the age of wisdom, it was the age of foolishness, it was the epoch of belief, it was the epoch of incredulity, it was the season of Light, it was the season of Darkness, it was the spring of hope, it was the winter of despair, we had everything before us, we had nothing before us, we were all going direct to Heaven, we were all going direct the other way—in short, the period was so far like the present period, that some of its noisiest authorities insisted on being received, for good or for evil, in the superlative degree of comparison only.

Moby Dick begins with a three-word sentence, and is also memorable:

Call me Ishmael.

Ultimately, you will need to decide when you have a sentence that is the right number of words.

Here are five principles for improving the conciseness of your writing.

1. Eliminate redundant words.

    EXAMPLE Currently, what we need now is a novel new plan.
    REVISED What we need is a new plan.

2. Shorten chiché phrases:
    at this point in time = "now"
    at that point in time = "then"
    at this juncture = "now"
    at the present time = "now"
    in a relatively short amount of time = "quickly"
    (and many more!)

3. Eliminate weak modifiers: If you use any of the following words, check to be sure they add information to the sentence. If not, replace them with a more precise word, or get rid of them altogether.

    really, very, definitely, quite, awfully, fine, nice, just

    EXAMPLE *He is really a very tall man.*
    REVISED *He is six feet tall.*
                 He is very tall.

4. Replace wordy phrases.

    EXAMPLE At the time when she was trying to find her new book, she seemed quite upset. She had just bought it recently.
    REVISION She seemed upset while trying to find her new book, because she had just bought it.

5. Simplify sentence structures; use adjectives.

    EXAMPLE Pearl, who was a teacher, wanted to take a vacation in Hawaii.
    REVISION Pearl, a teacher, wanted a Hawaiian vacation.

6. Eliminate "it is . . . that" structures (sometimes called "deferred subjects").

    EXAMPLE It is the state of Washington that is most famous for apple production.
    REVISION The state of Washington is most famous for apple production.

7. Minimize the number of prepositional phrases per sentence.

EXAMPLE   The members of the committee for which I am the leader want to form a subcommittee devoted to the restructuring of the entire organization of our club.

REVISION   The committee, of which I am the leader, wants to form a subcommittee to restructure our club's organization.

8. Reduce unnecessary nominalizations.

Nominalization refers to changing a verb into a noun. Structures that rely on nominalization frequently rely too much on the verb "to be" as well, making for weak writing.

EXAMPLE   My realization of my procrastination is an alteration in my thinking.

REVISION   I realize that I procrastinate, which has changed my thinking.

ACTIVITY 13: WORDINESS

Make the following passages more concise.

1. It is not completely impossible, at the present time, to begin to develop an ample supply of monetary resources.
2. Each individual person in attendance should obtain the approval of his or her personal instructor before leaving the classroom area.
3. Three of my very closest friends just want to go to the party, but I much prefer a movie for the evening's entertainment.
4. Excuse me, but would you mind terribly much, if it's not too much trouble, opening the window just a little?
5. My grandmother is eighty-six years of age, but she has the capability of dancing the night away, just like people who are thirty years her junior in age.
6. The assistance of the three women was of great importance to our organization for alumni of our university.

Self-Correction: In a recent piece of writing, identify areas where you had difficulty with wordiness. Rewrite any sentences that were too wordy, and make them more concise.

Quoting and Referencing Sources

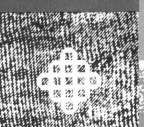

*T*his chapter presents two different citation formats: one for writing in the humanities and one for the social sciences. There are many other formats. You will find a list of references for other format types at the end of this chapter. You should use each type appropriately, depending on your paper, and your teacher's instructions. The following outline shows only the basic elements of these two formats. For more complete instructions, refer to *The MLA Handbook for Writers of Research Papers,* 3rd ed. New York: MLA, 1988, or to the *Publication Manual of the American Psychological Association* [APA], 4th ed. Washington, D.C.: APA, 1994.

All formats have two basic parts: referencing within the text, used when quoting, and a list of sources, known generally as a bibliography or reference list. Specific citation formats may have additional features.*

HUMANITIES: MLA FORMAT

MLA stands for "Modern Language Association," and its format is the preferred style for writing in literature.

Quotation References

When you quote or refer to an author within your text, you should include a **parenthetical reference.** Within the parentheses include the author's last name and the page number on which you found the reference. Look carefully at the punctuation conventions as well. Even if you only summarize or paraphrase another author, you still must give a reference:

> "Philosophy since Kant," he argues, "has purported to be a science which could sit in judgment on all the other sciences" (Rorty 141).

If you are quoting more than one source by the same author, then you need to include a shortened title as well.

> As Prichard writes, "Everything turns upon how the principles of criticism are applied" (Prichard, <u>Practical Critical Practice</u> 121).

When any of the information normally put within the parentheses is included in your sentence, you can omit that part from the citation.

> In <u>Principles of American Literary Criticism</u>, Prichard notes that the "theory of language is the most neglected of all studies" (261).

---

*Many of the references used in this chapter are fictitious; don't use them to conduct your own research.

When you quote a longer passage (usually more than three lines of your paper), that quotation should be indented and offset from the rest of the text. Notice in the previous examples that the parenthetical reference comes after the final punctuation instead of before. Do not put quotation marks around a block quotation.

In his essay, he writes:

> I am not sure that "phase two" marks a split with "phase one," a split whose form would be cut along an indivisible line. The relationship between these two phases doubtless has another structure. (Derrida 72)

If you omit part of a quotation, you should signal this omission with an **ellipsis,** . . . a series of three dots. If you need to rephrase a portion of the author's words or add a word in order to maintain the phrase's grammaticality or sense in the quotation, you can do so with **square brackets** [ ]. You should never omit important information or rephrase the author's words in a manner that changes the original meaning.

> According to Tanaka, critical reading "should offer a means of inducing constant habits of feeling . . . [and] the possibility of one's acting in accordance with the findings of one's improved intelligence" (29).

If the portion of text you omit is at the end of a sentence, you need to add a fourth dot, which is actually the final punctuation of the sentence.

> Wang notes that "every statement makes a claim to justice, sincerity, beauty, and truthfulness. . . . And these values are not defined by their relation to language, but by their relation to reality . . ." (123).

If there are two authors, they should be referenced in the order they appear on the cover of the book or in the title of the work.

> "American New Criticism also tended to surpass the British in the degree to which it was willing to formulate the objective form of poetry" (Davis and Schleifer 79).

If there are three authors, you should use the following form:

> Paton himself demonstrated that children's difficulties with conservation of length could be lessened by weakening the visual illusion involved (Paton, Regis, and Szeminska 43).

If there are more than three authors, in the text list the first author, then the abbreviation *et al.* (meaning "and the others") and the page number.

> The authors found no difference in the two situations (Terrace et al. 891).

SOME SPECIAL CASES

If your work does not have an author listed, use a shortened version of the title in the parenthetical reference.

("Bridges in the Night" 111).

If the entire reference is only one page long, you do not need to list a page number in the parentheses.

When something you read refers to another source, and you do not read the source referred to, use the abbreviation *qtd.* ("quoted") as part of your reference.

Miller said that literature and history "were inextricably entwined" (qtd. in James 15).

When you support a claim with more than one reference, cite each work as previously specified, but separate them with semicolons.

(Martin 123; Garcia 99)

If two authors you refer to have the same last name, include their first names or initials to distinguish them.

(John Smith 41) and (G. E. Smith 23).

If you are referring to a novel or a poem, it is helpful to give more information about where you found your information. You may include a chapter number.

In <u>A Tale of Two Cities</u>, Dickens begins with a very long sentence (1; chapter 1).

If you refer to, or copy, an author's figure or table, you must include that information at the bottom of the graphic material. Format the source line like this:

Source: Raul Jimenez, "A Guide to Poetry," <u>Journal of Poetry</u> 8 (1934): 33.

Source List

Every citation that you list in a parentheses in your text must appear, in alphabetical order, in a section called <u>Works Cited</u>, which you should place at the end of your paper. If you also want to include titles of works you read but did not reference directly in your paper, you should call your list <u>Works Consulted</u>. In general, in your bibliography you should underline the titles of books and other major works; but put double quotation marks around the titles of smaller works, such as articles, short stories, and poems.

The basic entry for each listing in your bibliography is made up of the following: the author's name, followed by a period and two spaces; the title, underlined and followed by a period and two spaces; the city of publication,*

---

*If the city of publication is small or not well known, include, if it is a U.S. publisher, the state as well. If the publisher is outside the United States and the city of publication is small or lesser known, include the country name.

followed by a colon and two spaces; the name of the publisher, followed by a comma; and the year of publication, followed by a period. The second line and any line after it in each reference should be indented.

BOOKS

Yeats, William Butler.   <u>Collected Poems</u>.   New York: Macmillan, 1956.

If the book has an **edition number,** that information should come after the title, followed by a period.

Yeats,   William Butler.   <u>Collected Poems.</u>   2nd ed. New York:
    Macmillan, 1958.

When the book has more than two or three authors, only the first author has the order of his or her name reversed. Enter the names in the same order that they appear on the title page of the book.

Marx, Karl, and Friedrich Engels.   <u>Capital: A Critique of Political Economy</u>.
    New York: Vintage Books, 1976.

When the book has three or more authors, use the abbreviation *et al.* (see the explanation on page 197).

Smith, Michael, et al.   <u>The Many Uses of Masking Tape.</u>   New York:
    Walkabout Press, Inc., 1991.

If you refer to two or more books by the same author, include the author's name only in the first entry. After that, use three dashes (---) followed by a period in place of the author's name. List the books, in this case, alphabetically by the title.

Norris, Christopher.   <u>Derrida.</u>   Cambridge: Harvard University Press,
    1987.
---. <u>Paul de Man</u>.   New York: Routledge, 1988.

If you refer to a specific volume (or volumes) of a multi-volume work, include the volume number in your reference, along with the total number of volumes available.

Smetana, Susan.   Vol. 4 of <u>A History of Nylon Carpets</u>. 16 vols.   Muncie,
    IN: IAP Press, 1992.

If the book you cite has an editor rather than an author, the citation form depends upon the information you use. If you use materials written by the editor, such as notes, introduction, foreword, and so forth, then refer to the editor in your bibliography.

Kovacs, Pilar, ed.   <u>For and Against: Famous Arguments.</u>
    By Charlene Monad.   New Brighton, MN: Snowpress, 1955.

However, if you are mostly concerned with the original material and don't refer to the editor's remarks, list it by the author's name.

> Ruetz, Anna.   For and Against: Famous Arguments.
> Ed. Pilar Kovacs.   New Brighton, MN: Snowpress, 1955.

If you use one essay or work out of a collection, list the individual essay, not the entire book. You will need to include the relevant page numbers as well.

> Sikorsky, Elena.   "Big and Little Ideas."   Catalogue of Different Theories.
> Ed. Bobby McGee.   Paris: Voila Press, 1994. 110-115.

The preface, foreword, afterword, or introduction to a book must be referenced if you cite it. Write the appropriate term before the title, followed by a period.

> Bolling, Simon.   Introduction.   Beginning Dutch. By
> Hans Hollander.   The Hague: The Press, 1983. i–xiv.*

If you are using a translation, list the translator's name after the title, using the abbreviation "Trans."

> Molina, Antonia.   Life and Death on Russian Hill.   Trans. Paula Herrera.
> San Francisco: Angel Press, 1906.

If you use an encyclopedia, you do not need to include the volume and page numbers. For major encyclopedias, you do not need to include publication information, either. If the item from the encyclopedia does not have an author, list it under the title of the entry.

> "Ellis Island."   Encyclopedia Americana.   1988 ed.

If an author or authors are listed for the entry, include the name(s) as you would any other entry. If you use a smaller, less well-known encyclopedia, you should include publication information.

When you use a government document and no author is listed, use the name of the government agency in place of the author's name.

> United States Dept. of Agriculture.   Six Hundred Species of Garden Peas.
> Washington: GPO, 1933.

ARTICLES

A citation to an article contains the following information: the author's name, followed by a period and two spaces; the title, followed by a period, enclosed in quotation marks and followed by two spaces; the title of the

---

*If the page numbers are Roman in the original text, you must use Roman numerals in your citation as well.

periodical, underlined and followed by the volume number; the date of publication in parentheses, followed by a colon and a space; and the full page numbers* of the article, followed by a period.

A professional journal:

LeMonde, Alain R.   "French Bicycles throughout History."   <u>The Journal of Bicycle Studies</u> 14 (1984): 21-39.

When you refer to an author's review of another writer's work, include the phrase "*Rev. of*" by the work that is reviewed, and then after the title, the phrase *by* plus the original author's name.

Smith, Chris.   Rev. of <u>A Tale of Two Cities</u>, by Charles Dickens.   <u>The Annual Review of Really Old Books</u> 14 (1995): 23-35.

A popular magazine:
1. Weekly: List the complete date and page numbers.

Walla, Jamal.   "A Word on Patios."   <u>New Jersey Life</u> 13 Oct. 1989: 56+.

2. Monthly: Include only the month and year. Do not include volume or issue numbers.

Thomsen, Paul.   "Life on Fiji."   <u>Travel Today</u> May 1988: 19-21.

If an article in a magazine has no author, list it alphabetically by the title.

A newspaper: List the name of the newspaper as it appears on the first page, without any articles to start it (for example, <u>San Francisco Chronicle</u>, not *the* <u>S.F. Chronicle</u>). Give the date it appeared, the edition (found at the top of the front page), and if the sections are numbered or lettered, that information along with the page numbers.

Carman, John.   "'Tales' a San Francisco Treat."   <u>San Francisco Chronicle</u> 10 Jan. 1994, final ed.: sec. D: 1-2.

If the item is an editorial, include the word "Editorial" followed by a period, after the title. Again, if there is no author identified, use the title as the item to list.

"State Needs Help to Pay Alien Costs." Editorial. <u>San Francisco Chronicle</u> 10 Jan. 1994, final ed.: sec. A: 22.

---

*If an article does not appear on consecutive pages—that is, if there are "skips" in the printing—state the first page number of the article, followed by a plus sign (40+, for example, for an article beginning on page 40).

If you want to cite a letter to the editor, include the word "Letter" after the author's name.

Sias, Laura. Letter. <u>San Francisco Chronicle</u> 10 Jan. 1994,
    final ed.: sec. A: 22.

NONPRINT REFERENCES

Films and videos: You may use different formats for citing films and videos, depending on whom or what you wish to emphasize. (For example, you can list one by the director's name, if that is important to your paper.) However, it is probably simplest to list all video and films by their titles. Include date and production information, including the director's name.

<u>Annie Hall</u>. Dir. Woody Allen. United Artists, 1977.

Personal interviews:

Jordan, Michael. Personal interview. 21 Jan. 1993.
Barkley, Charles. Telephone interview. 14 Dec. 1992.

Lectures: Include the name of the lecturer, the title, location, and date. If there was a sponsor or series name, include that as well. If the lecture has no title, provide a descriptive name yourself.

Lao, Pufang. "The Cultural Revolution." Asian Studies
    Colloquium, Dept. of Chinese, University of Illinois,
    23 June 1986.

Personal letters: If you want to quote a letter someone wrote to you, refer to yourself as "the author":

Clinton, Bill. Letter to the author. 20 Feb. 1993.

Information from a computer service: Cite this information just as you would an article, but include the name of the file and any identifying numbers with it.

Jersey, Delia. "The Newest Information Trends."
    <u>Information News Weekly</u>, 10 Aug. 1985: 121+. INFONET
    file 22a, item 85.08.10.

Computer software: Include the company that produced the software, the title of the program, and the year of publication. Also include the type of machine for which it was written.

<u>SimFarm.</u> Computer Software. Maxis, 1993. IBM.

Television/Radio: Record the underlined name of the program, the network or cable station that produced it or showed it, the local station, city, and date of the program.

<u>New Horizons in Bonsai</u>. KCSM-60, San Mateo. 11 Jan. 1994.

Explanatory Notes

MLA style also allows explanatory notes. If you need to include information that doesn't fit clearly into your text or doesn't use a standard reference citation, include it in a note. Number these notes sequentially in your paper, and then list them on a separate page at the end of your paper just before your <u>Works Cited</u> list.

In your paper:

Television has reached new heights of violence, according to some experts.[1]

On your "Notes" page:

[1]For more information about recent polls, see the article "The Real Story of Violence," in <u>TV Guide</u>, January 1, 1994.

SOCIAL SCIENCES: APA FORMAT

The American Psychological Association (APA) format is a popular format for the social sciences and other areas of research. It uses short references, including the last name of the authors and the year of publication, put within parentheses inserted in the text. The following references are the same as those in the MLA section, but they have been changed to the APA format.

Quotation References

APA also uses **parenthetical reference.** It is different from MLA in that a comma is used in the parentheses.

"Philosophy since Kant," he argues, "has purported to be a science which could sit in judgment on all the other sciences" (Rorty, 1976, p. 141).

If you are quoting more than one source by the same author, the date usually tells the one to which you are referring. However, if the author has two different publications in the same year, in your reference list and your citations follow the year date with the letters *a* for the first one, *b* for the second, so on, alphabetized according to the title.

As Prichard writes, "Everything turns upon how the principles of criticism are applied" (Prichard, 1991a, p. 121).

When any of the information normally put within the parentheses is included in your sentence, you can omit that part from the citation.

> In <u>Principles of American Literary Criticism</u>, Prichard notes that the "theory of language is the most neglected of all studies" (1991b, p. 261).

When you quote a longer passage (more than 40 words), that quotation should be indented and offset from the rest of the text. Notice that the parenthetical reference comes after the final punctuation. Do not put quotation marks around block quotations.

> In his essay, Derrida writes:
> I am not sure that "phase two" marks a split with "phase one," a split whose form would be cut along an indivisible line. The relationship between these two phases doubtless has another structure. (1972, p. 72)

If you omit part of a quotation, you should signal this omission with an **ellipsis.** See the instructions in the previous section page 197.

If there are from two to six authors, they should be referenced in the order they appear on the cover of the book or in the title of the work, and joined with an ampersand (&).

> "American New Criticism also tended to surpass the British in the degree to which it was willing to formulate the objective form of poetry" (Davis & Schleifer, 1991, p. 21).

If there are more than six authors, in the text list the first author and then the abbreviation *et al.* (meaning "and the others").

> The authors found no difference in the two situations (Terrace et al., 1891).

SOME SPECIAL CASES

If your work does not have an author listed, use a shortened version of the title in the parenthetical reference.

> ("Bridges in the Night," 1911).

When something you read refers to another source, and you do not read that source, use the phrase 'cited in' as part of your reference.

> Miller said that literature and history "were inextricably entwined" (cited in James, 1991, p. 15).

When you support a claim with more than one reference, cite each work as previously specified, but separate them with semicolons. List them in alphabetical order.

> (Garcia, 1982; Martin, 1923).

If two authors you cite have the same last name, include their initials to distinguish them.

(J. Smith, 1941) and (G. E. Smith, 1923).

If you are referring to a novel or a poem, it is helpful to give more information about where you found your information. You may include a chapter number. Abbreviate words such as "section" and "chapter."

In <u>A Tale of Two Cities</u>, Dickens begins with a very long sentence (1900; chap. 1).

If you refer to, or copy, an author's figure or table, you must include that information at the bottom of the graphic material. Use the following format:

Source: Jimenez, 1934, p. 33.

Source List

Every citation that you list in a parentheses in your text must appear, in alphabetical order, in a section called <u>References</u>, which you should place at the end of your paper. In general, in your reference list, you should underline the titles of books and other major works; but do not put double quotation marks around the titles of smaller works, such as articles, short stories, and poems. In titles, capitalize only the first letter of the first word, first letters of proper nouns, and the first letter of the first word after a colon.

The basic entry for each listing in your bibliography is made up of the following: the author's last name, followed by his or her initials; the year of publication in parentheses, followed by a period and two spaces; the title, underlined and followed by a period and two spaces; the city of publication,* followed by a colon and two spaces; and then the name of the publisher, followed by a period. The second line and those following should be indented.

BOOKS

Yeats, W. B.   (1956).   <u>Collected poems</u>.   New York: Macmillan.

If the book has an **edition** number, that information should come after the title, in parentheses and followed by a period.

Yeats,   W. B.   (1956).   <u>Collected poems</u>   (2nd ed.).   New York: Macmillan.

---

*If the city of publication is small or not well known, include, if it is a U.S. publisher, the state as well. If the publisher is outside the United States and the city of publication is small or lesser known, include the country name.

When the book has more than two to six authors, all authors have the order of their names reversed. Enter the names in the same order that they appear on the title page of the book.

> Marx, K., & Engels, F. (1976). <u>Capital: A critique of political economy</u>. New York: Vintage Books, 1976.

When the book has three or more authors, use the abbreviation *et al.* (see page 197).

> Smith, M., et al. (1991). <u>The many uses of masking tape.</u> New York: Walkabout Press, Inc.

If you refer to a specific volume (or volumes) of a multivolume work, include the volume number in your reference.

> Smetana, S. (1992). <u>A history of nylon carpets: Vol. 4.</u> Muncie, IN: IAP Press.

If the book you cite has an editor, and you want to refer to the editor's comments, rather than an author, use the following organization.

> Kovacs, P. (Ed.). (1955). Introduction. In A. Ruetz, <u>For and against: Famous arguments.</u> New Brighton, MN: Snowpress.

If you use one essay or work out of a collection, list the individual essay, not the entire book. You will need to include the relevant page numbers as well.

> Sikorsky, E. (1994). Big and little ideas. In B. McGee (Ed.), <u>Catalogue of different theories</u> (pp. 110-115). Paris: Voila Press.

If you are using a translation, list the translator's name after the author's name (in parentheses) using the abbreviation "Trans."

> Molina, A. (Trans.). (1906). <u>Life and death on Russian Hill</u>. San Francisco: Angel Press.

If you use an encyclopedia, you need to include the volume and page number, and include publication information as well. If the item from the encyclopedia does not have an author, list it under the title of the entry.

> Ellis Island. (1988). <u>Encyclopedia Americana</u> (Vol. 4, pp. 300-344). New York: Americana Publishers.

If there is an author or authors listed for the entry, include their names as you would any other entry. If you use a government document, and there is no author listed, use the name of the government agency as the author. Include the government document number.

> United States Dept. of Agriculture. (1933). <u>Six hundred species of garden peas</u>. (NTIS No. P880-14333). Washington: U.S. Government Printing Office.

ARTICLES

A citation to an article contains the following information: the author's name (last name, initials), followed by a period and two spaces; the year of publication in parentheses, followed by a period and two spaces; the title of the article, followed by a period and two spaces; the title of the periodical, followed by a comma; the volume number, underlined and followed by a comma; and the full page numbers* of the article, followed by a period. The first line is indented.

A professional journal:

NOTE All major words in a journal or magazine name should be capitalized.

LeMonde, A. R. (1984).   French bicycles throughout history.   The Journal of Bicycle Studies, 14, 21–39.

When you refer to an author's review of another writer's work, include the phrase "*Rev. of*" by the work that is reviewed, and then after the title, the phrase *by* plus the original author's name.

Smith, C. (1995).   An old favorite.   [Review of A tale of two cities, by Charles Dickens]   The Annual Review of Really Old Books, 14, 23–35.

A popular magazine:

Weekly: List the complete date and page numbers.

Walla, J. (1989, October 13).   A word on patios.   New Jersey Life, pp. 56–78.

Monthly: Include only the month and year. Do not include volume or issue numbers.

Thomsen, P. (1988, May).   Life on Fiji.   Travel Today, pp. 19–21.

If an article in a magazine has no author identified, list it alphabetically by the title.

A newspaper: List the name of the newspaper as it appears on the first page, without any articles to start it (for example, San Francisco Chronicle, not *the* S.F. Chronicle). Give the date it appeared, the edition (found at the top of the front page), and if the sections are numbered or lettered, that information along with the page numbers. If the pages are not consecutive, give all the page numbers, separated by commas.

Carman, J. (1994, January 10).   'Tales' a San Francisco treat.   San Francisco Chronicle, pp. D1–2.

If you want to cite a letter to the editor, include the word "Letter" after the author's name.

Sias, L. (1994, January 10).   In support of Bosnian intervention [Letter to the editor].   San Francisco Chronicle, p. A22.

---

*If an article does not appear on consecutive pages—that is, if there are "skips" in the printing—state the first page number of the article, followed by a plus sign (40+, for example, for an article beginning on page 40).

NONPRINT REFERENCES

Films and videos:

Allen, W. (Director) & Joffe, C. H. (Producer). (1977).   Annie Hall [Film].
Culver City, CA: United Artists.

Personal Interviews: Unpublished interviews should not be listed in your references. Instead, explain the interview in your text, or in a note.

Published interviews:

Smart, J. (1993, January 21)   [Interview with Micha   ~dan].   Sports
Illustrated, p. 34.

Information from a computer service: Cite this information just as you would an article, but include the name of the file and any identifying numbers with it.

Jersey, D. (1985, August 10).   The newest information trends. Information
News Weekly, pp. 121, 123, & 135.   [INFONET file 22a, item 85.08.10].

Computer software: Include the company who produced the software, the title of the program, and the year of publication. Also include the type of machine for which it is written.

SimFarm. (1993). [Computer Software].   Orinda, CA: Maxis. IBM.

Explanatory Notes

APA style also allows explanatory notes. If you need to include information that doesn't fit clearly into your text or doesn't use a standard reference citation, include it in a note. Number these notes sequentially in your paper, and then list them on a separate page at the end of your paper which you place just before your References list.

In your paper:

Television has reached new heights of violence, according to some experts.[1]

On your "Notes" page:

[1]For more information about recent polls, see the article "The Real Story of Violence," in TV Guide, January 1, 1994.

American Chemical Society. <u>Handbook for Authors of Papers in the American Chemical Society Publications</u>. Washington: American Chemical Soc., 1978.

American Institute of Physics. <u>Style Manual for Guidance in the Preparation of Papers</u>. 3rd ed. New York: American Inst. of Physics, 1978.

<u>The Chicago Manual of Style</u>. 13th ed. Chicago: University of Chicago Press, 1982.

Council of Biological Editors. <u>CBE Style Manual</u>. 5th ed. Bethesda, MD: CBE, 1983.

Irvine, Demar B. <u>Writing About Music: A Style Book for Reports and Theses</u>. Seattle: Univ. of Washington Press, 1968.

Turabian, Kate L. <u>A Manual for Writers of Term Papers, Theses, and Dissertations</u>. Chicago: Univ. of Chicago Press, 1973.

Preparing your Papers

Most students dread the prospect of writing under pressure within a set time limit. With practice, planning, and preparation, however, you will find writing in class or for examinations can be easier.

This section will give you some strategies for preparing for in-class writing.

Quickwrite

What experiences, good or bad, can you recall regarding writing under pressure? What aspects of the process were most troublesome? What elements do you do well?

Before the Essay

There is no substitute for being ready for an in-class essay. Being ready means reading the required material, attending class, taking notes, participating in discussions, reviewing, and—most important—asking questions.

Another useful preparation technique is to try to predict the questions that might appear on your essay examination. As you review your notes, imagine that you are the instructor, and create essay questions you think could be on your examination. Then take some time to freewrite answers to your sample questions. Share your questions with classmates and practice writing in study groups.

The following table lists some common complaints students have about their experiences with in-class writing. Which of these problems do you share? Can you propose a solution to each of these problems? Discuss your answers with your classmates.

TABLE 10.1 TEN COMMON COMPLAINTS ABOUT IN-CLASS WRITING

1. "I read the questions carefully, but often I don't understand what I am supposed to write about."
2. "I start out okay, but I get off the topic easily."
3. "I am so nervous that I can't think of a thing to say."
4. "I always run out of time and don't finish my essay."
5. "Everyone else seems to write faster than I do; they hand in their essays before I'm done."
6. "My essays are so messy when I finish that I'm sure the teacher won't be able to read them."
7. "Every time I look at the clock, five more minutes have passed, and I know I'll never finish on time."
8. "When I get my essays back, there are always too many stupid mistakes— misspellings, errors in grammar, omitted words—things that I know are wrong."
9. "Last time, I didn't know I was supposed to write in ink or that I could bring a dictionary. I never seem prepared."
10. "I have done poorly on all my in-class essays."

What solutions did you arrive at? Here are some suggestions, some of which you may have already discussed.

1. "I read the questions carefully, but often I don't understand what I am supposed to write about."

   What you can do:

   a. Identify the important elements of the question. A good essay question has two parts: the **strategy** and the **topic.** The strategy is the word or words that tell you what technique to use. The following table lists some strategies and examples of how to address them.

   EXAMPLE

   Explain the role of Liu Shaoqi in the Chinese Cultural Revolution.

   strategy   topic

TABLE 10.2 STRATEGIES FOR IN-CLASS ESSAYS	
STRATEGY TERM	**MEANING**
Analyze	One common approach to "analyzing" is to divide an event, idea, or theory into different elements and examine each one separately. However, the word "analyze" is used differently in different subject areas (for example, literary analysis is different from historical analysis). Make sure you know the meaning in your particular field of study.
Compare/Contrast	Demonstrate the similarities and/or dissimilarites between the named topics. Sometimes an essay question may say "compare," but the instructor is expecting "compare and contrast." If you see "compare" alone, ask if you should also contrast.
Define	Identify the important traits and characteristics of the topic. Clearly differentiate it from other similar topics.
Describe	Tell about a person, place, or event in detail. Create a clear image of it for your reader.
Discuss	See *analyze*. (*Note:* "Discuss" does not mean to talk about a topic as you would in a typical discussion.)
Evaluate	Assess the significance of the topic. Give your opinion on its importance.
Explain	Make the topic clear and understandable to a reader by offering reasons and examples.
Summarize	State the major points of the topic comprehensively and concisely.

    b. Ask your instructor! She or he may be willing to explain what the question is asking. However, if your instructor won't give you additional information, it means you are expected to know the terminology that is troubling you; that is, you should answer your own question as part of your essay. First, define the word or phrase in the way you understand it; then write your essay based on your understanding.

2. "I start out okay, but I get off the topic easily."

    What you can do:

        Plan your essay. How much time do you have? Give yourself at least five minutes (more if you have two hours or more in which to write) to plan your essay. Write a brief outline or notes, and refer to them frequently while you write your essay. Think of the examples you want to use before you start writing.

3. "I am so nervous that I can't think of a thing to say."

    What you can do:

    a. One way to reduce nervousness is to "warm up." Give yourself ten or more minutes before class to freewrite. You can write about any topic you want, whether it's a topic you think might appear on the essay or what you ate for breakfast. But, like playing the piano or running a marathon, a little "stretching" exercise will help prepare you for the real thing.

    b. Relax. Before the essay, listen to music that you enjoy, go for a swim or a walk, talk to friends. It won't eliminate your nervousness but it may lessen it somewhat.

4. "I always run out of time and don't finish my essay."

    What you can do:

    a. Plan ahead. Similar to the suggestions in #2, make a time schedule for yourself, given the amount of time you have. Allow yourself enough time to complete all the stages.

    b. Don't waste time. Come to class prepared—pencils sharpened, needed materials readily available, and your mind on the essay. And be on time!

    c. Be concise. In-class essays have certain limitations: although an out-of-class essay may require you to explain a lot of background material from an article or book, an in-class essay typically requires you to write for an audience that already knows your subject matter. You can spend less time summarizing and restating the topic and more time getting right to the point with your answer.

5. "Everyone else seems to write faster than I do; they hand in their essays before I'm done."

    What you can do:

        Stop comparing yourself to everyone else! Each person writes at a different speed, in a different way. Unless you have trouble finishing on time (if you do, see #4), it really doesn't matter how quickly you write. Don't rush just because others seem to be finishing first.

6. "My essays are so messy when I finish that I'm sure the teacher won't be able to read them."

    What you can do:

    a. Ask your instructor if you can write in pencil. Use a good eraser.

    b. If you must write in ink, use an erasable ink pen or bring white correction fluid.

   c. Double-space your lines, leave wide margins, and allow extra space between paragraphs. That way, if you need to cross something out, you'll have room to write in your new text neatly.

   d. Although it usually isn't practical to write a draft and then rewrite a whole paper, for particularly difficult parts of the paper—the introduction and conclusion, for example—you may want to write a draft on scrap paper before you write those parts out on your essay.

7. "Every time I look at the clock, five more minutes have passed, and I know I'll never finish on time."

   What you can do:

   Don't bring a watch, and don't sit where you can see a wall clock clearly. Instead, ask your instructor to write the remaining time on the board periodically (every 20 or 30 minutes).

8. "When I get my essays back, there are always too many stupid mistakes— misspellings, errors in grammar, omitted words—things that I know are wrong."

   What you can do:

   Leave time to proofread your paper. One proofreading technique that some find effective is to read the paper backwards, that is read the last sentence, then the next to last, and so on. This way you can focus on your grammar and spelling and not on the content.

9. "Last time, I didn't know I was supposed to write in ink, or that I could bring a dictionary. I never seem prepared."

   What you can do:

   a. Read your assignment carefully. Write on your planner or calendar the dates essays are due and the necessary materials to take to class.

   b. Confirm with classmates your understanding about the essay requirements.

   c. Ask your instructor what you need to bring and if there are any special instructions you need to know (Can you use a dictionary? Do you need a blue book? and so on).

   d. Write down all the necessary information to help you remember it.

10. "I have done poorly on all my in-class essays."

   What you can do:

   a. Stop thinking about the past! You didn't know as much then as you do now about preparation and planning. You can't change the past—but you *can* improve on your future essays.

   b. See your instructor during office hours to discuss problems you have had with in-class writing. Ask his or her assistance and advice in how you can address your specific problems. If you have a copy of an old in-class paper you've written, bring it along.

   Finally, once you have completed your in-class essay, be sure to make an appointment with your instructor to discuss your paper. Go to office hours prepared with specific questions about your paper and about how you can improve the next one.

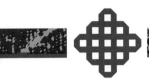
A computer or a word processor can simplify many of the steps of writing. If you don't have your own, ask your instructor whether you can get access to one at your school. (Maybe a friend or roommate

will let you use his or hers if you don't have one.) Most colleges and universities have some general-access computers, but the competition for them is often very high.

Quickwrite

If you could design a computer that would help you write, what would it be able to do? Be specific—which tasks would you like help with?

What Word Processing Software Can Do

Look at the following list of some of the tasks that word processing software can accomplish. Compare it to your quickwrite response. Are some of your wishes answered?

A wordprocessor can:

- check spelling
- check grammar*
- create outlines and tables of contents
- automatically set margins
- place footnotes correctly
- underline, boldface, italicize easily
- format bibliographies more easily

Every word-processing program, such as WordPerfect, Microsoft Word, and so on, deals with these tasks differently and may not do all the ones on the list. Many new word-processing programs include "tutorial" programs that help you learn how to use the program quickly and easily. Also, many campus computing centers offer

BIZARRO   By DAN PIRARO

YOU CORRECT MY GRAMMAR, MY SPELLING, MY PUNCTUATION! I CAN'T STAND THE PRESSURE OF LIVING WITH A PERFECTIONIST.

workshops to let you learn the system that is used there. Take advantage of these opportunities—they will help you not only in your coursework but can teach you essential job skills as well.

---

*The grammar checkers that are available are not very sophisticated. It is fine to use them, but don't rely on their advice exclusively. They give a lot of useless (and wrong) suggestions.

How You Can Use the Computer

Freewriting: You can write directly on the computer if you are comfortable doing so. If you are trying to explore ideas for writing, sit down and type at the keyboard. The advantage to writing at the keyboard is you don't waste paper by throwing out drafts you don't like—you need only to erase them. It's also easy to correct mistakes and rewrite text. Later, it's also easier to rearrange paragraphs, move sentences, and do other kinds of editing that are harder by hand or with a typewriter.

Organizing: Write an outline for your paper on the computer, and then go back to fill in the paragraphs or sections under each heading. An outline will help you stay organized. Some programs have an outline system built in.

Revising: All programs will allow you to delete and move sections of text. It is also easy to insert new material if you were told your draft needed more examples or support.

Editing: The spelling checker will help you look for misspelled words. However, you shouldn't rely on the spelling checker alone. If you, for example, type "mush" instead of "must" the spelling checker won't catch it because "mush" is a perfectly spelled English word.

Printing: Explore the different typefaces (called fonts) and other formatting possibilities of your software.

Use the following instructions to create a sample page of text on your word processor.

CREATING A SAMPLE PAGE

1. Set the margins to one inch on the top, left and right, and one-and-a-quarter inches on the bottom.
2. Turn off the page numbering and right justification. Set the line spacing to double-space.
3. Set the font to Courier, 12 point size, bold-faced type.*
4. On the first line, type the words **Test Page** and center them.
5. Set the font to Courier, 10 point size, not bold-faced.
6. Space down four times (8 lines) and type the following passage (including the mistakes).

> Every country and culture is unique, and the "Asian" economic system naturally is something different in Singapore from whak it is in Thailand or Japan. There are comparable variations among European and North American styles of capitalism. In their emphasis on industrial guidance and national policy, France and Germany are more Asian than they are American. In their approch to leisure and the good life, the Europeans are less like the new Asian model than like Americans.

7. Space down two times (4 lines) and type the following reference for the preceding passage:

> Fallows, James. "What Is an Economy For?" The Atlantic Monthly, January 1994: 76.

---

*If your printer does not have fonts that are scalable—that is, fonts that can be made very large or very small, complete all the instructions using 12-point size (most computers have a choice of 10-point and 12-point).

8. Run the spell-checking program. Correct any misspellings.
9. Print one copy of your page.
   Your page should look like the following:

Test Page

Every country and culture is unique, and the "Asian" economic system naturally is something different in Singapore from what it is in Thailand or Japan. There are comparable variations among European and North American styles of capitalism. In their emphasis on industrial guidance and national policy, France and Germany are more Asian than they are American. In their approach to leisure and the good life, the Europeans are less like the new Asian model than like Americans.

Fallows, James. "What Is an Economy For?" <u>The Atlantic Monthly</u>, January 1994:76.

PREPARING A FINAL DRAFT

Whether you use a word processor, write by hand in class, or use a typewriter, your work must meet the specifications set by your instructor. The following guidelines give you some general specifications; ask your instructor for further instructions.

Handwritten Papers

Handwritten work should be neat, written in dark ink on lined white paper. Ask your instructor if you should skip lines and if you can write on the back of the paper. Many instructors don't like paper that has been torn out of spiral-bound notebooks—use loose-leaf paper instead.

Typewritten Papers

Use standard size, white paper. Paper labeled "erasable" is not a good choice; the ink smears. Instead, use correction fluid for correcting typing mistakes.* Type on one side of the paper, double-spaced. Select either 10- or 12-point† type, and if you have a choice, use a typeface that is bold and easy to read. Leave one-inch margins on all four edges of the paper, being particularly careful not to type too closely to the bottom of the page. Number your pages according to the specified format.

Word-Processed Papers

Use the same directions as for typewritten manuscripts. When printing out your manuscript, if you use a dot-matrix printer, be sure your ribbon is dark and not dried out. (If it is, and you don't have time to get a new one, set your printer to "double strike" to darken the print.) If you are using an ink-jet or laser printer, use a font that is clear and legible. Although there are some very attractive and artistic fonts available, such as script or cartoon-like writing, they are not good choices for academic papers as they may be hard to read.

For All Papers

Clip or staple your papers together. It is generally not necessary to have them bound or to put them in a special folder. If you aren't sure, ask your instructor. If you are going to do an in-class essay on looseleaf paper, be sure to bring your own clip or stapler. Don't expect your instructor to supply them.

Finally, think what your final product says about your pride in your work. If you turn in a paper filled with hand-corrections and your breakfast stains on its pages, it sends a message that you don't value your work much. Take a little extra time to present a manuscript that looks as good as it reads.

---

*If you have used a lot of correction fluid on a page, you may want to photocopy it before handing it in. The correction fluid won't show on the copy.

†Type-sizing on word processors is completely different from that on typewriters. On most word processors, the larger the number, the larger the type. However, on a typewriter, 12-point type is smaller than 10-point. On a word processor, it may say "cpi" (characters per inch) rather than "point." If it does, 12 cpi is smaller than 10 cpi.

Appendix

The **bold-faced** items are terms you might hear or read in your studies. The *italicized* words, phrases, or sentences are examples of the terminology. You can find more complete explanations for some of these terms in *The Tapestry Grammar* by Deakins, Parry, and Viscount (Boston: Heinle & Heinle, 1994). The chapter and page number are in parentheses (for example: TG 6, 140 refers to *The Tapestry Grammar,* Chapter 6, page 140).

Absolute construction   (also called a sentence adverbial) a word or phrase that is grammatically independent from the sentence in which it is found. It is not joined to the rest of the sentence by a conjunction or a relative pronoun, but it modifies some element of the sentence or the entire sentence. (TG 3, 44)

> *To be perfectly honest,* I would like to go home.
> *Hopefully,* everyone will be quiet.

> *NOTE* some traditional grammarians consider this an improper usage because "hopefully" can be interpreted as an adverb.

Abstract noun   a subclass of nouns that express concepts that are not observable or measurable. (TG 5, 96)

> *Freedom* is our goal.
> We wanted to increase our *happiness*.

Active voice   refers to a sentence in which the agent is doing something expressed by the verb. (compare its opposite, *passive voice*) (TG 8, 177)

> The dog *ran* away.
> Melissa *ate* dinner late.

Adjective   a word that is used to modify the meaning of a noun or noun phrase. (TG 6, 120)

> The *blue* plate is my favorite.
> It's a very *hot* day today.

Adverb   a word that is used to modify the meaning of a verb, adjective, sentence, or even another adverb. (TG 11, 263)

> She drove *slowly*.
> *Suddenly,* the boy jumped up and screamed.

Agent   the "doer" of the action of a verb.

> *The cat* chased the mouse.
> Willy was kicked by *his horse*.

Anaphora   a word or phrase that refers to another word or phrase found earlier in the sentence or text. (The underlined words are the <u>antecedent</u>; see later entry.)

> Yoko wants to visit <u>San Francisco</u>, but I don't want to go *there*.
> <u>Jun</u>'s shirt looks nice on *him*.

Antecedent   the word or phrase to which a pronoun refers.

> *Juan* was studying when <u>his</u> phone rang.
> Measure *an ounce of chocolate* and put <u>it</u> in the cup.

Appositive (also called an "insert") a noun or noun phrase that follows another noun or noun phrase and identifies or explains it. The two noun phrases must refer to the same thing. (TG 14, 336)

> Susan, *a woman in my class,* studies very hard.
> Mystery novels, *my favorite type of reading,* are exciting.

Article a, an, or the.
Definite article: the word the, which indicates a specific object or idea that both the speaker and hearer (or reader and writer) recognize. (TG 5, 94)

> *The* moon is full next Wednesday.
> Bring me *the* book, please.

Indefinite article: the words a or an, used when not referring to specific things or people. Use a before a word that begins with a consonant sound; use an before a word that begins with a vowel sound.

> *An* apple a day keeps the doctor away, so they say.
> *A* university student sleeps very little.

Zero article: places where no article is used before the noun. A | below shows where an article might be expected.

> | Horses are smarter than | cows.
> There's a good program on | television tonight.

Auxiliary verb (sometimes called a "helping verb") a type of verb that supplements the main verb, typically forms of be, have, and do. (TG 8, 184)

> We *are* going to the movies at eight tonight.
> Ping *doesn't* like chicken.
> Ronny *had* gone by the time we arrived.

Clause any group of words that has a subject and a verb.
Dependent clause (or subordinate clause): a sentence within a sentence, which is introduced by a subordinating conjunction. It cannot stand on its own because of this conjunction. (TG 3, 45)

> I ate pizza *while I studied for chemistry.*
> The huge traffic jam, *which hadn't moved for hours,* was caused by the snowstorm.

Independent clause: a clause that can stand on its own. (TG 4, 63)

> *It is sunny today.*
> When we get home, *we will cook a big meal.*

Relative clause: a dependent clause introduced by a relative pronoun. (TG 6, 134)
Restrictive relative clause: a phrase that makes a noun phrase more specific. (TG 6, 134)

> The program *that I watched last night* was terrible.

Nonrestrictive relative clause: a clause that adds information about a noun phrase. (TG 14, 336)

> That tall man, *who is standing by the door,* is my brother.

Collective noun   a noun that is used to refer to all the members of a group that is considered to be one unit. (In U.S. English, collective nouns are generally considered singular, but in British, some are considered plural.) (TG 5, 91)

> My *family* is very large.
> The *committee* meets on Thursday night.

Comma splice   combining two sentences into one by using a comma instead of a conjunction or semicolon. This usage is considered incorrect, but is sometimes used in fiction and creative writing for stylistic reasons. (TG 4, 64)

> *Julia was talented, she could dance very well.*
> *I am tired, I think I'll go home.*

Comparative   an adjective or adverb showing the second degree of comparison. (TG 6, 122)

> Frank is *taller* than Sally.
> That restaurant is *more expensive* than the cafeteria.

Concrete noun   a noun that refers to a material thing—something that can be seen, touched, smelled, etc. (TG 5, 96)

> Chuck was happy with his new *car*.
> Teresa put her *hands* on the *table*.

Conditional sentence   a complex sentence that expresses a hypothesis or a statement contrary to fact. A conditional sentence includes an independent clause and a conditional clause. (TG 8, 195)

> *If it rains, we will stay indoors.*
> *If Pedro hadn't studied so hard, he wouldn't have gotten an 'A' on his examination.*
> *I would bake a cake if I knew how.*

Conjunction   (also called a coordinator or subordinator) a word that joins words, phrases, or clauses. (TG 4, 64)

> I like sugar *and* cream in my coffee.
> Kim can't sing *or* dance.
> Saïd says he likes to travel, *but* he hasn't any money.

Copula   the verb "be" and its forms, used as a main verb.

> Jamal *is* a serious musician.
> You *are* energetic today.

Countable noun   a noun that can be preceded by a number indicating how many. (TG 5, 91)

> There are four *books* on my desk.
> There are *ships* in the harbor.

The opposite is a "uncountable" noun and includes words such as <u>water</u>, <u>rice</u>, or <u>mud</u>. However, many uncountable nouns have countable versions that refer to a type, class, or species.

> I ate *fish* for dinner.
> There are many *fishes* [= species of fish] in the aquarium.

Dangling modifier   any modifier that is misplaced so that it appears to be modifying something other than what the author intended. (A "*" means an incorrect usage.) (TG 10, 249)

>*Hanging in the closet, he found his tie.
>*We saw the building, running around the corner.

Demonstrative adjectives or pronouns   the words <u>that</u>, <u>this</u>, <u>these</u>, and <u>those</u>. When placed before nouns, they act as adjectives; when used alone, they are pronouns. (TG 5, 100)

>I'll eat *these* papayas and you eat *those*.

Diminutive   a form that indicates small size, sometimes used as a term of endearment. These forms are: *-en, -ette, -ie, -kin, -let, -ling, -ock,* and *-y.*

>Bill calls his son Bill*y*.
>I'd like a room with a kitchen*ette,* please.
>Don't call me "lamb*kin*"!

Double negative   two negative words used in the same clause, typically considered nonstandard usage in written English.

>*I *don't* want *no* more lunch.
>*Joan *didn't* do *none* of the things you said.

Emphatic   also called an "intensive." A form of emphasis by use of an additional verb "do" or reflexive pronoun.

>Auxiliary: I *do* hope you will enjoy the meal.
>Pronoun: Einstein *himself* couldn't have solved this problem.

Expletive subject   the words "it" or "there" used as a subject, and not referring to a specific noun. (TG 12, 302)

>*It* is raining.
>*There* are a lot of frogs in the pond.

Fragment sentence   a group of words that does not constitute a full sentence, although the writer intended them to. Fragments can be used in writing intentionally to create a specific style. (TG 3, 48)

>*Three boys eating dinner while watching television.
>*Because I want to go to the movies.

Future time   a phrase indicating an action that will begin or be completed in the future. In English, there is no true "tense" marking on the verb for future tense. There are a number of ways to indicate future, however. (TG 8, 200)

>Fernando *will* go to the library.
>I *shall* leave my shoes outside.
>Yin *is going to begin* a new class.
>Paolo *leaves at noon.*

Gender (grammatical)   a property of eight pronouns that show whether the noun is feminine, masculine, or neuter: *(fem.) she, her, hers; (masc.) he, him, his; (neut.) it, its.* There are a few nouns that are considered to have gender; for example, ships and countries are sometimes referred to as "she," but this usage is inconsistent. (TG 7, 159)

>*He* carried *his* books. Did you see *him*?

Gerund and **participial noun**   a verb with an -ing ending that functions as a noun. (TG 10, 245)

> *Reading* is my favorite activity.
> I am tired of your *complaining*.

> *NOTE*   since the gerund is a type of noun, it requires a possessive pronoun. However, you will probably hear or read this construction with a subject pronoun: *I am tired of *you* complaining.

Historical present   a present-tense verb used when telling a story that took place in the past. The historical present gives the reader or listener the sense of being part of the action.

> William *walks* in and *sits* down and *starts* talking.

Idiom   a word or phrase in English whose meaning is not regular or predictable from the meaning of the individual words.

> I'd like to *hit the sack* early tonight.
> The criminal *gave himself up* to the police.

Imperative   a sentence that gives an order or command. In English, imperatives usually do not have an expressed subject. (TG 8, 199)

> *Shut the window!*
> Please, *make me some dinner.*

Indirect question   a statement that reports a question in a dependent clause. (TG 13, 321)

> I wondered *when the play would begin.*
> Barbara asked him *where his jacket was.*

Infinitive   a verb form that is not marked for tense or person. It sometimes is preceded by the word "to". (TG 1, 8)

> He wanted *to go* dancing on Saturday.
> She made us *finish* our lunch before leaving.

> Split infinitive: In traditional grammar, it was considered incorrect to "split" an infinitive—that is, to put a word between "to" and the main part of the verb phrase. However, this "rule" is not adhered to strictly in current usage.

> Sung had *to completely finish* his homework before eight.

Intransitive verb   a verb that does not take a direct object. (TG 11, 288)

> She *slept.*
> Dodi's baby has really *grown,* hasn't she?

> *NOTE*   some verbs can be both transitive and intransitive.

> Farley *ate* at ten last night.
> He *ate* fish and rice.

Irregular plural   a noun whose plural form is not created by adding *s* or *es.* (TG 5, 88)

> The *children* washed their *feet* in the stream.
> I saw the pictures of the *oxen, geese,* and *mice.*

Irregular verb   a verb whose past tense or past participle is not formed by adding *ed* or *en*. (TG 8, 180)

> He *ran, fell,* and *broke* his leg.
> We *swam, sang,* and *ate* a picnic lunch.

Modal auxiliary   a class of verbs that show necessity, ability, possibility, permission, or obligation: <u>can</u>, <u>could</u>, <u>would</u>, <u>should</u>, <u>might</u>, <u>may</u>, <u>must</u>, <u>ought to</u>, <u>have to</u>, and <u>had to</u>. Verbs that follow model auxiliaries are infinitive in form. (TG 8, 200)

> Jermaine *can* ride horses very skillfully.
> I *ought to* exercise more regularly.

Noun   a word that indicates a person, place, thing, or idea. (TG 5, 85)

> *Kahlil* likes your new *house*.
> *Laziness* is my *specialty*.

Object   a noun or noun phrase that receives the action of a verb or follows a preposition. Objects may be direct or indirect. (TG 11, 265)
Direct object:

> Sabina carried *her suitcase.*
> Please hand <u>*that pencil*</u> to <u>*me*</u>.
>   D.O   I.O.

Participle   a form of a verb used with an auxiliary. (TG 10, 245)
Present participle: a form made by adding *-ing* to a verb.

> Carlo is *weeding* the garden.

Past participle: a form made by adding *-ed* or *-en* to a verb.

> Fatima has *stopped* smoking.

Passive   a verb construction that focuses on the object of an action rather than the agent. In a passive sentence, the verb phrases consists of a form of "be" plus the past participle. If the agent is included, it follows a phrase beginning with the word "by". (TG 9, 225)

> The wall *was painted by Marco.*
> Mirella's chair *had been designed* in the 14th century.

Perfect tense   an aspect of a verb that indicates that the action is completed in relation to a specific point in time. (TG 8, 204)
<u>Present perfect</u> shows that the action is completed at the time of the statement.

> We *have packed* our bags.

<u>Past perfect</u> shows that an action was completed at some time in the past.

> I *had taken* a shower before you arrived.
> Ali didn't know who *had taken* his scissors.

<u>Future perfect</u> shows that an action will be completed by a time in the future relative to the time of the statement.

> I *will have finished* my lunch by the time you get here.
> Donna doesn't think *she will have graduated* by December.

Person   the grammatical person who is the speaker or writer. (TG 7, 154)
First person: "I" or "we"
Second person: "you"
Third person: "he," "she," "it," "they"

Phrase   a group of words that functions as a part of speech.
Noun phrase: a noun and all of its modifiers (TG 5, 86)

The big red apple is on the teacher's desk.

Prepositional phrase: a preposition and its complete object

The big red apple is *on the teacher's desk.* (TG 1, 9)

Verb phrase: a verb and its complete complement

The big red apple *is on the teacher's desk.* (TG 8, 184)

Plural   more than one noun or pronoun, usually indicated by *-s* or *-es.* (See the entry on irregulars for those without *-s* or *-es* page 169.) (TG 5, 90)

There are many bee*s* by the swimming pool.
Three church*es* were built last year in our city.

Possessive   a grammatical relationship between an object and its owner. This relationship is shown by a possessive pronoun, a possessive marker (*'s* or *s'*) or the preposition "of". (TG 5, 102)

Our class is small.
The *boy's* brother is taller than he.
The leg *of* the table is broken.
Their *houses'* addresses are not clear.

Possessive pronouns do not use apostrophes.

That car is *theirs*; where is *yours*?
The dog wagged *its* tail.
Is that coat *hers*?

Predicate (complete)   a verb and all of its complements in a sentence (TG 1, 3)

The furniture *stood in the middle of the room.*
The white cat and the black dog *ran away.*

Preposition   a word indicating a relationship between two things, which may be spatial, temporal, grammatical, or metaphorical. The prepositions include: <u>about,</u> <u>above,</u> <u>across,</u> <u>after,</u> <u>against,</u> <u>along,</u> <u>amid,</u> <u>among,</u> <u>around,</u> <u>at,</u> <u>before,</u> <u>behind,</u> <u>below,</u> <u>beneath,</u> <u>beside,</u> <u>between,</u> <u>beyond,</u> <u>by,</u> <u>down,</u> <u>for,</u> <u>from,</u> <u>in,</u> <u>into,</u> <u>like,</u> <u>near,</u> <u>of,</u> <u>off,</u> <u>on,</u> <u>out,</u> <u>over,</u> <u>past,</u> <u>since,</u> <u>through,</u> <u>to,</u> <u>towards,</u> <u>under,</u> <u>until,</u> <u>unto,</u> <u>up,</u> <u>upon,</u> <u>with,</u> and <u>within.</u> (TG 1, 9)

Present tense   a verb tense indicating action occurring at the time of statement. (TG 8, 181)

I *am* unable to attend.
Walter *hears* music coming from the stadium.

Progressive (or continuous) verb   a verb that shows continuing action. It is constructed of a "be" verb and a present participle. (TG 8, 207)

> Iggy *is cleaning* his apartment from top to bottom.
> Zoltan *was trying* to listen to the lecture.

Pronoun   a form that takes the place of a noun or noun phrase. (TG 7, 155)

> *She* isn't happy with *her* grade.

Reflexive pronoun   a form of personal pronoun that refers to the grammatical person of a statement: myself, yourself, himself, herself, itself, oneself, ourselves, yourselves, themselves. (TG 7, 155)

> John shaves *himself* every morning at seven.
> You have to ask *yourself* why this happened.

Run-on sentence   in written English, two independent clauses that are inappropriately joined. (See also comma splice.) It is considered nonstandard in most writing, although it may be used for certain effect in fiction and creative writing. (TG 4, 63)

> *I ate my lunch he polished my shoes.
> *Hiromi went to the baseball game and she bought a hotdog.

Sentence   a group of words, properly ordered, containing at least a main verb, although typically other elements as well. (TG 3, 39)

> *Run!*
> *He is nice.*
> *Sal cannot read French, nor can he write it.*

Subject (of a sentence)   the noun or noun phrase that is the originator of the main verb in the sentence. (TG 3, 39)

> Art is my favorite subject.
> *Cows* graze on grass all day long.
> *Kennedy* died before I was born.

Subjunctive   a type of verb that suggests doubt, wish, regret, possibility, hypothesis, or something contrary to fact. It is used irregularly and often inconsistently in current English. The subjunctive is formed either by the verb "were" or by a bare form of a verb after another verb of regret, concession, etc. (TG 8, 201)

> If I *were* rich, I'd buy a new car.
> I asked that the appointment *be* postponed.
> Tom suggests that Mary *return* her library books.

Superlative   the extreme degree of comparison, referring to the maximum quality. (TG 6, 125)

> That was the *worst* movie I have ever seen.
> Federico is the *tallest* man in our class.
> The *most* food I have ever eaten was at the deli on 4th.

Tag question   a question formed from a statement plus a tag, a short question which uses the appropriate auxiliary verb. If the statement is positive, the tag is negative, and vice versa. (TG 2, 23)

> You are very tired today, *aren't you?*
> Sandrine enjoys skiing, *doesn't she?*
> Andrew can't play the violin, *can he?*

Tense shift   the inappropriate mixing of verb tenses in one sentence or passage of writing.

> *Cindy knew that we are content.
> *We saw how quickly he completes his work.

Transitive verb   a verb that requires a direct object. (See also intransitive verb.) (TG 11, 265)

> The cat *ate* the salmon.
> David's friend *kicked* the soccer ball.

Verb   a word that shows action or state of being (TG 8, 177)

> Many horses *are* shy and easily frightened.
> My calendar *shows* all of the holidays.

Index

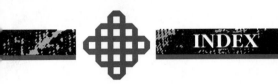